Plotting Terror

Plotting Terror
Novelists and Terrorists in Contemporary Fiction

Margaret Scanlan

University Press of Virginia

Charlottesville and London

The University Press of Virginia

Printed in the United States of America
First published 2001

Frontis art: *Hostage* by Peter Scanlan (courtesy of the artist)

∞The paper used in this publication meets the minimum requirements
of the American National Standard for Information Sciences—Permanence
of Paper for Printed Library Materials, ANSI Z39.48-1984.

Library of Congress Cataloging-in-Publication Data

Scanlan, Margaret, 1944-
  Plotting terror : novelists and terrorists in contemporary fiction
/ Margaret Scanlan.
    p.   cm.
  Includes bibliographical references and index.
  ISBN 0-8139-2031-0 (alk. paper) — ISBN 0-8139-2035-3 (pbk. : alk. paper)
   1. Fiction — 20th century — History and criticism. 2. Terrorism in
literature. I. Title.

 PN3352.T35 S28 2001
 809.3'9355—dc21   00-065434

For
Lois Thompson Trieschmann
Theodore Baker Trieschmann
in loving memory

Contents

Acknowledgments

would like to thank Indiana University South Bend for supporting my research with two sabbaticals and two summer faculty fellowships. I also thank the National Endowment for the Humanities for allowing me to spend part of the summer of 1994 at Yale in a seminar directed by R. W. B. Lewis. Patrick Brantlinger of Indiana University Bloomington provided encouragement in the early stages, and I am especially grateful to him for bringing Mick Taussig's essay on "Terrorism as Usual" to my attention. As chairs of the English department, Jim Blodgett and Eleanor Lyons provided help in dozens of ways, and I want to thank them for that otherwise thankless task. Elizabeth Cotter of the IUSB Interlibrary Loan department and her successor, Maureen Kennedy, made dozens of obscure books and articles almost instantly available.

Friends and family provided support, reading lists, and laughter. As always, my husband, John, read every draft of every chapter, providing invaluable advice on everything from pronoun references to legal citations. Our sons, Christopher, Patrick, and Andrew, were resolutely partisan at every stage and learned fortitude from years of Kraft dinners and frozen pizza. I owe a great deal to my colleagues at Indiana University South Bend, but particularly to those who often lunch in the faculty lounge of Wiekamp Hall: Jim Blodgett, Linda Chen, Margarete Feinstein, Pat Furlong, Roy Schreiber, Monica Tetzlaff, Lesley Walker, and Tammy Fong Morgan. At those Socratic symposia only the purest English is spoken, the loftiest topics entertained, viz. the fortunes of the Chair-Tossing coach on the mother campus, the suitability of the Better-Known University across Town for our graduation, and ways of finding international films and food in northern Indiana.

The longer I spend in college teaching the more grateful I am to my own teachers, whose patience seems in retrospect to have been infinite. In particular, I would like to thank Jane Sherwin Schwartz and the late Robert Dalziel, extraordinary undergraduate teachers I still try to emulate.

This book is dedicated to my parents. My mother was a great reader, the only one I knew before college. She read aloud to me, when I was nine and ten and eleven, books that might otherwise have been encountered much later, as an obligation, but were pure pleasure then. I still hear her accents, and even detect her occasional bowdlerisms, in the texts of Willa Cather, the Brontës, and Mark Twain. My father, like many another immigrant's son, loved American public education and was never happier than when regaling us with stories about working his way through college or coaching basketball and teaching in small Iowa high schools. As it is much easier to contract an enthusiasm than to follow advice, I remain grateful not only for their love, but for what they loved.

Earlier versions of the following chapters appeared in the following journals, and I thank their editors for permission to reprint: chapter one: "Writers among Terrorists: Don DeLillo's *Mao II* and the Rushdie Affair," *Modern Fiction Studies,* 40.2 (summer 1994): 229–52; chapter three: "Terrorists, Artists, and Intellectuals: Mary McCarthy's *Cannibals and Missionaries,*" in *Twenty-Four Ways of Looking at Mary McCarthy: The Writer and Her Work,* ed. Eve Stwertka and Margo Viscusi, Westport, CT: Greenwood, 1996, 35–42; chapter four: "Language and the Politics of Despair in Doris Lessing's *The Good Terrorist,*" 23.2 (winter 1990), *NOVEL: A Forum on Fiction,* copyright NOVEL Corp. © 1990; chapter five: "Incriminating Documents: Nechaev and Dostoevsky in J. M. Coetzee's *The Master of Petersburg,*" *Philological Quarterly* 76 (fall 1998): 463–77; chapter six: "Terror as Usual in Friedrich Dürrenmatt's *The Assignment,*" *Modern Language Quarterly* 52.1 (March 1991): 86–99; chapter eight: "Literature at the Margins: The Terrorist as Novelist in Antoine Volodine's *Lisbonne dernière marge,*" *New Novel Review* 3.1 (October 1995): 67–82.

Scholarly conferences provided the first opportunities to test many of the ideas in this book; I especially want to thank Tony Jackson for organizing the history and literature panel at MLA in 1995 and Alex

Houen for inviting me to lecture at the Political Violence and Literature Conference at King's College, Cambridge, in August 1997.

I would also like to thank Cathie Brettschneider of the University Press of Virginia for her help in bringing this manuscript to press. Jane Curran edited the copy expertly and graciously, saving me from many an error.

Finally, I am grateful to my talented brother-in-law, Peter, for permission to reproduce "the Hostage."

Plotting Terror

Introduction

I n the wake of the Second World War, as our Japanese and West German enemies turned into model citizens working economic miracles, the fear and loathing that fascism had so recently inspired were channeled into Communism. Some forty years later, the collapse of the Berlin Wall and the evil empire called for a "new public enemy number one," and terrorism stepped into that role (Said 149). Now it is terrorists who lurk in every shadow, images of terrorist attacks that fill our television screens, and fears of new varieties—nuclear, biological, cyber-terrorism—that drive calls for increased surveillance and larger defense budgets. If such Orwellian transformations in the identity of the enemy do not make us skeptical, an element of construction in political and journalistic rhetoric about terrorism, even in terrorist acts themselves, seems inescapable. Bombings and hijackings begin with a few people plotting violence for maximum exposure, come to us on television, where distinctions between news and entertainment are ever more tortuous, and quickly pass into the popular imagination, into blockbuster movies and paperback thrillers. Yet however mediated and manipulated it may be, the terrorist story chronicles actual deaths; however low its casualties in comparison with those exacted by terrorizing states, they are real enough; they have historical and social origins and consequences. This paradoxical affiliation between our violence and our fictions lies at the heart of those complex novels about terrorism sometimes called "literary thrillers," as vital to them as gore and mayhem are to the blockbuster.

Plotting Terror is a study of contemporary novels in which terrorist themes lead to questions about writing and violence. In each of these novels, writers and terrorists encounter each other, resuming a motif of the writer as terrorist's victim, rival, or double, which first appears in Dostoevsky's *Demons*, James's *The Princess Casamassima*, and Conrad's *Under Western Eyes*. I ask why so many writers have been drawn to terrorists and what affinities they find between literary and terrorist plots, between literature and violence. I see both writers and terrorists in these novels as remnants of a romantic belief in the power of marginalized persons to transform history. I argue that serious terrorist fiction develops an increasingly pessimistic account of the novel's social power, a pessimism that some recent novelists extend to the revolutionary impulse itself. All the same, and because, as a Don DeLillo character puts it, "Writers know how reality is created," such fictions elucidate the process that allows militants, journalists, and politicians to construct terrorism as a political reality.

The theoretical conception of my topic—that terrorism is both actual killing and a fictional construct, that fiction embodies an acute critique of the power of discourse as opposed to the power of the individual's self-assertion—owes a great deal to deconstruction and neo-Marxism and will be familiar to readers with a grounding in the New Historicism and cultural studies. In contrast both to a New Criticism that once dismissed history and politics as "themes" or "background" irrelevant to the literariness of the literary text, and to an old-fashioned Marxism that insisted that an economic base determines the superstructure of the literary text, New Historicists assert a "reciprocal concern with the historicity of texts and the textuality of history" (Montrose 20).

This conception of the historicity of texts owes much to neo-Marxists such as Louis Althusser and Pierre Macherey, who argued that literary texts generate rather than simply reflect an ideology. Althusser called attention to the "displacements and substitutions" in texts and Macherey to their silences. Although deconstruction often seemed ahistorical, even Paul de Man emphasized, as did the neo-Marxists, that what we take for history or reality is often fictional: "What we call ideology is precisely the confusion of linguistic with natural reality . . . the linguistics of literariness is a powerful and indispensable tool in the unmasking of ideological aberrations, as well as a determining factor in accounting for their occurrence" (363). Eight years later, Jacques Derrida argued even more strongly that deconstruction introduced into literary studies a new "multidisciplinarity" and was "set into motion by a concern with history, even if it leads to destabilizing certain concepts of history" (376).

No theorist, however, is more central to understanding the relations of terrorists and novelists than Michel Foucault, who thoroughly destabilizes conventional accounts of political history. Discounting such traditional staples as Great Men, Books, and Events, Foucault constructs genealogies of discourse, freely mixing the evidence provided by, say, a Velázquez painting with long-forgotten medieval medical treatises and lists of regulations for controlling school children or prisoners. Foucault famously argues that medieval people saw power emanating from the king, who as God's representative quite literally held power over the bodies of his subjects. At some point after the middle of the eighteenth century, people abandoned this view: power ceased to be identified with a single office, the crown, and was no longer exerted in scenes of public torture. Power was dispersed and control internalized; speech and thought were "policed" by disciplinary "discourses" that marked what the speaker says as "in the true" or beyond its margins. Humane developments, such as public education, psychiatric counseling, and the replacement of public executions with reform-oriented prisons, were in Foucault's view only more elaborate and effective efforts to control deviants. In Foucault's account, even the novel, a "discourse of infamy" disposed to incur "the charge of scandal, of transgression, or of rebellion," forms "part of that great system of constraint by which the West compelled the everyday to bring itself into discourse" ("Life" 91).

But who is plotting these moves? Is it still the king, or is it the merchants who control the wealth, or the church, or some secret organization like the Freemasons or the New World Order? This is a question Foucault refuses to answer, except to tell us how naive we would be to think that the state could "occupy the whole field of actual power relations . . . or operate [independently of] already existing power relations." Power as Foucault imagines it circulates everywhere and is amazingly resilient when attacked: "the State consists in the codification of a whole number of power relations which render its functioning possible. . . . Revolution is a different . . . codification of the same relations. . . . one can perfectly well conceive of revolutions which leave essentially untouched the power relations which form the basis for the functioning of the State" (123). If the later Foucault wanted to argue that yes, change is possible, the tendency of his thought stresses the futility of individuals and revolutionary movements struggling against the nets of power that enclose us.

Foucault's work thus allows us to formulate, and ultimately challenge, one deeply held tenet of literary romanticism, the alliance between the writer and the revolutionary. Traces of this alliance, which writers such as Byron, Hugo, Thoreau, and Lamartine exemplified for the nineteenth century, are still visible today. We find them in the very phrase "creative writing," in our tolerance, even encouragement, of eccentric or self-destructive behavior in writers; every story of a poet locked up or executed in Nigeria or Iraq confirms our sense that writers are enemies of tyranny. Yet the idea of the writer as revolutionary implies an extraordinary faith in that writer's power to act in the social world. The unacknowledged legislator of mankind must articulate a vision of a better world and set it down in unambiguous language, must persuade many readers to accept that vision as authoritative, and, moreover, must motivate them to act in ways that ensure change. Even in the mid-nineteenth century, when crusaders such as Elizabeth Barrett Browning and Harriet Beecher Stowe were widely read, it must have seemed a great deal to ask.

As the nineteenth century wore on, and the first terrorist novels began to appear, writers seem increasingly drawn to depicting their society as a Foucauldian nightmare, a formidable blank like the Siberian wastes that Dostoevsky and Conrad depict, or the vast impersonal city that overwhelms James's would-be terrorist and ignores his suicide. Assassins do not know whom to assassinate or discover that the bureaucracy simply replaces the hanging judge. Foucault's view of the novel as "part of a system of constraint" would have been anathema to Henry James, and yet the possibility that every original act is only a repetition of an old pattern stalks his hero throughout *The Princess Casamassima*. The journals and letters of James and Conrad demonstrate their own struggles against a sense of futility, their fears that they had few readers. Doubtless the growth of empires and the centralization of state power played a role in fostering this "agency panic," this "sense of *diminished human agency,* a feeling that individuals cannot effect meaningful social action and, in extreme cases, may not be able to control their own behavior" (Melley 11, emphasis in original).

But so too did the rise of mass journalism, of illustrated newspapers and magazines that offered such direct competition to the novel. Owned by powerful families, supported in part by sales and advertising, and regulated by the state, the popular newspaper is a site where Foucault's "relations of power" become visible. What goes into the newspaper is what most people will accept as the chronicle of their public life; the mass newspaper normalizes certain behaviors and stigmatizes others; even its silences (about hijackings in the Soviet Union, or about the marriages of U.S. citizens of color before 1960) signify. While some nineteenth-century novelists served an apprenticeship in popular journalism, most saw it as a competitor, a threat to their own sales, cheapening language and shortening the reader's attention span. Revolutionaries, on the other hand, gradually learned how to use the mass media to disseminate their message. Dynamiters could seize the headlines, if only they could assassinate the czar or blow up the Houses of Parliament or kill enough innocent bystanders.

It is this link to the mass media that leads most scholars to conclude that the insurgent terrorism that evolved in the second half of the nineteenth century was something new and not merely a repetition of the violent conspiracies that marked political history long before Brutus stabbed Caesar.[1] Scorned by Lenin and Trotsky alike as representative action undertaken by the intelligentsia on behalf of a distrustful proletariat, terrorism is more a violent means of communication than a direct strike at militarily significant targets. In a widely cited definition, the terrorist deed is "a symbolic act designed to influence political behaviour by extranormal means, entailing the use or threat of violence" (Thornton 73). As we shall see, this definition raises some questions; yet it has the merit of distinguishing insurgent terrorism from state terrorism and even guerrilla warfare: the insurgent group chooses a symbolic target because it cannot hope to overpower by force alone.[2] Terrorism in this definition is a behavior of small groups alienated from conventional ways of influencing the political process; of people, for example, who are either unable or unwilling to participate in elections.

Terrorists succeed when they seize headlines. Yet this very success means that they and their causes are understood in terms set by popular journalism. If television "coproduced" the Palestinian hijacker of the 1970s, it also ensured that for a global audience a few images and sound bites would constitute Palestinian history.[3] As importantly, the media's incessant repetition of the word *terrorism* has given it an emotional resonance that Thornton's sober definition of strategy, "the symbolic act of violence," fails to suggest.

As one result, the word *terrorist* has only the briefest of histories as self-description. Although in the late 1860s Sergei Nechaev "defiantly embraced the word 'terrorist,'" by 1876 the Russian "Land and

Freedom" movement preferred the euphemism *disorganizer* (Miller
"Origins" 77);[4] Johann Most's "Advice for Terrorists," published in the
German-American newspaper *Der Freiheit* in 1882, seems one of its last
instances. *Terrorism* soon denoted other people's violence, illegitimate
violence: Conor Cruise O'Brien, no friend to the Irish paramilitary, argues that "'Terror,' 'terrorism,' 'terrorist'—isolating the element of fear
which all violence must inspire—necessarily evoke all our negative feel-
ings about violence, and place at a distance the calming concept of legit-
imacy" (quoted in Hocking 103). In practice, to call people terrorists is
to condemn them; those of whom we approve are, of course, soldiers,
liberators, partisans, freedom fighters, or revolutionaries; even *guerilla*
remains more neutral.

Moreover, as Joseba Zulaika and William Douglass remind us, the
term is so flexible that Menachem Begin, Yassir Arafat, and Nelson Man-
dela, all once labeled as terrorists, have been rehabilitated as statesmen
and awarded the Nobel Peace Prize. As an umbrella term, *terrorism* includes pro-state groups such as France's Secret Army Organization
(OAS) and Northern Ireland's Ulster Volunteer Force (UVF), as well as
the familiar revolutionary groups; it describes acts ranging from hijacking and hostage-taking to the destruction of public property to street
fighting; what it does exclude are atrocities, such as the bombing deaths
of refugee children, committed by legitimate governments.[5] "Terrorist
exudes generic or universal overtones. . . . If all sorts of murders, kid-
nappings, threats, civil wars, government crimes, killings by secret or
underground organizations, paramilitary executions, and so on, were
simply called by those names without ever using the word 'terrorism,'
would there be something missing in the description of the real world?"
(Zulaika and Douglass 103).

As heirs to the revolutionaries of 1776 and 1789 and 1848, terrorists
retain their traditional affinity to writers. However, as a special case of
the old alliance between romantic writer and revolutionary, the relation
of writers with terrorists does not "go without saying"; it is no longer
assumed, but contested. Since *terrorist* has negative connotations, to figure the writer as terrorist is quite different from figuring him or her as
revolutionary. Far from being a ritual acknowledgment of originality
and power, it is an imputation of violence or underhandedness. Thus
within contemporary fiction, we find terrorists both as rivals and as
doubles of the novelist. The terrorist acts a writer describes may take

place in his or her homeland and may be of great immediate importance to the novelist. On the other hand, literary depictions of terrorism often displace some other scene of violence. In the imagined act of terrorism, a writer may assess his or her own political commitments, actions, and failures. Thus the terrorist novel opens itself up to more general questions about the writer's ability to understand, respond to, and influence politics.

Between 1871 and 1914, Dostoevsky, James, and Conrad all wrote novels in which writers consort with revolutionaries. The relations between writers and terrorists in *Demons, The Princess Casamassima,* and *Under Western Eyes* are stifling: of father to son, of sycophant to celebrity, of double, rival, and secret sharer. Put schematically, Dostoevsky argues that intellectuals engender revolution and naively adulate the men of violence who, when they have the opportunity, will be as ready to kill them as to burn their books. James shares Dostoevsky's sense of the artist's vulnerability, to the point of suggesting that those who love art must side politically with the aristocracy. But more critically, he undermines the romantic model of revolution, in which strong-willed individuals pit themselves against authority, suggesting that in the end both writer and terrorist fail. Like James and Dostoevsky, Conrad also sees writers and intellectuals as potential victims of revolution, but their own violence and guilt intrigue him further.

Dostoevsky, as we all know, was sent to Siberia in 1850 after the czar commuted his death sentence for taking part in a plot to democratize Russia. His fascination with revolutionary movements, as they increasingly turned to violence in the 1860s, grew out of his experiences, and though his own politics grew increasingly conservative, he never forgot why revolution attracts idealistic young people. In *Demons* (1871), he traces the connections between an otherworldly intellectual, Stepan Verkhovensky, and his neglected son Peter, a thinly disguised version of the terrorist Sergei Nechaev. Just as the liberal pamphleteer is father to the arsonist, the novelist is the terrorist's dupe. The Europeanized novelist Semyon Yegorovich Karmazinov, a stand-in for Ivan Turgenev, shamelessly curries the young activist's favor, even lending him the single handwritten copy of his newest novel. In a painful scene Peter has helped to orchestrate, a drunken crowd humiliates Karmazinov at a public reading timed to usher in an apocalyptic night of murder and arson. Roundly jeered, "red as though he had been boiled," Karmazinov must remain on stage just long enough to receive "a magnificent wreath of laurels" from the governor's formidable wife. Knowing Yulia Mikhailovna's flirtation with his revolutionary tormentor makes this gift all the more ironic to the beleaguered writer, who tells her he has "suddenly become so much of a realist" that he considers it more fitting to give laurels to a cook than to himself (482). The proletarian dictatorship in which cooks outrank writers menaces the humiliated novelist, to whom nobody listens, even while he still wears the classic symbol of his vain ambition.

Unlike Dostoevsky, Henry James passed his life in middle-class comfort, and the prefaces to the New York edition of his novels became basic texts for New Critical pronouncements on the techniques and values of a formally scrupulous fiction. He seems perhaps the least likely of men to write a terrorist novel, yet the commonplace about *The Princess Casamassima* that no one wants to challenge is that its protagonist, the would-be assassin Hyacinth Robinson, shares many qualities with its author. Like James, he has a facility with French, a propensity for agonizingly platonic relationships, a reverence for the monuments of high culture, and a distaste for the smudges and smells of poverty. Hyacinth is a bookbinder and aspiring poet, torn between his revolutionary sympathies and a desire to cultivate the friendship and patronage of the eponymous princess. Having promised to assassinate a duke on behalf of a revolutionary cell, Hyacinth kills himself rather than betray either the movement or the aristocracy that nourishes high culture.

To Hyacinth, the Houses of Parliament loom "as a fortress of the social order which he, like the young David, had been commissioned to attack with a sling and pebble" (583). Dostoevsky saw visions of such fortresses falling, but James hardly imagines that marginalized people like Hyacinth can scratch their surface. Indeed, the police do not need to stalk James's unpublished poet and suicidal terrorist. A revolutionary act may disappear into empty space as readily as an unnoticed novel, *The Bostonians,* for example: "not a word, echo, or comment . . . have come to me . . . from any quarter whatever. This deathly silence seems to indicate that it has fallen flat" (Anesko 104; James, *Letters* 3: 102).

James's Foucauldian vision of a silent and unreachable social power that simply absorbs every rebellious voice and reassembles itself after every revolutionary assault echoes as well through Conrad's *Under*

Western Eyes. Russia in this novel is a vast frozen landscape hiding prison camps where half-starved wretches labor for a state against which they once raised some futile protest. Such places were no figment of the imagination to the son of Apollo Korzeniowski, translator of Shakespeare, poet, and revolutionary, who took his wife and four-year-old son with him into exile in the remote Russian province of Vologda after one more abortive Polish uprising. Green or white, wrote Conrad's father, it was always winter in that dreadful place; both parents contracted tuberculosis and left their son an orphan. As stories of assassinated czars and dynamited railways filled the London papers, they could not help reminding the expatriate novelist that he had declined to continue his father's struggle against the czar.

But in *Under Western Eyes*, the writer's desperate struggle to extricate himself from the trammels of violent revolution is doomed from the beginning. When the scholar Razumov returns to his room, he finds the assassin Haldin waiting for him, demanding protection. For perhaps one moment they confront each other, opposed figures, the man of action and the writer. But within hours Razumov has beaten a drunken peasant within an inch of his life and has betrayed Haldin to the state, which tortures and executes him. Evidently Haldin was right when he told Razumov, "It's you thinkers who are in everlasting revolt" (18). Conscripted as a police informer, Razumov goes to Geneva representing himself as Haldin's friend and fellow revolutionary. In an age of information, storytelling quickly becomes tale bearing and lethal; the journalist who finally reveals Haldin's fate to the readers of the *Evening Standard* delivers a deathblow to his mother.

The ease with which writers become adjuncts of some larger system, the state or mass journalism, demonstrates how problematic the romantic idea of a self-contained individual becomes for Conrad. Haldin is not the writer's only secret sharer; rather, the novel offers Razumov a number of more or less disturbing relationships with people who invade his privacy, supervise him, reinvent him as the son or lover or hero they need. In what Karl Miller in a different context calls a "slew of reciprocal identity," neither the writer nor the terrorist occupies an uncontaminated space from which to oppose power (136). These and other distinctions, what Derrida would call the binary oppositions enabling Western thought, are collapsing into each other. Russia is a place where brutality has already effected some Nietzschean transvaluation of values, a place where the "Christian virtues themselves appear actually indecent," where "virtues themselves fester into crimes in the cynicism of oppression and revolt" (Conrad, *Under* 56, 300).

From such a place, England, like the tolerant city of Geneva, ought to offer a refuge. But the novel, in its repeated insistence on the incompatibility of its implicit male, English reader with its Russian characters, repeatedly figures him as unimaginative, politically naive, and easily shocked. The narrator assures us that "our Western ears" are not "attuned to certain tones of cynicism and cruelty, of moral negation, and even of moral distress already silenced at our end of Europe" (138). Yet he leaves unanswered the question of whether it is progress that has "silenced" the "moral distress" of Europe, or whether we ought really to congratulate ourselves on our inability to feel it. Perhaps Western indifference, like the vast Russian landscape, swallows up every voice and makes the new century a "monstrous blank page awaiting the record of an inconceivable history" (26).

Dostoevsky, James, and Conrad pressure the commonsense distinction between writers and terrorists, between stories and violence, without entirely accepting some view, deconstructive *avant la lettre,* that they are indistinguishable. Their novels anticipate many of the questions about representing violence that late-twentieth-century theorists have pressed—the alliance between storytelling and power, the tendency of art to convert violence into an enthralling spectacle, and even, in the case of Conrad's Peter Mikulin, the distortions of the victim's narrative-become-bestseller.[6] They issue an invitation to see in insurgent terrorism an occasion for exploring the romantic idea of the writer as rebel and for questioning romanticism's optimism about literature's social power.

We might also think they had issued an invitation for the next generation of writers, the ones who came after the Russian Revolution and the First World War, to find new legitimations for the social role of literature. Yet for reasons about which we can only speculate, few if any of their immediate successors took up that challenge. The New Critical response, that it was not the function of literature to change the world, merely claimed that the problem was insoluble, perhaps beneath notice. The question of literature and history was even easier in Stalinist Russia, where the state, as Dostoevsky and Conrad had predicted, simply jailed and murdered dissident writers, ensuring that its presses churned out nothing that appeared to contradict its will. In the West, progressive, even Marxist, writers—George Orwell and Graham Greene, Jean-Paul

Sartre and André Malraux—continued to write about poverty, injustice, and violence, implying that literature could at least be part of the movement for a better world. Though even Sartre was less confident than Shelley, the figure of the guilty writer brooding over unwritten or futile texts seems to disappear.

We cannot say for sure why that was so. Dostoevsky, James, and Conrad ended their lives as conservatives and perhaps seemed too reactionary to serve as models of political thought even for writers, such as Greene, who admired them. Then, too, James and Conrad were absorbed into the modernist canon. The apolitical author of *The American* and *The Wings of the Dove* became, as it were, the real Henry James. Conrad's political themes proved harder to dismiss, but the New Criticism turned *Heart of Darkness* into an allegory of light and dark, or a search for some abstract evil in "the heart of man," and ignored the colonial themes of *Lord Jim* and *Victory*. But surely the historical context was at least as important as trends in literary theory.

After the Great War, with notable exceptions such as Malraux's *La Condition humaine,* the number of terrorist novels diminished, as did the frequency of terrorist incidents, to the point that in 1933 Jacob Hardman declared in *The Encyclopedia of Social Sciences* that terrorism had become "outmoded as a revolutionary method" (Zulaika and Douglass 17). Hardman was not arguing that political terror and violence had ended in 1933, of all years, but that the labor movement had learned that sustained strikes were more effective than sporadic violence. Much more recently, Martin Miller argues that the increasing numbers of socialists elected to British and continental parliaments in the 1920s suggest that many old revolutionaries found they could work within the increasingly democratic postwar regimes (56). On the other hand, he notes, both Communist and Fascist governments might be seen as extensions of older terrorist movements whose "leaders, once in power, introduced state terrorism on an unprecedented scale" (57). By 1939, a massive world war between well-armed states once more swallowed up any thought of small insurgent movements threatening large governments.

After the Second World War, the guerillas of the past, such as Malraux's Chinese Communists, sought power in many of the former colonies. As they did so, the colonizers at least regarded their tactics as terrorist: the blowing up of the King David Hotel by Begin's Irgun, for example. Yet the nationalist movements of the immediate postwar period tended to confine their activities to the homeland, and the old specters of international terrorism, of men with foreign accents planting bombs in London and Paris, resurfaced only with the student revolutions of 1968. As they did, the word *terrorism* reappeared, as Ronald Crelinsten shows in his analysis of four major indexes to newspapers and periodicals published between 1966 and 1985.[7] Before 1970, only the *Reader's Guide* included *terrorism* as a heading; by 1972, all four did. Prior to 1970, *assassinations, bombing, torture, repression,* and *massacre* appeared as separate headings; after 1972, many such events were subsumed under *terrorism* (Crelinsten, quoted in Zulaika and Douglass 45).

As the number of skyjackings, car bombings, and hostage-takings climbed, television became the primary medium for the terrorist story and brought the anxieties generated by terrorist acts to a fever pitch. After all, its images were available in the home, more or less around the clock; it threatened to drive out not only novel reading but newspapers and conversation as well. It was only three years from the world's first live global television broadcast, the moon landing of 1969, to the first global terrorist broadcast. In the summer of 1972, perhaps 800 million viewers around the world tuned in for the Olympics and instead watched a day-long hostage drama that ended with Black September killing eleven Israeli athletes just off camera (Schlagheck 68).

As terrorists grew more savvy about television, they threatened to take control away from broadcasters. A German television journalist noted that during the Baader-Meinhoff organization's kidnapping of Peter Lorenz in 1975, "We lost control of the medium. We shifted shows to meet their timetable. [They demanded that] our cameras be in a position to record each of the prisoners . . . and our . . . coverage had to include prepared statements of their demands" (Hickey, quoted in Picard 54). In 1985, when TWA Flight 847 was hijacked to Beirut, the Amal militia made five hostages available at the airport for interviews with journalists (52). At the Commodore Hotel in Beirut, Howard Stringer of CBS News recalled that "one of the first things we saw was the Amal sign . . . telling us, 'All coverage is pool coverage'" (quoted in Picard 53).

Losing control, almost everyone agreed, meant playing into the terrorists' hands. Charles Fenyvasi, a reporter who in 1977 was one of 134 hostages seized by members of the Hanafi sect, emerged from captivity feeling that he and the others were part of a "high impact propaganda exercise programmed for the TV screen. . . . Reporters . . . help create [the news]. They are not objective observers, but subjective participants—actors, scriptwriters and idea men" (Schmid and de Graaf 42). Terrorist acts, argues N. C. Livingstone, are custom-made for the medium; they are relatively concise, dramatic, and "not so complex as to be unintelligible to those who tune in only briefly. . . . terrorism is so ideally suited to television that the medium would have invented the phenomenon if it had not already existed" (Weimann and Winn 95).

Popular terrorist fiction, too, came back in earnest: published in 1975, filmed in 1977, *Black Sunday* was only the most prominent "blockbuster thriller" to exploit public anxieties. But a new generation of more serious novelists was also ready, as Dostoevsky, James, and Conrad had been, to brood over the resemblance between "the men in small rooms" who write novels and those who plot terror. Like their illustrious predecessors, writers such as Doris Lessing and Don DeLillo, Mary McCarthy and Friedrich Dürrenmatt, find terrorist themes congenial for exploring the influence of fiction on history and politics, the relation between language and violence, the nature of power, and the impetus to resist. Unlike their predecessors, however, the new generation of writers had to cope with global electronic media, with a technology that could transmit its images around the world instantaneously, threatening all printed texts with extinction.

This is the story that the following chapters tell in detail, about how the contemporary terrorist novel conceives terrorism as a constructed phenomenon and measures terrorism's impact against its own possibilities for changing political and social reality. In the first section, "The Terrorist Rival," I look specifically at the phenomenon of televised terrorism in Don DeLillo's *Mao II* and Eoin McNamee's *Resurrection Man*. DeLillo once mused in an interview that television news was superseding the novel: "The news is fiction, the news is the new narrative—particularly, the dark news. . . . I think that from this kind of news people find a kind of narrative with a tragic stamp which in another time they found in fiction" (DeLillo, "Interview" 92). Or, as a character in his *Mao II* puts it, "Beckett was the last writer to shape the way we think and see. After him, the major work involves midair explosions" (157). This sense of the limitations of writing echoes through the novel's account of an exhausted writer offering himself as a hostage to Lebanese terrorists. The theme of rivalry is even more intense in *Resurrection Man*, set in a phantom Belfast where the death of literature already seems taken for granted. In both novels, the distinction between shooting with a camera or machine gun, or between a occupying a city with foreign troops or the international press corps, breaks down. Political reality is driven by images and shaped by the narrative conventions of television and film; the novel, tied to an outdated belief in the personal voice, is simply beside the point.

As both DeLillo and McNamee suggest, with their alertness to the bookishness of imprisoned terrorists and the writer's outbursts of violence, rivals have a way of becoming alter egos. In the second section of this book, "Displaced Causes," I turn to terrorist novels written by two women long associated with Leftist politics: Mary McCarthy, for years a contributor to the *Partisan Review* and later a highly visible opponent of U.S. involvement in Vietnam, and Doris Lessing, who joined the Communist Party as a teenager agitating for racial justice in Rhodesia and remained a member until the Soviet invasion of Hungary in 1956. The terrorist plots in *Cannibals and Missionaries* and *The Good Terrorist* displace the authors' own political histories. McCarthy's writers and intellectuals fly off to Iran to investigate the shah's regime and end up hostages of a Palestinian cell. Attractive and courageous as they are, the hostages' capacity for rationalization and self-criticism deter them from acting and blind them to the suicidal despair of their captors. The model of writer as activist blows up with the bombs that destroy the terrorists, their paintings, and most of their hostages. A similarly disillusioned and newly conservative Lessing suggests that radical action sooner or later leads the most idealistic rebels to ally themselves with a repressive power.

The writers in terrorist novels are nearly always guilty: of being radically chic, or of complicity with the repressive state, or, at the very least, of treating people around them selfishly, even violently. As a DeLillo character lectures one novelist, "It's the novelist who understands secret life, the rage that underlies all obscurity and neglect. You're half murderers, all of you (158)." In the third section, "Novelist as Terrorist: Terrorism as Fiction," I trace what J. M. Coetzee portrays as an inevitable logic that links Dostoevsky to Sergei Nechaev, the real-life model for the terrorist in *Devils*. Coetzee's Dostoevsky recognizes his own violence and understands writing as aggression—as plagiarism, appropriation, and perversion. Coetzee imagines the great writer working under humiliating restraints, unable either to change or transcend history.

All of the novels considered in this book demonstrate a sensitivity to the constructed nature of terrorist plots. But in Friedrich Dürrenmatt's *The Assignment*, the central terrorist incident, the kidnapping of a Swiss psychiatrist's wife, is pure invention, a hoax. Suggesting the difficulty of distinguishing between the victims and practitioners of terror, Dürrenmatt undermines the usual story of sinister Islamic terrorists preying on the West. Terrorism in his novel belongs as much to the illusory order as to its half-imagined opposition; it is dispersed through government and business and can be found as well in high culture and in the representational practices taken for granted in realistic novels and mass journalism. Yet although he thoroughly recognizes the popular critique of the letter as terrorizing, Dürrenmatt implicitly argues that a novel about terrorism can present what is otherwise "unrepresentable, incommensurate" in our experience of public violence (Lyotard 81).

The fourth section, "Is Terrorism Dead?" notes that although novels about terrorists and writers often express a loss of confidence in the power of art, they usually show terrorism, however crudely, making its mark on London, Belfast, czarist Petersburg. But Philip Roth's *Operation Shylock* and Robert Stone's *Damascus Gate* suggest that art and terrorism are equally illusionary and politically ineffective. It is a theme taken even further by Antoine Volodine in his *Lisbonne dernière marge*, where the terrorist *is*, quite simply, the novelist. The private imagination, the solitary brooding of DeLillo's "men in small rooms," does not drive public events, and terrorists are as powerless as writers.

Throughout this study, I note variations on the terrorist as the writer's rival, double, or secret sharer, tracing them from their origins in the romantic conviction of the writer's originality and power through a century of political, social, and technological developments that undermine that belief. This theme leads back and forth between actual bombs and stories about bombings, from the world to the electronic image, from the exercise of political power to fiction that meditates on the writer's power in the world.

Part I

The Terrorist Rival

1

Don DeLillo's
Mao II and the Rushdie Affair

Terror, like a toxic airborne event, floats across the deceptively shiny surfaces of Don DeLillo's fiction, turning the reassuring rituals of even suburban life—filling up at the self-service pump or playing golf—into desperate acts. The intersecting planes of that world, even at its glossiest, always include nameless dread, the possibility that the banal will erupt into violence, the clichés of the tabloid come to life. Not surprisingly, terrorists, cult murderers, assassins, and hit men have always been at home in that world, but *Mao II* (1991) marks a new phase, DeLillo's first extended exploration of the relationship between terrorists and writers. More starkly than his predecessors in the genre, DeLillo displays a contemporary world in which terrorism's televised narrative has replaced the novel, transforming the writer into an anonymous and voiceless hostage.

Whatever other influences may be at play in *Mao II*, since 14 February 1989, when the Ayatollah Ruhollah Khomeini issued his *fatwa*, or decree, it has been impossible to think about terrorists and writers without thinking of the Rushdie affair, that enormous political and media event that threatens to swallow up the actual Salman Rushdie, the actual *Satanic Verses*. Although *Mao II* contains no direct references to it, the questions the affair raises about the enmeshment of contemporary writers with electronic journalism, fundamentalism, and terrorism provide DeLillo's novel with its most pressing themes. Rushdie's novel and the author's fate make an inescapable context for reading *Mao II*.[1]

The Satanic Verses (*SV*) begins with Rushdie's characteristic mixture of documentary realism, literary allusion, and magic: two Indian actors, who will share the interchangeable identities of the angel Gabriel and

Satan, fall into the English Channel from a jet exploding at precisely 29,002 feet, the height of Mount Everest. Victims of a terrorist bombing modeled on the blowing up of an Air India Boeing 747 off the coast of Ireland in 1985, they survive miraculously to undergo more fantastic sufferings: one metamorphoses into a horned and hoofed Beelzebub, while the other, increasingly haunted by nightmares and pathological jealousy, is diagnosed as a paranoid schizophrenic and commits suicide. To those familiar with postmodern art, the novel's subsequent juxtapositions of *Othello* allusions with advertising jingles, or of fantasies about medieval Arabia with quasi-journalistic exposés of police brutality in contemporary England, scarcely seem surprising. Blurring history and fiction to make the historical appear fantastic is the stock in trade of such books. The 1983 Hawkes Bay incident, for example, in which a Pakistani woman, Naseem Fatima, led thirty-eight Shiah pilgrims to their deaths in the sea out of the mistaken belief that it would part to allow them to pass safely to the holy city of Kerbala, needs little fictional transformation to fit into the phantasmagoric world of Gibreel Farishta's unwelcome dreams.[2]

Similarly, to imagine the possibility, which lurks in an apocryphal tradition, that the Qu'ran might be an edited text, that Muhammed might briefly have allowed into it a few verses of satanic origin, seems harmless enough; retelling stories in new registers is, to those schooled on *Ulysses*, unastonishing.[3] If we could read the novel innocent of all knowledge about book burnings and murdered translators, we would turn to leisurely explications—of its debts to James Joyce and *The Thousand and One Nights*, or its diversion of *Our Mutual Friend* into a musical called *Friend!* or *"The Chums*, as it was known in the business" (421).

This perspective, however, has largely been denied us. Operating in the best postmodern manner, history has violated the boundaries of this fiction. The Ayatollah Khomeini, mentioned once by name in the text and travestied in an extended episode as an exiled imam who returns to his homeland to stop time and wreak apocalyptic damage on his people, seemed to rise from its pages to condemn the author to death. And as he did so, as the protestors screamed and fell under police gunfire, the text seemed to offer its own sardonic commentary: "Fiend, the Imam is wont to thunder. Apostate, blasphemer, fraud"; "Those who listen to the Devil's verses, spoken in the Devil's tongue . . . will go to the Devil"; "Burn the books and trust the Book"; "Your blasphemy, Salman, can't be forgiven" (*SV* 209, 484, 211, 374).

Compelled to focus on its political and religious themes, and on the episode of the satanic verses especially, the well-trained Western reader has no difficulty agreeing with Rushdie's remarks in *Imaginary Homelands* (*IH*) that his novel "dissents . . . from imposed orthodoxies *of all types* . . . from the end of debate, of dispute, of dissent" (*IH* 396, emphasis in original). Rushdie's political aim is familiar: through modestly experimental devices—multiple narrators, time shifts, the violation of realistic decorum by improbable coincidences, magical events—to liberate the reader from the tyranny of an inerrant text. As in DeLillo's *Libra*, Robert Coover's *Public Burning*, or J. G. Farrell's Empire trilogy, storytelling in *The Satanic Verses* is meant to act on a world already saturated by narratives, urging the reader to consider an alternative perspective, hoping to free up some space in the real world for another interpretation of the patriotic myth, the official version, the sacred text. Though familiar to those of us who actually read such works, and for whom their views are already congenial—the Rosenbergs should not have been electrocuted, the Warren Commission Report is untrustworthy—the assumption that postmodern or experimental texts can transform the world is seldom tested in the world of actual politics. It is oddly touching, then, to read Ziaddin Sardar's observation that "since *The Satanic Verses* . . . we have had a long line of bearded academics telling us that magical realism is a new and liberating form of literature that benefits Third World folk" (305).

The Rushdie affair has become the exemplary instance of the postmodernist political novel encountering actual politics, actual violence. The deaths of Rushdie's Japanese translator and of at least fifteen protesters, and the miserable life imposed on the author, are elements that do not usually figure in reception studies. Nor is any Western branch of criticism prepared to read a text on the terms Muslim tradition regards as appropriate for the Qu'ran. According to believers, it is the perfect transcription of the voice of God; "as an 'uncreated' part of the godhead [it] cannot be translated" (Ruthven 55). Thus even the strictly verbal responses to Rushdie disorient one trained in the pieties of academic criticism. In the stream of outrage, the most fundamental assumption of literary discourse, that one actually reads the text one criticizes, was repeatedly flouted because, as the member of parliament who led the fight to ban the book in India, Syed Shahabuddin, pointed out, one "does not have to wade through a filthy drain to know what filth is" (153).

Context, and the whole series of Western conventions surrounding parody and satire, fell by the wayside. Quite typical is the complaint of one Islamic critic quoting another's article in *India Today:* "Ayesha, the youngest wife of the Prophet . . . is shown, in the words of Madhu Jain . . . 'clad only in butterflies' leading 'an entire village, lemming-like into the Arabian Sea" (Dixit et al. 83), a view that conflates Rushdie's contemporary holy woman with the Prophet's wife because both are called Ayesha. The perception that Rushdie "portrays [the wives of the Prophet] as prostitutes" because he describes a brothel where twelve women assume the roles and names of the Prophet's wives was commonplace (Mustapha 38; see *IH* 397).[4] Polemicists unfamiliar with the Jamesian injunction to grant the writer his donnée claimed that *The Satanic Verses* is blasphemous because Rushdie deliberately ignores such facts as the "mathematical proof that the Quran came directly from the Supreme Being because it is the only book in the world with an intricate mathematical interlocking formula" (Mustapha 56). In the United States, where the separation of church and state makes blasphemy laws unconstitutional, two men equally unpracticed in the folkways of literary criticism, Jimmy Carter and the late archbishop John James O'Connor, entered the lists to express their solidarity with militant Islam against what the former called "an insult to the sacred beliefs of our Muslim friends" (Appignanesi and Maitland 236–38; Dooley 127). Evidently a threat to one orthodoxy threatens them all.

But it was not only that the Rushdie affair made visible the yawning gulf that separates postmodernist fiction and the well-schooled critic from the struggling immigrant Muslim in Bradford or a Baptist former president of the United States. It also revealed, as Islamic spokespersons were quick to point out, the extent to which some of those practiced Western attitudes had themselves become orthodoxies.[5] In an essay responding to the blasphemy charges, Rushdie quoted Western writers and intellectuals from Joyce and Beckett to Foucault and Lyotard. His arguments, reasonable and indeed moving as they are to those who share his assumptions, recall the *suras* of the Qu'ran his critics cite to defend their positions, authorities whose authority is not universally conceded. In language that later seemed naive, Rushdie expressed a sense of outrage that must have been shared by many literary scholars: "It has been bewildering to learn that people *do not care about art*" (*IH* 397, emphasis in original). Although often measured and gracious about Islamic tradition, at times he seemed patronizing; his plaintive remark that he had been rejected "by [his] own characters" has a proprietary ring (*IH* 395). Many earnest defenses of Rushdie's right to publish seemed considerably less aware of Islamic sensibilities than the author was; the most notorious remarks, the comments of the novelist Fay Weldon, called the Qu'ran "food for no-thought" and characterized the Bradford Muslims as "primitive folk . . . mad fundamentalists" (Weldon 6, 8).[6]

It is surprisingly difficult to find a middle ground between Islamic orthodoxy, as represented by the protesters if not by the *fatwa,* and the Western literary orthodoxy represented by Norman Mailer's heroic declaration that "maybe we are even willing, ultimately, to die for the idea that serious literature . . . is the absolute we will defend" (Appignanesi and Maitland 164). One could, of course, simply concede to the protestors, as the editors of *Public Culture* did, when they challenged "the post- Enlightenment assumption . . . that all intelligent criticism must *follow* the individualized act of reading" and defended "the rights of people to resist reading" (iv, emphasis in original). If Westerners continued to find reading books before burning them desirable, they could not deny their own inability to master the history and culture that shape other people's unwillingness to do so. Although Edward Said, a friend of Rushdie's, defended "the brilliance" of his "deliberately transgressive" novel, his conception of "Orientalism" was frequently used to brand the book and those who defended it as heirs to a thousand years of Western stereotypes about the fiendish Turk (Appignanesi and Maitland 166, 164).[7] Western readers' probable ignorance, not only of Islam, but of everything from Urdu to Indian cinema, was evoked as the only possible explanation of sympathy for the satanic novelist.[8]

Indeed, Western readers, unable to pin down the facts and thus incessantly told that they do not understand, may hesitate to speak at all.[9] In this case they can defer to those readers with more knowledge of the cultural context who encourage Westerners to look for Islamic diversity. Rushdie himself persuasively argues that the book burners represent only one strand of Islamic tradition, which "contains ribaldry as well as solemnity, irreverence as well as absolutism" (*IH* 409). Even more compelling is Gayatri Spivak's troubled evocation of the suppressed voices of Islamic women in India with its warning that cultural relativism not become an excuse for abetting their suppression. Sara Suleri's brilliant reading notes Rushdie's "profound cultural fidelity" even though *The Satanic Verses* represents "specific acts of religious betrayal" (60). Each urges us to consider the multiple perspectives of Indian, or Islamic, people, to understand their traditions of dissent and self-division, and to distrust official spokespersons.

Yet if Western readers do well to exhibit some diffidence about their expertise in Islamic theology and to consider the history of colonialism and racism that fuels the resistance of many Muslims to Western cultural innovations like postmodern fiction, they are on safer ground when they ask what the Rushdie affair says about the fate of the novel. For really two distinct, yet oddly complementary, features of contemporary life worked against *The Satanic Verses:* the resurgence of religious fundamentalism and the explosion of the electronic media.[10] On the one hand, we note the extreme literalism of Rushdie's opponents, their unwillingness to accept "the fictionality of fiction" (Rushdie *IH* 393). The "death of the author," in the West a philosophical proposition, became in Iranian hands a large cash incentive, and a promise of paradise, for the assassination of a Booker Prize winner. Yet in a sense the literalism of the British Muslims who burned the book in the streets of Bradford was a tribute to the printed page that is rare indeed in the West; they did not regard the novel as an inconsequential imaginative exercise but as a powerful expression of ideas deeply engaged with reality.[11]

On the other hand, the familiar enemy of the print text, the electronic media, arouses Baudrillardian anxieties. As Daniel Pipes points out, the 14 February *fatwa* has all the marks of a media event; had the ayatollah simply wanted Rushdie dead he could have dispatched a hit squad months earlier, when British Muslims began their protests.[12] "Broadcasting his intentions allowed Rushdie to take cover, so Khomeini's real goal must . . . have been . . . something quite different" (97).[13] An apocalyptic vision of all solid ground disappearing, to be replaced by a vertiginous mass of images, attaches itself to the phenomenon of the writer who disappears into the spy fiction world of safe houses and Secret Service protection. Surely the text of *The Satanic Verses* also seems to disappear, in spite of phenomenal sales, into televised images created by angry men who pride themselves on not having read it.[14] Surely, too, the claims of political fiction to act on the world seem overwhelmed by the world's evident ability, especially when kept instantly up-to-date by satellite, to act on novel and novelist.

Of course, it is possible to say that Rushdie's rejection by Muslim immigrants resembles Joyce's rejection by the Irish and to hope "a rising generation of British Asians" will discover "that Rushdie has been writing to their own interests" (Murray 51). One can assert that "words go deep, that stories last." But as one critic and practitioner of postmodern political fiction goes on to say, in our day "such propositions are frankly theological" (Pfeil 38). A real virtue of Don DeLillo's *Mao II* is that it moves beyond such testimonials to imagine the implications of the Rushdie affair for novels and novelists.

"If I were a writer," remarks a character in Don DeLillo's 1982 novel *The Names*, "how I would enjoy being told the novel is dead. How liberating, to work in the margins" (77). How hopeful this remark seems, assuming that the death of the novel is only a cliché, perhaps even an opportunity. In *Mao II*, as in the Rushdie affair, worn-out metaphors have a way of becoming ominous. In this 1991 novel, the old literary system seems thoroughly dead; writers are blocked, taken hostage, lose their identities, die. A new information technology creates the desire for, then enables, the features of contemporary life most hostile to the novel: terrorism, a resurgence of fundamentalism, a crowd psychology characterized by longing for authority.

Though *Mao II* contains no direct allusions to *The Satanic Verses*, it shares many of its themes and motifs. Like Rushdie, DeLillo continually displays the objects and effects of the electronic revolution: television is omnipresent, Muzak plays in the bookstore, terrorists watch a VCR in their hideout near Beirut. Key characters in both books make their living in the post-Gutenberg world: DeLillo has his photojournalist, Rushdie his cinema star and his television actor, the voice of the talking ketchup bottle and the garlic-flavored potato crisp. Benign technologies reveal a sinister side: Rushdie's voice-over actor drives his cinema star mad by doing impersonations over the telephone whereas DeLillo's writer worries about the role of answering machines in terrorist bombings: "You enter your code in Brussels and blow up a building in Madrid" (91). National boundaries are frequently crossed in these books where international jet travel is a tedious reality, not an adventure; both writers contemplate the in-flight movie as an emergent genre. Characters in both speak the global or Third World English of those who come to it with an imperfect education gained far from English-speaking countries; both note the saturation of Third World countries by First World advertising, itself a new language, the "esperanto of jet lag" (DeLillo 23). Both books portray the desire for fundamentalism, for purity of doctrine and strong authorities who override the fragmented contradictory self; and although they criticize mass movements bitterly, they convey the intensity of that desire, as it is experienced by the believer, sympathetically.

Similarly, although DeLillo avoids dates and never mentions the Rushdie affair directly, *Mao II* is set in 1989, the year of the *fatwa*. Three public events from that year flit across television screens: the deaths of ninety-three people in Sheffield, suffocated or trampled at the soccer stadium; the funeral of the ayatollah; and the Tiananmen massacre. To underscore this point, part 1 is introduced by a photograph taken at Sheffield, part 2 by a photograph of the Khomeini funeral. These events and photographs, which associate large crowds with death and mass hysteria, seem to evoke a missing fourth, the famous book burning.[15] And if there is no fictionalized Rushdie, DeLillo's protagonist is a novelist who dies on his way to Beirut, where he had hoped to exchange himself for a poet held hostage by terrorists.

If the Rushdie affair dramatizes the conflict between postmodern conceptions of political fiction and current political realities, DeLillo's novel provides a larger context in the by-now familiar conflict between actual late-twentieth-century life and romantic notions about the writer. "Born under the old tutelage," to use a phrase he admires, Bill Gray seems part J. D. Salinger, part Thomas Pynchon, and perhaps part Don DeLillo as well (215).[16] Grown rich and famous from two early novels, Bill has spent twenty-three years writing and rewriting a third, "struggl[ing] for every word" (52). To reduce the pain of this struggle, he has, of course, taken to drink, and to a whole rainbow of prescription drugs as well. As if to parody the romantic role, he freely chooses the elaborately policed seclusion into which the ayatollah drove the sociable Salman Rushdie: guests are driven to see him at night, on back roads without signposts. His isolation reinforces radical individuality; all but literally a self-made man, he conceals his unpoetic real name, Willard Skansey, even from his best friends. His individuality is deeply connected to his claims about the novel itself, which expresses a unique personal vision. Writers, in his view, have a high calling, are supposed to transform "the inner life of the culture," tell us stories that "absorb our terror" (41, 140). Novels, perhaps especially when they do not take politics as their theme, implicitly support a liberal political system: "the novel . . . [is] a democratic shout" (159).

The old romantic view of novelists and novels always risked declining into self-pity and self-indulgence; as Bill's daughter puts it, "writing was never the burden and sorrow you made it out to be but . . . your convenient alibi for every possible failure to be decent" (114). Worse yet, the romantic role could simply become a "lifestyle." Reemerging into New York, finding himself lost in the new talk of audiocassettes and miniseries, Bill reminisces about parties held in the 1950s and pleads for the old system: "Remember literature, Charlie? It involved getting drunk and getting laid" (122).

Whatever Bill Gray's self-indulgence and violence, they pale beside his apparent victimization and his realization of the "failure" of contemporary novelists "to be dangerous" (157). In his hideaway, Bill seems already hostage to Scott Martineau, the hero-worshiping Midwesterner who moved in eight years ago to help out. Scott's arrangements suggest a new version of the old academic devotion to text, a private archive rivaling the University of Texas's vast collection of manuscripts, in which the meaning of words is less important than their physical embodiment in manuscript, quarto, and folio. Their house is an archive; one room contains galleys, manuscripts, correspondence, reviews; another holds copies of the two published novels in all of their editions and translations; a third, bunker-like room in the basement contains two hundred thick binders filled with drafts and revisions for the novel-in-progress. Such worship has a sinister side.

Scott sees himself not only as enabling Bill to write but also as the guardian of his image. Convinced that the essentially completed third novel is a failure, Scott urges Bill to withhold it; another publication "would be the end of Bill as a myth, as a force" (52). He brings a photographer, Brita Nilsson, into the house, telling her that her photograph of Bill is all the public needs: "the book disappears into the image of the author" (71).

Brita's project is archival, too; she has spent years creating a "planetary record" of the world's writers, photographing as many of them as possible (25). Once a photographer of war and famine, she condemns the aestheticizing tendencies of the photographic image: "no matter what I shot. . . it was all so fucking pretty in the end" (24–25).[17] Now she has a "disease called writers," and as she photographs Bill, she seems convinced of their old claims to social importance. Bill, however, suspects that her project is a memorial: "a portrait doesn't mean anything until the subject is dead" (42).

Scott also brings home Karen, who, in Bill's words, "carries the virus of the future" (119). Simple, gentle, and compassionate, she nonetheless is infected with the postmodern world, as seen in Jean Baudrillard's apocalyptic vision. A former member of a cult led by a charismatic Korean "master," she yearns for clarity and authority. Hers is the sensibility through which we understand the appeal of fundamentalism and the difficulty of distinguishing between images and reality. She is the character who wanders through an exhibit of contemporary art, bewildered that an actual spoon has been glued to canvas; she is the character who watches the televised scenes from Sheffield, Tehran, and Peking. Scott muses that she is "thin-boundaried" and believes everything that she sees on television, making no distinction between hard news and advertisements (119). Yet her easy identification with the delirious mourners at Khomeini's funeral also suggests that, even in Bill's hideaway, she participates in a global culture every bit as much as Gibreel Farishta does. When, still later, she wanders the streets of Manhattan urging the homeless to think of "God all minute every day," we realize that she even speaks the new global English (193).

The criticism she implicitly offers of romantic isolation, with its foundations in a solidly bourgeois notion of the private life, may or may not contribute to Bill's decision to go to Beirut. More certainly, her tendency to conflate televised images becomes ominous. We have a disturbing sense that her master, the "chunky man in a business suit from the Republic of Korea" (186), and the ayatollah responsible for the Rushdie *fatwa* are almost interchangeable in her mind, their followers, like the Chinese in Tiananmen Square dispersed by troops, "one crowd replaced by another" (177). Her association of the "light inside of her" that shines when Khomeini dies with the "beautiful-sounding Shining Path" (187), the Peruvian *Sendero Luminoso*, suggests how short the distance between enthusiastic fundamentalism and the practice of terror can be.

Through Karen, too, DeLillo suggests that artists like Bill bear some responsibility for the dazzling world of simulacra in which we currently live. No one, remarks Charlie, knows better than a writer "how reality is invented," and DeLillo's text seems to entertain an ancient suspicion of artists (132). Between Plato's distrust of the artist as a liar and magician, a man who can paint the bed he could not build, and Baudrillard's distrust of the hyperreal, "the generation by models of a real without origin or reality," there is a clear line of descent (166). Seen through Brita Nilsson's eyes, a Warholish Russian painting called *Gorby II* illustrates the political implications of simulacra. It is a "maximum statement about the dissolvability of the artist and the exaltation of the public figure, about how it is possible to fuse images, Mikhail Gorbachev's and Marilyn Monroe's, and to steal auras, Gold Marilyn's and Dead-White Andy's" (134). What is the connection between the artist who painted *Gorby II* and a political world driven by such images? Between that artist and Karen, who conflates Korean messiahs with Khomeini and Mao, or between the artist and a magazine editor in Chile who published caricatures of General Pinochet and then is sent to jail for "assassinating the image of the general" (44)?

Bill's growing realization of the centrality of such images to contemporary culture is a major reason that his Thoreauvian life rings false even at the beginning of the novel. To be a celebrity in an age of paparazzi is to realize that privacy has been redefined: he is not "the woodsman-writer" but the "hunted man" (102). "In the mosque, no images": Bill finds the hostility to representation on which Rushdie transgressed appealing, yet he also recognizes the grandiosity of refusing the world one's image. After all, it is Allah and his Prophet who must not be depicted: a writer who "won't show his face" is "playing God's own trick" (37). But if, by consenting to be photographed, he agrees to engage his culture on its own terms, he also recognizes its dangers. Half realizing that Scott intends to substitute his image for his new book, he escapes to meet Charlie Everson, his agent, in New York and discovers the "new culture, the system of world terror" (112).

Plot developments reinforce theme: Charlie, thriving participant in the new literary scene that he is, belongs to a committee on free expression that has been contacted by the kidnappers of a Swiss poet, Jean-Claude Julien. At Charlie's instigation, Bill flies to London to read the poet's work before an audience of journalists; the terrorists promise to release the poet simultaneously "on live television in Beirut" (98). The poetry reading, however, is canceled when a bomb blows up its site, but for Bill the die is cast. As part of his effort to help his fellow writer, he agrees to meet with George Haddad, a Lebanese political scientist "photographed in the company of known terrorist leaders," who has frequently acted as their apologist and intermediary with the West (131). Haddad—the resemblance to Edward Said as he might be imagined by George Will is striking—convinces Bill to go a step further, to continue talks about releasing the poet privately, in Athens.

When Bill Gray moves into the shadowy world of international terrorism, he is not entirely a stranger to it; like other fictional writers we have seen, he occasionally behaves like the terrorist's alter ego. The old idea of the writer produced "men in small rooms" plotting to change the world and was also accompanied by an emotional violence that makes Charlie speculate that writing not only comes out of "bitterness and rage" but actually produces them in the writer (101).[18] One notes Bill's dependence on an IRA man to forward his mail and that his eyes become "rifleman's slits" when Scott accosts him (60). Driving to meet Bill, Brita Nilsson remarks that she feels as if she is "being taken to see some terrorist chief at his secret retreat" (27). As Haddad says, "It's the novelist who understands the secret life, the rage that underlies all obscurity and neglect. You're half murderers, all of you" (158).

But in Bill's view, the old affinity between terrorists and novelists, as solitary rebels and plotters, has turned into a corporate takeover of art by violent people who manipulate the media. Information technology, which increases the publicity on which terrorism has always depended, becomes almost inseparable from it: "There were the camera-toters and the gun-wavers and Bill saw barely a glimmer of difference" (197). The public is addicted to "news of terror, to tape recorders and cameras, to radios, to bombs stashed in radios. News of disaster is the only narrative people need. The darker the news, the grander the narrative" (42). Haddad adds, "the more clearly we see terror, the less impact we feel from art" (157).

As modish intellectual par excellence, Haddad sees this process as benign and inevitable and urges Bill to recognize that terrorists are the "only possible heroes" for our time. They are the only people left who have not been "incorporated"; they use the media, they speak "the language of being noticed, the only language the West understands" (157). While it is true, Haddad concedes, that terrorists operate on behalf of authoritarian regimes and are not really romantic, solitary outlaws, he urges Bill to accept the purity and necessity of those regimes. If Bill's fear is that the world no longer offers a role for writers, Haddad is all optimism. As willing as the editors of *Public Culture* to transcend the Enlightenment model, he argues that books are necessary to totalitarian regimes. Bill should think like a Maoist, hoping to write one of those little red books that give a culture its "unchanged narrative" (162). Moreover, as he urges Bill to take up word processing, even this blameless tool acquires a sinister side, enabling writers to dispense with the constraints of reality: "You don't deal with heavy settled artifacts. You transform freely, fling words back and forth" (164).

But for Bill, "total politics, total authority, total being" (158) require mass murder, the death of the spirit, and certainly the end of the novel. Like Rushdie, and also like Mikhail Bakhtin and Milan Kundera, Bill sees the essence of the novel as skepticism, the representation of conflicting voices, a tolerance of ambiguity. Writing must "increase the flow of meaning, be a "reply to power" (200). These beliefs, and a love of the well-turned phrase, are ones for which this reclusive man is willing to die; as Haddad speaks, Bill loses his usual sardonic detachment and begins to say no. Jean-Claude's image looming large in his mind, he fixates on the possibility of rescuing him. When negotiations break down, he decides to travel to Beirut independently, though the more realistic Haddad tells him that doing so will be futile.

Of course, this heroic, almost Byronic, mission fails in a manner calculated to illustrate the forces that oppose such romantic and humanistic narratives. Bill, suffering from an injury incurred in a hit-and-run accident, dies on a freighter bound for Lebanon. The cleaner who finds his body steals his passport and other identity papers in order to sell them to "some militia in Beirut" (217). Abu Rashid sells Jean-Claude to a fundamentalist faction. Meanwhile, back at the hideout, the archival enterprise purrs on indefinitely, without the author, thanks to a check automatically deposited in Scott's account every month by computer. But before this ignominious end, DeLillo measures the effects of terrorism on the living writer.

Jean-Claude's situation invites comparison with the rich tradition Victor Brombert's *Romantic Prison* articulates. For the Swiss poet, being held hostage by terrorists is a descent into anonymity, not an opportunity to nurture uniqueness in the womb-like cell of a Stendhalian "happy prison." Forced to wear a hood in a small room in a location his captors never disclose to him, Jean-Claude suffers from sensory deprivation. At first he thinks to save himself by the traditional means; he tries to memorize details that might someday allow him to identify his location, plans to learn Arabic. As his sense of self fades, he begins to suffer from Stockholm syndrome, identifying with the boy in charge of feeding and torturing him. In this flat world outside history he has no time for originality; even his sexual fantasies, the stories he tells himself, must be banal and predictable, the same as the boy's. His VCR-watching captors forbid him to write, though he longs to do so: "written words could tell him who he was" (204). As Bill sees it, Jean-Claude disappears into "his own wan image" (161); to have been a writer was simply to have been more vulnerable to guerrillas: "It was writing that caused his life to disappear" (215).

Even Bill, theoretically free to keep writing himself into existence, loses the heart to do so. At first the culture of terror seems to give him purpose. By locking innocent people in rooms, terrorists act like bad artists; they "empty the world of meaning . . . replacing real things with plots and fictions" (200). He will use fiction to restore meaning; he will write about Jean-Claude in order to "bring him back" (200). It is an old-fashioned purpose, more Zola than Salinger or Bill Gray, and appropriately he is forced to carry it out with a pencil and pad, regretting the typewriter that belongs to his phase of literature: "it was the hand tool of memory and patient thought . . . he could see the words better in type" (160).

But Bill has too little strength left to carry out the project. Like any liberal, he is vulnerable to other people's burning convictions. As the Rushdie affair illustrates so well, skepticism can become an orthodoxy, but self-doubt stalks genuine skeptics. Thus although Bill can formulate the old humanistic claims for literature, that it is a reply to power, for example, he also can imagine valid objections to them: "George would have said that terrorists do not have power" (200). After his accident, he refuses to go to a hospital, becomes exhausted, and gives up writing: "It was harder than major surgery and it didn't even keep you alive" (198).

What is left for the writer who cannot write, who has lost faith in literature, is the sterile impulse to make up stories and to bring the narrative of his life to that conclusion toward which a DeLillo character once argued that all plots tend, death (*Libra* 221). Early in the novel Bill describes the pleasure he felt as a child when, like the protagonist of Robert Coover's *Universal Baseball Association*, he amused himself by making up whole baseball games. It was a "pure game of making up"

(46), a model for literature as simulacrum, renouncing transcendent claims, giving up its urgency about meaning, its desire to transform consciousness. It was invention without the pressures of originality, its goal to manipulate the clichés of broadcasting while remaining within a perfectly orderly structure. Despairing of his work in Athens, Bill looks up and says aloud: "Keltner takes his time, tipping a glance at the baseball. Hey what a toss. Like a trolley wire, folks" (198). If this is not the madness of living in a rule-bound world with no meaningful connection to reality, it is certainly close, and whatever its theoretical virtues, it fails to give Bill a reason to live.

The last use Bill makes of his talents is to transform himself into a character in an imaginary novel. Having lost his high calling, he seems reduced to the basic suffering animal self; as pain in his side and shoulder worsens, he refuses to seek medical help. When he meets a group of British veterinarians at a bar, he poses as a novelist needing a credible diagnosis for a character's mysterious injury. Falling into the game with well-liquored enthusiasm, they assure him between roars of laughter that his character is on the verge of acute infection from a lacerated liver and will soon fall into a coma and die if he does not see a doctor. Bill buys a ticket to Lebanon instead.

Though Bill Gray can scarcely be seen as a double for Don DeLillo, the death of this author suggests that if the novel is not dead, its circumstances at least are highly troubled. It is no accident that this death is a virtual suicide, and *Mao II* explores the failures of a romantic conception of writing: the isolation, self-importance, and self-pity for which it often provided a cover. But it also looks at the forces that led to the ayatollah's *fatwa* not as a bizarre concatenation of specific circumstances—a Bombay-born Muslim educated at Rugby and Cambridge provokes Islamic fundamentalists by representing their prophet in a postmodern novel just as their most "televisible" *mullah* comes to the inconclusive end of a devastating war—but as representative of the conditions of contemporary writing.

According to this novel, modern society is an inflammable mixture of the voiceless and invisible poor and a middle class that can only see what appears on the television screen: for Karen's mother, the "city nomads" of New York are "more strange . . . than the herdsmen of the Sahel, who at least turn up on the documentary channel" (4). Both groups, though for different reasons, are susceptible to the appeal of any

master who can offer "total vision, total politics"; both will find it easy
to excuse the violence necessary to execute his plan. Terrorists use the
latest information technology to promote medieval theologies and des-
potism. This technology permeates our lives, naturalizing even guerilla
war: at a bar in Athens, the dying writer notices "fashion references,"
women wearing "skull jewelry" and men in "camouflage sunglasses"
(211). When the addiction to televised terror becomes great enough, the
novel loses its power to move: no wonder that Bill finds it so easy to
identify with Jean-Claude the hostage. No wonder either that he suffers
a momentary hallucination in the bar where terrorism makes a fashion
statement: "he saw his book across the room, obese and lye-splashed,
the face an acid spatter, zipped up and decolored, with broken teeth
glinting out of the pulp" (210).

We can always say about DeLillo, as people tend to say about despairing writers, about Conrad at his most acerbic or Beckett as his most
nihilistic, that their willingness to keep on writing demonstrates some
well-concealed optimism. Yet little in this actual text consoles. In the last
chapter, we find Brita Nilsson in Beirut, having abandoned her project
of photographing writers. Going off to meet a real terrorist chieftain, the
same Abu Rashid that Bill hoped to meet, she observes that Beirut is a
"millennial image mill" (229). The intense red of advertisements for
Coke II contributes to the fantasy that they are promoting a new Maoist
group—Mao II, no doubt. Local militias have taken to a new form of
fighting, shooting up pictures of each other's leaders; Rashid's boy soldiers wear his picture on their shirts to "teach them identity . . . one man
every man" (233). History is dead, or at least can be remade at will after
lunch; in the midst of hopeless misery, Rashid echoes George Haddad's
platitudes about Mao. What might in another novel seem like a gleam of
hope, the wedding party Brita witnesses from her apartment window,
seems simply another testimony to human perversity, a belief that the
right pastel tuxedo will protect one from bombs. With both of the
novel's writers missing and presumed dead, the image alone remains as
Brita watches the flash from someone else's camera: "the dead city photographed one more time" (241).

DeLillo's pessimism about the circumstances that afflict contemporary writers is in many respects understandable; certainly the Rushdie
affair offers ample evidence that writers and texts can be made to disap-

pear, at least for a time, in a media blitz. Charlie Everson's prostate surgery, which has left him able to perform "enthusiastically" but without issue ("nothing comes out") seems a disquieting analogue for the literary scene as DeLillo imagines it (127). The kind of attention paid the book, the busy activity of getting movie rights, producing audiocassettes, merchandising in the mall, even storing up its successive drafts in an underground archive, may well be a sterile deflection from the vital transaction between a reader and a text.

In developing the implications of the novelist's encounter with terrorism and information technology, DeLillo has written a thoughtful book and has helped open up the wider implications of the Rushdie affair. But *Mao II* also seems complicit in the process it criticizes. If Bill's identity ends up being sold to Lebanese militia, we might be disturbed at the ease with which he has already absorbed Jean-Claude's identity. Early passages describing the Swiss writer appear to have the same ontological status as the passages describing other characters, but once Bill starts writing about Jean-Claude the passages describing him seem to come from his pencil rather than from the omniscient narrator. It is a familiar trick of modern fiction, not very different conceptually from what Faulkner does in *Absalom, Absalom!*, but it has the effect in *Mao II* of undermining belief in Jean-Claude as a distinctive personality. As Jean-Claude is reduced to being one of Bill's symptoms, his plight seems less significant.

Similarly, as he flashes from New York to London to Athens to Beirut, DeLillo seems so intent on reproducing the forces that homogenize the world that he gives up on the possibility of reproducing its heterogeneity. If Karen conflates the ayatollah and Mao with her Korean master, so does the novel, in its own rigorously synchronic portrayal of the Christian cult, Chinese Communism, and Islamic fundamentalism. Nothing about George Haddad seems especially Lebanese; nothing about Brita Nilsson seems Swedish. If Karen, roaming the streets of New York, stumbles into a world that television has not prepared her mother to find familiar, she has an answer: "It's just like Beirut" (176). Brita, visiting that city, finds it the "lunar part of us that dreams of wasted terrain": "Our only language is Beirut" (239). For the novel, this is a true insight. Everything in DeLillo's portrayal of Beirut, from its boy terrorists with "slightly murderous" eyes to its sandbagged shops to its Coca-Cola placards, could have been worked up from *Sixty Minutes*.

Yet surely we cannot help noticing, when we look at the fate of
Salman Rushdie and his *Verses*, that London is not Islamabad; Beirut is
probably not midtown Manhattan either. The Rushdie affair put a
whole complex of Western assumptions about the politics of postmodern art, about the nature of reading and of satire, up against traditional
Muslim assumptions about, among other matters, the nature of representation and the obligation to revealed truth, and found them, if not
wanting, at least not universal. "Cocacolonization," however objection-
able on any number of grounds, has not yet succeeded in erasing the
heterogeneity of history, religion, language, and culture. DeLillo's spec-
ulations about the effects of the esperanto of jet lag on global travelers
like Brita Nilsson or its implications for the future are intriguing, but he
does not broach the difficult history separating the wretched of Manhattan from the wretched of Beirut. The notion that reducing homelessness
in the United States would require different strategies and might be
marginally easier for Americans to accomplish than ending religious hatred in the Middle East is one the text is equally unable to address.

What one misses in *Mao II* finally is an old-fashioned novelistic virtue,
the attempt to communicate the distinctive accents of a culture, of a
time and place. Bill Gray expresses nostalgia for the novel that shows us
"one thing unlike another, one voice unlike another" (159), but the book
in which he appears seems to have abandoned that goal. Certainly the
degree of realism in *The Satanic Verses* is much greater, and the attempt
to render the differences between, say, Bombay and London or between
English as spoken by Pakistanis and by the native British is both more
obvious and more successful. It is this realistic texture as well as a mor-
alizing ending, complete with a father's deathbed and the spiritual re-
generation of one of its leading characters, that justifies Sara Suleri's
remark that the book "begins as Joyce and ends as Dickens" (606). If
DeLillo's vision of the world as a "millennial image mill" is accurate, if
books do not really matter very much, then no view of fiction can matter very much either. Yet, as opposed to the grandiose claims DeLillo
satirizes, which do seem to have come to grief in the Rushdie affair, this
very modest one—that fiction might help us distinguish Beirut from
New York and respect the nuances of difference as well as deplore universal disasters—seems well worth pressing.

2

Eoin McNamee's
Resurrection Man

urking behind Bill Gray's encounter with terrorism is the possibility that writers are so powerless, their books so seldom read,
as to render the question of their political influence moot. In *Resurrection Man*, a 1994 novel about the Northern Irish Troubles, Eoin Mc-
Namee also seems to assume the death of the novel as a social force. His
writers are two journalists, one dying of cancer and the other drifting
into alcoholism; his terrorists are secondary school dropouts, Protestant
boys from the Shankill Road. If McNamee's grim city contains poets
delusional enough to consider themselves its unacknowledged legislators, they remain silent. Yet, paradoxically, in this world cut off from high
culture, characters close to illiteracy brood over the power of language,
and a trained sensitivity to the nuances of public relations rhetoric and
an acuteness about the strategies of fictional plotting allow a journalist to
predict the course of political events with astonishing accuracy.

McNamee's novel has a strong postmodern bent, to be detected in the
paranoia that informs its plot, in a tone that allows irony to shade into
parody and pastiche, and perhaps also in its preoccupation with the images of film and television at the expense of such features of the older
realistic novel as fully developed characters and a thoroughgoing interest in history. The application of such techniques to a novel set in
the midst of Northern Ireland's contemporary troubles is surprising,
even disturbing, because it forces readers to look at the conflict in a new
context.

After all, for a long time it has been axiomatic that Irish politics are an
anachronism. In a celebrated image, Churchill saw the "dreary steeples
of Fermanagh and Tyrone" reemerging as the deluge of the Great War
subsided. Along with the massive political and social changes wrought

by war, Churchill argued that elsewhere "the mode and thought of men
. . . have encountered violent and tremendous change." Yet such fundamental transformations scarcely touched Catholics and Protestants in
the North of Ireland; the "integrity of their quarrel" was one of the few
"institutions" to survive the "cataclysm . . . unaltered" (329).

Churchill's view has had a long life. Familiar features of Northern Ireland's cultural landscape, whether wall posters of King Billy accompanied by exhortations to "Remember the Boyne" or nationalist ballads
about the brave Wexford men and Kevin Barry answering no, have rein-
forced many a newspaper columnist's sense of the current troubles as a
"tribal" war. In this view, Northern Ireland today is in but not of the
early twenty-first century, and the most relevant context for explaining
its conflicts is the distant past.

McNamee suggests, on the contrary, that contemporary Northern Ireland is just as much a part of the global electronic culture as Pynchon's
Los Angeles or, for that matter, Rushdie's New Delhi. Whatever their
origins, the "tribal" hatreds of the North are now modulated through
sensibilities shaped by cinematic and televised violence. Irish history,
McNamee suggests, is less present to the relatively uneducated foot soldiers in its sectarian wars than America's mythic urban ganglands and
Wild West. Though his story often seems fantastic, it sticks surprisingly
close to the documented public record; McNamee never denies the force
or reality of public history but instead emphasizes the power of elec-
tronically transmitted myths to influence our perceptions of reality and
to act on that reality. Northern Ireland as he presents it is a place that
confirms the aptness of Baudrillard's argument about the contemporary
electorate: "It is the football match or film or cartoon which serve as
models for perception of the political sphere" (37). Movies, television,
and popular journalism are media through which McNamee's grim
"city" acquires its knowledge of itself; they help it make sense of its violence and its pathologies and direct the actors in its political dramas.

A foreign reader is in some danger, given the novel's modestly "postmodern" elements, of concluding that the story he tells is invented. To
stage torture murders in the back rooms of pubs, where an audience
cheers each knife cut, seems barely probable; for the murderers to call
these places "Romper Rooms" after a local television program for children seems like a satirical touch, the invention of some jaded relic of the
Gutenberg era. The inference that the murders are tolerated, even abet-
ted, by some dim receding series of politicians and officials who are
covering up their own participation in a homosexual ring, organized by

one of the terrorists, that molests boys from state homes seems even more fantastic. Yet as any longtime reader of the *Belfast Telegraph* could testify, McNamee's story is well grounded in the public record.

The ringleader of McNamee's terrorists is Victor Kelly, a figure closely modeled on Lenny Murphy, a young Protestant with a Catholic name from the working-class Shankill neighborhood of Belfast.[1] Between 21 July 1972, when he was one of several men who participated in the murder of Francis Adams, and 16 November 1982, when Murphy was machine-gunned to death in front of his girlfriend's house in Glencairn, he was either actively involved in terrorist activities or in prison because of them. He and his unit killed perhaps as many as two dozen people: most of the victims were randomly selected men assumed to be Catholic because of the pubs they frequented or the neighborhoods in which they lived; a few were UVF (Ulster Volunteer Force) men killed in retaliation for such disciplinary violations as selling a gun to a Catholic or robbing an elderly Protestant woman. Some crime scenes were littered with the victims' teeth and fingernails; most victims had multiple stab wounds; some had nearly been decapitated. Although large numbers of working-class Protestants knew the identities of the "Shankill butchers," who after all did some of their "rompering" in public, their activities continued for a decade both because they had thoroughly intimidated the community and because Murphy's wiles matched his brutality.

Like McNamee's Victor, Murphy attended trials of other terrorists, later making good use of legal tips he acquired. Having learned, for example, that a witness's identification of a suspect can be discounted if the suspect has drawn attention to himself, he avoided a murder conviction by pitching a scene in a police lineup. On another occasion, when he was jailed on suspicion of having murdered a man named Pavis, authorities injudiciously assigned Murphy to work in the pharmacy. There he stole the cyanide he poured down the throat of the only witness against him, a fellow prisoner named Mervyn Connor, after first forcing him to sign a confession claiming responsibility for Pavis's murder and exonerating Murphy. Murphy's ability to enter Connor's cell undetected strongly suggests that he had help from a sympathetic guard; a police file containing records of an investigation into the poisoning later went missing. Afterward, one of the "police officers placed in charge of conducting the enquiry in the prison was . . . connected with files which went missing in relation to the enquiry into the homosexual abuse of young boys at the Kincora home in Belfast" (Dillon 30).

Since this suspicious circumstance may be the only shred of evidence linking the historical Murphy to the Kincora scandal, McNamee diverges from the public record most sharply by creating a character named Billy McClure, who welds the two stories together. In *Resurrection Man*'s paranoid plot, McClure is both Victor Kelly's associate, "the first to use the Romper Room," and a convicted pedophile who arranges for a series of parties to be held at the flat of Victor's girlfriend, Heather Graham (28). At these parties, "well-spoken Englishmen in suits, off-duty policeman, senior figures in the UDA," and media figures, men "from the Gibraltar," take boys McClure has procured into a wire-tapped bedroom. After manipulating Victor into leaving his last hideout to visit his family, McClure watches his execution; Heather, seeing McClure on television that night, observes a "custodial expression" on his face (231).

The Kincora scandal, however, needs no elaboration, being itself one of those real occurrences that seem drawn from the pages of an unusually sensational tabloid. Located in Belfast, the state-run Kincora home housed boys fifteen to eighteen years old; two of its male employees had been molesting residents since the early 1960s. In 1971, William Mc-Grath—the figure on whom Billy McClure is loosely modeled—was hired as a social worker at Kincora, where he molested "perhaps dozens of school-aged boys"; in spite of numerous complaints filed by the residents of the home, he was not arrested until 2 April 1980, more than two months after a newspaper in the Republic of Ireland ran a story alleging molestations and "recruitment of boys . . . for homosexual prostitution" at the home (C. Moore 147).

What has caused endless speculation about this all-too-familiar story of abuse, however, is that McGrath was also the founder of a right-wing Protestant organization called Tara, whose members saw themselves as a shadow government preparing to take over in the event of a "doomsday" scenario when a Northern Ireland abandoned by the British would have been invaded by troops from the Irish Republic. Though the group disavowed terrorism, it was committed to a radical agenda—outlawing the Catholic Church, for example—and allegedly worked with arms dealers in both South Africa and the Netherlands sympathetic to the Orange cause.

More spectacular allegations followed: Chris Moore, author of a book on McGrath and Kincora, interviewed several intelligence agents and civil servants who claimed that McGrath had actively worked for MI5, the British Security Service, and that Tara had been conceived by British intelligence as a means of gathering information about, and then manipulating, Protestant extremists. A former army intelligence officer reported that he had been warned in the strongest terms not to follow up stories about "McGrath's homosexuality and pederasty" (Moore 224). On the BBC's *Public Eye* program Peter Taylor reported that when the Royal Ulster Constabulary directed a series of written questions about McGrath to MI5, even they could get no answers, and argued that the whole case raised "a fundamental question of accountability" (Moore 227). East Belfast City Councillor Joshua Cardwell committed suicide in 1982 shortly after the police questioned him about weekend visits to Kincora recorded in a desk diary Moore had found there. The same year, the *Irish Times* printed a story alleging that a "homosexual vice ring" centered on the home had involved many prominent citizens. The story continues to unravel: on 10 October 1996 the *Irish Times* reported on the quashing of Colin Wallace's conviction for manslaughter. A former British army intelligence officer stationed in Northern Ireland in the 1970s, Wallace had always claimed that he was dismissed and then framed for murder "because he had exposed details of the British government's disinformation campaign" and had also threatened to "publicise how the security forces had deliberately covered-up systematic sexual abuse at the Kincora boys' home." By 1996, an English judge apparently found Wallace's allegation plausible.

Evidence that British intelligence, or at least what the *Irish Times* story characterizes as its "rogue right-wing agents," worked hand in hand with a Protestant extremist organization certainly confirms the worst fears of Northern Ireland's Catholics, who have often suspected the British Army and Unionist politicians of abetting Protestant violence. After all, the Protestant paramilitaries have historically seen themselves as supplementing rather than opposing the regular army and the police, and the Northern Irish government was much slower to proscribe them than the IRA and other militant nationalist groups. In general, this suspicion that the government colludes with Protestant paramilitaries may be unfounded, as Steve Bruce argues; governments do not necessarily "tolerate terrorist groups of the same political complexion" as themselves: he notes as one example that in 1982 the conviction rate for accused Loyalist murderers approached twice that for IRA killers (270, 275).

But although hardly typical, William McGrath's putative career underscores the fault lines within Protestant extremism. Along with familiar contradictions of all Christian violence, the Protestant paramilitaries exhibit the contradictions inherent in pro-state terrorist organizations, which break the state's laws in order to preserve the state's rule. These contradictions, to allude to a history McNamee's novel suppresses, were visible in 1912, when Protestant Ulster mobilized for war against England rather than accept Home Rule, and they were still visible in the spring of 2000, as Loyalist feuds and punishment beatings continued.[2]

If McNamee's terrorists are drawn from recent history, in their conception his writers, Ryan and Coppinger, owe more to fictional figures, such as the hard-drinking newspaperman of the American detective story, and to the literary tradition of the writer as the terrorist's alter ego, than to the public record. Coppinger, the older, a Protestant, is dying of throat cancer, "a cheap metaphor," as he says, for an investigative reporter whose editor has taken him off the political beat and assigned him to cover sports (183). Ryan, a Catholic, recently separated from his wife and is slipping into alcoholic isolation; like Coppinger, he finds his editor reluctant to publish stories about the city's terrorists. Both men become obsessed with the "Resurrection Men," a name given to Victor's unit by local citizens remembering a gang of grave robbers and murderers who once sold bodies to medical colleges. With Coppinger feeding him information from confidential Protestant sources, Ryan meets with Billy McClure and follows his telephoned directions to find the body of a rival terrorist Victor has tortured to death. Long before Ryan watches Victor's execution, McNamee has woven together the lives of his journalists and his terrorists, suggesting that both are players in a larger plot directed from the shadows by nameless men sanctioned by the British government and its intelligence agencies. In the final paragraph, Ryan is headed back to the hospital for Victor's autopsy report, with no certainty that he will learn anything or be allowed to publish his findings if he does. The narrator's ambiguous comment that "he was of the city now, part of its rank, allusive narrative," suggests that he may be even more deeply woven into the conspiracy that created and destroyed Victor Kelly (233).

Just as the deliberately "postmodern" tone of *Resurrection Man* belies its dependence on documented fact, so too does the author's refusal to name the grim city in which he sets his story. Although the text names innumerable Belfast streets, parks, prisons, hotels, and bars—the Shankill, Crumlin Road, Ormeau Park, the Europa—it never once names Belfast. One can think of political explanations for McNamee's decision: the desire to show that, at least for working-class citizens, "the Shankill" and the "Crumlin Road" have real political meaning, whereas "Belfast" suggests an illusory unity. Certainly, as we shall see, McNamee wants to stress the unusual weight that names bear in a place where a decision to say "Ulster" instead of "Northern Ireland" marks one as Protestant as clearly as a decision to say "Derry" instead of "Londonderry" marks one as Catholic. But a more immediate effect of McNamee's emphasis on the names of streets and buildings is to stress fragmentation, nostalgia, the remains of a colonial day: "The city . . . has withdrawn into its place-names. Palestine Street. Balaklava Street. The names of captured ports, lost battles, forgotten outposts held against inner darkness" (3). The place-names carry traces of a past that the city's contemporary inhabitants have forgotten: not an Irish nationalist's idea of the past, nor even an Ulsterman's, but an imperial, Victorian past.

Indeed, with one notable exception McNamee also defamiliarizes Northern Ireland by avoiding references to the better-known events of Irish history. A couple of references to the *Titanic* and one to the Dreadnoughts recall the city's once-thriving shipbuilding industry; Victor listens to street preachers' sermons recycling "sectarian history," but the narrative suppresses their historical content, focusing instead on a catalog of anti-Catholic slogans (24, 117, 9). The one concrete reference to the Ulsterman's fabled obsession with the Battle of the Boyne is strategically located at the end of the novel's seventh chapter. Meeting in a house on Crimea Street, McClure and Victor share the contents of a Benzidrex inhaler, dipped in milk, as the narrator explains in DeLillo-flavored language, "to deaden its bitter chemical taste with overtones of dumped chemicals, slow leakage and genetic damage" (64). Beginning with their shared detestation of Catholics, the conversation moves to McClure's admiration for Nazis; he shows Victor a book filled with pictures of naked boys published in Berlin in 1940. Already disoriented by evocations of the Crimean disaster, Nazi Germany, and unmistakably contemporary drug habits in a space of four paragraphs, the reader's time sense boggles as the sounds of drum and flute echo through the street and the men move to the front door to watch the passing parade where men in bowler hats carry a "banner showing William of Orange on a white charger" (65). The Protestant victory of 1690, the culmination of the seventeenth-century religious wars that is commonly read as setting the stage for Catholic grievance and Protestant intransigence, loses its place in the chain of cause and effect. The Dutch king with his white charger seems hopelessly irrelevant, less connected to Victor Kelly and Billy McClure than Nazi pornography or a mid-Victorian defeat in Russia.[3]

The events of Irish history seem to bear little connection to the lives and psychologies of McNamee's terrorists, and that history, like present-day politics, can only be glimpsed in fragments—street names and sudden outbreaks of violence for which the available rhetoric offers no plausible explanation. When Ryan hears McClure go on about his birthright being sold out, about "the boys [who] built the Empire" being unwilling to "stand idly by for much longer," he experiences the speech as part of a familiar ritual, but he also detects "something fraudulent . . . a tone of mockery" in the delivery (151). Where even an extremist can no longer fully credit his side's version of the historical imperatives, he naturally enough will turn to the only force still able to generate collective myths, the electronic media, represented in the novel by American movies and BBC newscasts; the local newspaper, while clearly playing a secondary role, contributes to shaping the sense of the real. Both McClure and Ryan take it for granted that they will interrupt their interview to watch the television news.

For Victor Kelly at least, the primary myths, the stories that "explain the present and predict the future," as Lévi-Strauss put it, come from Hollywood. Gangster movies and Westerns encourage him to see the cinema as inherently violent.[4] Little Victor, touring the projection room, sees it almost as an arsenal, with "asbestos chimneys," "long Bakelite fuseboxes," and a smell of "phosphorous, chemical fire"; the projectionist has "a long white scar" where a "hot casing," coming into contact with his arm, "laid it open to the bone" (4). Just as McNamee himself plays with such clichés as the hard-drinking journalist obsessed with a criminal or the killer's mother who believes that her boy "wouldn't hurt a fly," his characters self-consciously embrace roles created by popular journalism and, especially, film. As a schoolboy Victor obsessively imitates the gangster walk, gestures, and speech he has seen in Edward G. Robinson and James Cagney films, an act he is still using five minutes before his death to disarm his mother's fears. Evidently his tastes are widely shared. When the detective Herbie interrogates Victor in Castlereagh, both men, knowing that "ordinary speech was inadequate," adopt "the tones of flawed irony employed in gangster films" (52). Willie's scheme to package stolen raw alcohol in Smirnoff's bottles and sell it to Catholic pubs is, Victor recognizes, a "boot-leg scheme" that belongs "on celluloid" (62). Coppinger, noting how many of Victor's associates have nicknames that recall Chicago in the 1920s, suggests calling in the FBI or Pinkerton's.

Deliberate imitation and half-conscious influence give way to a more serious interplay between cinema and life. When the leader of a rival unit taunts Victor with the old rumor that his father was born a Catholic, Victor shuts out dank Belfast to imagine himself in a Western showdown, complete with dusty streets, heat, and the smell of leather; he's on the verge of making a quick draw when he realizes that he's surrounded by men holding guns and allows himself to be guided to a waiting car. But in Victor's city, where the lines between reality and the movies are blurry, it's not always advisable to insist on separating them. In his desperate last days, when Victor is "holed-up," a phrase he knows comes from the movies, he turns to them for guidance: "from the films he knew that outlaws sometimes got lost in romance, and that it could become necessary to return to the basics of a savage, haunted existence" (205). "Romance," "savage," "haunted"; of course, we have to notice that Emma Bovary used words like that, that they hardly suit Victor's sordid career, but then in his film-saturated world the cinema's knowledge cannot be absolutely denied. A truly "savage, haunted" hero should know that giving in to the impulse to visit his paralyzed father will be fatal; killers always stake out the home.

Similarly, we can, of course, deplore the process by which a Hollywood version of World War II dominates the imagination of men like Big Ivan, whose parents after all must have lived through Belfast's own blitz and can hardly have experienced it as a scene in "an underground room . . . with scattered maps" where a "grim-faced" general plots "campaigns with hairs-breadth precision" (137). Yet the novel's omniscient narrator, speaking in the second person, urges the reader to share the perception that Long Kesh looks like a Second World War POW camp with "evidence of military nostalgia, a secret ache for wartime captivity, Red Cross parcels and daring escape attempts" (110). That this is the stuff of *The Great Escape, Stalag 17*, or even *Hogan's Heroes* hardly cancels out the more serious observation that such camps are "achievements of the century, maintained on the point of abandonment" (110).

It is not just that images made familiar by television and movies, such as the wintry prison camp huddled behind barbed wire, point toward an actual history and tell us something about how far it must be transformed to be made bearable. In McNamee's postmodern take on Northern Ireland, media clichés even become a tool of investigation, since they put the speaker in touch with a world where many people define reality by what they have seen in movies or on television. Trying to

figure out what is behind the knife murders, Coppinger and Ryan vie
with each other to produce the most resonant journalist clichés: Ryan
wants to know if the police have questioned a woman walking her dog
near the scene: "A woman walking a dog'd be a good witness. It's something to do with kindness to animals and regular habits" (35). When
Coppinger argues that the paper's refusal to print his stories comes
down to the public's unwillingness to read about knife murders, Ryan
replies: "You're wrong there. . . . People love to read things like that. . . .
Sexual organs mutilated. Policemen with thirty years' experience controlling their emotions." "You're right," says Coppinger. "There's nothing like a set of mutilated sexual organs." From this insight they
progress to another: "Nothing like a good conspiracy theory," says Coppinger, to which Ryan responds, "A cover-up at the highest level'd be
better" (36).[5]

Coppinger and Ryan neatly diagnose the plot, the good conspiracy
theory, that encloses them. Indeed, the novel's paranoid plot, like its allusions to Hollywood, links McNamee's city to a global culture largely
excluded from more conventionally realistic novels about Irish terrorists
such as Benedict Kiely's *Proxopera* or Bernard McLaverty's *Cal*. Paranoia
has a highly distinctive place in one strain of postmodern fiction: to find
its terrorist variant, one has only to think of the complex conspiracies of
hit men and government officials in several of the DeLillo novels or the
insoluble questions of identity in Volodine's *Lisbonne dernière marge*. As a
wider phenomenon, no one has analyzed paranoia in postmodern fiction better than Christopher Prendergast. Where conventional realism,
like tragedy, offers us "dianoia," the security of resolution, of order renewed and mysteries solved, novels such as *The Crying of Lot 49* and
L'Emploi du temps "question the forms of the traditional . . . novel from
an inversion of the procedures of the detective novel" (Prendergast 223).
Such books imply a "relationship between fictional 'plotting' and the
syndrome of 'paranoia'" and suggest that "once the process of perceiv-
ing and decoding clues has been launched, there is no possibility of 'ar-
resting' it" (224).[6] Ryan will identify Victor Kelly, he will watch Victor's
body being trundled off to the morgue, but at the end of the novel he
will still be hunting for clues; where the terrorist, in some sense never
clearly explained, has been a pawn of the government, its security
forces can achieve only an inconclusive, ominous victory.

Yet, of course, any understanding of the world rooted in myth resists
analysis, and the danger of a global perspective is that it rides over his-

torical particulars; Ryan notices that the city's outsiders, its foreign re-porters and visiting professors, hardly know where they are. One of the dazed correspondents in safari jackets admits that "other wars" keep getting into his reports: "The presidential palace is surrounded. Armed gangs are roaming the commercial sector" (23). The professors' wives, gathered for coffee, have conversations Ryan imagines people having at "embassy parties in the eastern bloc": "The inadequate grasp of local politics, talk of staff becoming sullen and unco-operative, the belief in the army's ability to maintain order on the streets" (33). Film replaces experience of even the most naturalistic phenomena: Heather, accus-tomed to sleeping late, wakes at 4 A.M. and finds it "a fictional hour, de-rived from films . . . packed with menace and grainy" (205). And if films and television have shaped one's sense of the real, then the actual must often come up short. Thus the *deréalisation* of the city extends even into the Shankill's Pot Luck pub, where Victor shoots a supposed informer in front of an audience of local people: "To McClure it seems distant, a televised roadside execution coming intact from a far-off war"; the corpse appears "unconvincing" (166).

Even in the privacy of their homes, coping with their own emotions, several of the characters have come to think of themselves as players in a B movie. To tell Victor she was shocked that McGrath informed on him, his mother automatically puts herself on camera: "If you'd seen my face when they told me it was a mask of disbelief" (72). Lying in bed, Heather thought that "if there was someone else in the room they could see the whites of her eyes like a picture of fear" (175). A few sec-onds before his death, as snipers emerge from a parked van, Victor "felt an expression cross his face like in a film, something's wrong" (230). Ryan is more literary, but he shares the others' tendency to experience his emotions as someone else might see them: "When he was drinking alone in the house he could work up to an impressive sense of ruined dignity" (177).

If Hollywood seems not only to have shaped the values of ill-educated people like Victor and Heather but to have fundamentally altered the way more sophisticated people like Ryan and the professors' wives also understand local politics or their own emotions, its effects are even more visible in journalism. McNamee's terrorists, who time their bomb-ings to "synchronize with news deadlines," are ambitious to "have a job as first item on the news" and feel humiliated when journalists fail to turn up for their court hearings, confirm the worst fears of media critics

who see television as a "co-producer of hostage drama, co-producer
with the terrorists," and argue that "terrorists do what they do, at least
in part, because of the publicity [television] gives them" (58, 39, 109).[7]
Like virtually everyone else in the city, they are addicted to the news,
clustering around their radios in Long Kesh as they had gathered
around the television set in their pubs.

Terrorists who think of themselves as celebrities are only part of the
problem McNamee describes. The facts journalists are supposed to establish prove elusive, so much so that even when Coppinger is allowed
to write an accurate report of a killing he feels that the published version acquires "implications which he had not put there" and seems to
hint "at something covert, unexplained, dissatisfying" (83). Terrorists
directly manipulate journalists, shooting some and threatening others
(83); editors resist publishing known facts (77, 83, 146). When Ryan
wishes to write up a killing, he explains to his editor that he knows the
story is true because he has seen the body in the morgue; the editor
replies, "Get confirmation" (22). Coppinger and Ryan feel "obsolete,
abandoned on the perimeter of a sprawling technology of ruin"; print
journalists in an electronic age, they must cope with a "new species of
information" coming out of paramilitary organizations operating under
cover names, or from politicians who condemn violence ambiguously,
or from courts where unidentified witnesses give their evidence from
behind screens (83). As Coppinger's contacts with the police and UDR
(Ulster Defense Regiment) men teach him early on, some forms of
knowledge become "a form of suffering" to which "the information became almost incidental" (14).

Television news already incorporates this understanding about the
marginality of fact. Even Victor recognizes the "narrative devices" it
uses, from the announcers' "neutral haircuts and accents" to their "careful placing of stresses to indicate condemnation or approval" (39). News
readers are celebrities with sunlamp tans who make local people un-
comfortable when they show up in pubs; heard on the air, they have
"crisp and authoritative" voices that pronounce every sentence "as if it
were an edict to be imposed upon an unruly native population" (138).
Already associated with the British government, broadcasting figures
drift in and out of Heather's flat with civil servants and policemen, and
we easily assume that when their reports diverge from fact, they serve
some obscure political interest. The newspaper stories that get published when Ryan's and Coppinger's are rejected follow the same pat-

tern, using the same "familiar and comforting vocabulary to deal with violence." "Atrocity reports" eschew detail and "achieve the pure level of a chant. It was no longer about conveying information. It was about focusing the mind inwards, attending to the durable rhythms of violence" (58).

When journalism is no longer about conveying information, journalists like Ryan and Coppinger disintegrate, and even the terrorists whose actions form the ostensible subject of media stories feel disoriented, experience a loss of self. Big Ivan, watching television coverage of events in which he had taken part diverge from fact, feels that "rich portions of his memory were being snatched from him" and suddenly becomes convinced that he was an adopted child (39). Darkie Larche sees the same problem in its public dimension: news "errors were subversive," denying "sectarian and geographic certainties" (17). UVF propaganda changes to meet the new conditions: at the beginning of the novel, Loyalists mail glossy pamphlets featuring pathologists' photographs of bombing victims to journalists and politicians, hoping to further inflame anger against the IRA. But after a time they realize the pamphlets are no longer needed: "the violence had started to produce its own official literature. Mainly hardbacks, with the emphasis on the visual" (92). This "literature," like the television news coverage it resembles, is both documentary yet oddly fictional. Every book has a photo of a civilian victim, who is always male, always wearing a shabby grey suit and ill-matched socks; Darkie Larche, who obviously knows better, becomes "haunted by the idea that the photograph was always of the same man taken from different angles" (92).

If McNamee sees the dangerous side of this disappearance of history, this transformation of more than 3,300 victims of the current Irish Troubles into a single mythic and anonymous victim, he also understands that television did not create the impulse to fictionalize unmanageable political histories. The legends created around the Resurrection Men remind Heather of the old rumors about "satanic rites in the graveyard" in her hometown, "lurid and necessary small-town fictions" (174). In the age of television, rumor's "complex networks of dubious information" continue to function as they did in medieval times. Rumor, says Coppinger, was always "an essential factor in historical events, situations which lent themselves to powerful fictions: soothsayers, exhausted riders at the city gates with tales of strange happenings, signs and portents" (82). In the immediate context, Coppinger is arguing that the truth about the knife murders will not be discovered by conventional investigative reporting techniques, such as questioning witnesses; rather, what he and Ryan must do is to get to "the source of all the rumours, the fear" (82). And while this source remains as elusive and undiscoverable as the "originary moment" that deconstruction counsels us to distrust, Coppinger's view that powerful histories summon powerful fictions seems to be borne out in the novel. Nothing will alter the human tendency to react, when confronted with the "raw, untransformed facts" of atrocity, by constructing stories "betraying their origins in older stories or in the adaptable myths of television" (191). Heather experiences television coverage of Victor's death as if she were watching a story from "archive footage," the same analogy Ryan had used for his father's funeral, "the documented past painfully reconstructed and enacted to purge a troubling historical reminder" (231, 123). The persistence of an oral culture, and the quite primitive magic of names, suggest that the decline of print journalism should not be taken as a sign that the electronic images of film and television have diminished the cultural force of language.

Street names and surnames play a critical role in *Resurrection Man*. McNamee capitalizes on a basic fact about Northern Ireland, the immense significance attached to the division between Protestants and Catholics and the lack of physical characteristics distinguishing the two Celtic groups. The acculturation produced by increasing "secularism, linguistic homogenization," and the "communications revolution" has, as John McGarry and Brendan O'Leary point out, failed to produce significant assimilation in Northern Ireland;[8] "as long as groups have *any* way of telling each other apart—names or clothes can be substituted for religion or language—ethno-national divisions can be maintained" (357). Indeed, residents of Belfast's poorer neighborhoods have developed an elaborate system of classification in which habits of dress, speech patterns, and preferences in sports, as well as names, addresses, and such biographical data as the schools one has attended, make "telling" Protestants from Catholics possible (Burton).[9] The harder it is to police the division between Protestant and Catholic, the more McNamee's characters insist on it, to such an extent that Victor Kelly's "Catholic" name is assumed to produce permanent scars because during his childhood the family moved whenever the "suspicion would arise . . . that they were Catholics masquerading as Protestants" (3). Like their real-life counterparts, McNamee's Protestant terrorists primarily operate through random sectarian killings, which after 1969 accounted for 78 percent of all deaths caused by Loyalist paramilitaries, though for Republicans the comparable figure was only 6 percent (McGarry and O'Leary 87).[10] Therefore, the ability to distinguish Catholics by their names, or the streets on which they walk, or the pubs from which they emerge, is crucial; and since none of these methods is foolproof, the Resurrection Men's victims soon include Protestants.

In a society where giving someone your name or address may give him the license to kill you, people learn to guard their addresses "as if the words themselves possessed secret talismanic properties" and to regard their names as "replete with power and hidden malevolence" (85). Victor is especially sensitive to them; the streets come alive for him in 1969 when their names begin "to appear in the mouths of news readers, obscure and menacing, like the capitals of extinct civilizations," evoking the feeling of the broken glass, bullet holes, and "burnt timber doused by rain" that the city's violence has left behind (10). "Victor," says the narrator, "got a grip on the names." He develops a deep knowledge of the city's geography and drives obsessively along the borders between Catholic and Protestant ghettos. Yet Victor's response to names deepens, as later in the novel he realizes that just as streets are not simple, names are not transparent: "India Street, Palestine Street. When he spoke them they felt weighty and ponderous on his tongue, impervious syllables that yielded neither direction nor meaning" (163). His father's retreat into almost pathological silence is a "condition of survival" in the sectarian atmosphere, and his revenge on his son is to accumulate a pile of newspaper cuttings about the Resurrection Men's activities. Reading them forces Victor to confront the full names of his victims and realize that the knowledge will have powerful consequences: "He realized that a name was accomplished and haunting, and that having read them he could not divest himself of them but they would come to him again like an old pain coming intact through the innuendo of years" (169).

Barely literate, Victor comes to share the view Coppinger acquired from memorizing lists of suspects whose names his informant refused to allow him to write down: that names conceal "elemental properties . . . dense tribal histories" (35). No wonder the one book Ryan finds in Coppinger's dusty terrace house is a city directory, sixty years out of date, which he must have pored over as if the "lamentation of the city was encrypted in its narration of street-names and dead inhabitants and

lost occupations" (220). As if driven by a distrust of rhetoric matched by
an equal faith in the magic of a few proper names, Coppinger's writing
style becomes increasingly bare, so that his sports copy evokes for Ryan
the "disciplined solitude of the prison diary" (176). Heather's faith in
language is more literal; she never quite gives up looking for the "word
or phrase with the exact conclusive property" to get rid of Darkie
Larche and is attracted to Victor in the first place because he looks "like
a man who carried within a tense coil of stored words capable of describing rare and dangerous sexual acts" (91, 42).

As Coppinger relocates the power of language, finding it in "words
devoid of their associations" rather than in books, the novel figures uneducated people, the terrorists and their hangers-on, rather than intellectuals, as the class most acutely aware of that power (35). Among their
other virtues, McClure admires the Nazis' skill with rhetoric and symbolism, "understood [their] extension of language into power" (30). In
prison Victor starts reading, drawn first by the strange words in medical
texts but later by their case histories; moving his lips, using a finger to
follow the words, he imagines the texts describing "a huge building beyond his comprehension," where the nameless case histories lie sunken
in crypts. Victor believes that "there was hidden power here, the voice
raised to an incantatory pitch" (74). In a scene based on Lenny Murphy's murder of the informer Mervyn Connor, Victor goes to the cell occupied by Hacksaw McGrath, the only gang member willing to testify
against him, and forces Hacksaw to sign a false confession before
smothering him. As Hacksaw cringes before his killer, he keeps alluding
to "words" where we might expect "knives" or "guns." Prison, he whim-
pers, is a quiet place, "no call for words at all"; he begs Victor to "put"
his "words away" and pleads "no more words" (103).

Modernist writers from Conrad to Beckett worried that language is
unreliable, but in *Resurrection Man* only Dorcas Kelly, the most self-
deceived character, briefly contemplates the possibility that "speech itself is a cruel deceiver or kind of hoax which could not be relied upon"
(56). The more pressing question for McNamee seems to be determining
what kind of language will be powerful, who will write the scripts, and
what their effects will be. Cringing from Victor's words, Hacksaw
equates pen and sword, as Victor also does when he regrets letting
Willie Lambe kill Smiley: "he regretted that he had not brought a knife
to work on him, to reveal the stony outlines of the silence within" (202).
Not surprisingly, then, McNamee collapses the distance between his

journalists and terrorists. Ryan and Coppinger not only drift through alcoholism toward unemployment or death, like so many habitués of the
Pot Luck bar, but even Coppinger's eyes change, become "a sniper's
eyes, deeply sunk, accustomed to range and distance" (78). Home for
his father's funeral, Ryan meets Heather in a bar and through her finally
comes face to face with McClure. Like many another journalist, Ryan realizes that he is not just reporting but participating in the story: "All of
a sudden I'm part of a conspiracy. I feel like I could be arrested" (183).
McClure takes to phoning him at odd hours, at 3 A.M. at his former
wife's house, for example, to tell him that members of the Resurrection
Men, but not their leader, are about to be arrested. Not seeming to realize Ryan's diminished role on the newspaper, McClure feeds him information confirming Coppinger's view that Victor is being written out of
the story and Ryan has been given the role of exposing him. After Victor murders Darkie Larche, McClure sends Ryan to the Tomb Street
baths to find the mutilated body; when nameless men execute Victor,
Ryan rushes to the scene and spends hours talking to Dorcas. At the end
of the novel, on the way to the hospital to check Victor's autopsy report,
Ryan stops by to see Heather; he is drunk, "looked as if he had been
drunk for days," weeping, and raving. Heather knows that he wants
comfort and feels "his desire that they should plead for each other as ac-
complices to events in the city" (233).

Just as Ryan's sense of complicity in the city's violence goes further than Representative Luken's indictment of the journalist as "co-
producer" of terrorist incidents, McNamee's implicit argument goes
beyond conventional debates about the ethical responsibility of the
press. Of course, publicity is one of the forces driving his terrorists, who,
of course, shape their violence around television deadlines; of course,
Ryan has information he does not share with the police. These are all serious issues if one believes that terrorists, police, and journalists function independently, in which case Ryan's decision about what kind of
coverage to give a terrorist or about what kind of information to pass on
to the police might actually affect the level of violence in his city. But as
we have seen, in Ryan's world decisions about what to publish are
made by unnamed editors for unexplained reasons, just as sympathetic
prison guards help one terrorist murder another, and terrorists themselves operate only as long as they have the sanction of more powerful
people. This thoroughly paranoid universe run by obscurely malignant
forces dwarfs Ryan, and the futility of his attempts to locate the power

that enmeshes journalist and terrorist hedges his attempts to establish personal responsibility.

If Ryan's responsibilities are less clear than Representative Luken might have them, they nonetheless remain too compelling to abandon. Midway through the book Ryan recalls the bitter quarrel that finished his marriage. Margaret, normally an elegant woman, had taunted him as a "shit, a pitiful fuck," and Ryan responded by hitting her under the eye, causing her head to strike a door frame as she slid to the floor (81). At the time, this eruption seemed too cataclysmic to talk about, but when Ryan confesses to Heather that he too is an accomplice of the city's violence, it is the only example he gives. But the novel's insistence on the barely concealed complicity of government officials in terrorism and on the influence of popular culture and journalism on terrorists suggests that the conventional distinctions between those who commit crimes and those who merely observe or police them does not work. What remains admirable in Ryan and Coppinger is that neither responds to that situation by abandoning the idea of responsibility. When Ryan, like any good Catholic, argues that the Diplock courts, where decisions are made without juries and where witnesses are allowed to testify without identifying themselves, represent a denial of justice, Coppinger neither agrees nor disagrees but raises another point that Ryan finds compelling. A judicial system where a person may be charged with "conspiracy with persons unknown to murder persons unknown" is strange but fitting: "it's all just a mechanism for dealing with different forms of complicity. . . . this town has invented new ways of getting involved, like it's all just one big experiment in human guilt" (183).

To think of McNamee's city as offering "new ways of getting involved" is to understand it as a highly contemporary site where the "new myths of television" and the new ways of understanding one's self and one's world that a global electronic culture fosters have been assimilated to inherited antagonisms. Doubtless the traditional explanations of Northern Ireland's violence—the careful political and religious histories, the economic studies of Catholic unemployment levels, and the sociologists' accounts of segregated housing estates and schools— have more meaning for Belfast than they do for McNamee's fictional city. But the parallel universe that *Resurrection Man* creates has the salutary effect of forcing readers to see Northern Ireland in a context that outsiders at least usually ignore, as vitally connected to London and

New York and Hollywood. In this context, the "tribal violence" English and American newspaper editors like to deplore in Northern Ireland begins to look a great deal like urban violence in Liverpool or Los Angeles—a perception that carries no suggestion of facile solutions but at least reduces the level of mystification. McNamee's city deserves to be contemplated; it is involved with the rest of us in new ways; it is our city; like Ryan we are written into its narrative.

A generation after Lenny Murphy's first documented murder, as a fragile peace is repeatedly violated by punishment beatings and arson, we are well placed to understand why *Resurrection Man* ends so bleakly, without the satisfactions of resolution. For all its postmodern elements, the novel's politics are anchored in an intractable world of fact, not magic. But novels where writers encounter terrorists are always to some extent about writing and language, and here McNamee may initially seem less pessimistic than, for example, DeLillo's Bill Gray remarking that after Beckett, "the major work involves midair explosions and crumbled buildings" (157). That Ryan, however damaged, is still doggedly seeking out the facts after the Resurrection Men are all dead or imprisoned suggests that terrorists are not supplanting writers. The more serious fear is that the shadowy, powerful figures who manipulated Victor will also succeed in making Ryan's efforts futile.

For a novel so centered on the themes of language and power, *Resurrection Man* is remarkable for having little to say about books. Coppinger's city directory, Heather's romance novels, and the medical cases Victor spells out in prison offer the only texts, other than daily newspapers, to which the characters have recourse. High literary culture is simply an absence; nobody, not even Margaret the university lecturer, talks about books; the omniscient narrator avoids literary allusions. Even for writers, the city is post-literate, exchanging its stories face to face over drinks or watching them on the screen. Yet in the wake of literature, in this novel that seems to assume the death of the novel, words and stories are so compelling that authorship is the chief metaphor for a terrifying social control. As the television camera captures McClure at the scene of Victor's murder, Heather sees that "this was his: the ambulance, the soldiers, the bystanders, Victor's outflung arm." Soon McClure will be feeding the news media "information, outlining a plot" and she imagines the "enthralled conversations of men in pubs . . . caught up in McClure's hypnotic fictions" (232). That we know McClure's fiction has its anonymous ghostwriters does not diminish the strength of that metaphor, nor the acuity of a man like Coppinger, who knows how to read the news as fiction. Noting the "new vocabulary" the media have adopted and the decreasing coverage of terrorist incidents that makes it "harder and harder to make the headlines," he knows Victor will have to be killed. Knife murders are too unpredictable; they "don't belong any more" (156).

Coppinger's insight will not defer his death, or Victor Kelly's, and whether Ryan's stories or for that matter McNamee's novel will lessen the miseries of contemporary urban violence remains unfathomable. When Ryan and Coppinger meet, they like to exchange small stories, observations about the city; on Sundays, for example, the only people who seem to be out are the "wee old men" standing on every street corner, wanting to share their reminiscences with strangers. To draw out such "small themes" to their limits is to make the oral story what romanticism has always wished literature to be, a vehicle for resistance, or a new creation, the model of a better world: "It was an attempt to create new levels, to resist the city's definition of itself as violent, divisive, pitiful" (78). But Ryan knows that such stories also contain "depths of parody" and may be nothing more than "a sideshow for good-humoured crowds at the place of execution" (79). If he were given to assessing the value of contemporary novels about terrorism, *Resurrection Man*, for example, his judgment might well remain the same. We can be quite clear that the novel's almost documentary accuracy about the Romper Rooms and the Crumlin Road prison and its witty parodies of bureaucratic rhetoric about acceptable levels of violence suggest that to focus meticulous attention on events while distancing ourselves from an official language that conceals them is a necessary condition of change. But violence, whether at Newgate or on the Shankill Road, always has a way of turning into a spectacle, and the good-humored crowd cannot be trusted to stop the hangman.

Part II

Displaced Causes

3

Mary McCarthy's
Cannibals and Missionaries

Both DeLillo and McNamee observe the mass media closely; DeLillo emphasizes the novelist's waning political influence, McNamee the possibility of the writer's complicity with terrorism. The career of Mary McCarthy illustrates how a writer's past political activism can engender this guilty sense of responsibility. By the early 1970s, Mary McCarthy had become that rare creature, the American woman of letters, famous for debating Diana Trilling about Vietnam on the pages of the *New York Review of Books* and being sued by Lillian Hellman for calling her a liar on the *Dick Cavett* show. Her career as a public intellectual began in the late 1930s, when the novelist James Farrell added her name to a letter from the Committee for the Defense of Leon Trotsky, and continued through the 1940s and early 1950s, when she was a regular contributor to the *Partisan Review*.

Yet for many years her political commitments seem halfhearted, even careless; the casual remark that led Farrell to take her for a Trotskyite was made by a woman who later admitted that "I knew nothing about the cause I had espoused; I had never read a word of Lenin or Trotsky, nothing of Marx but the Communist Manifesto, nothing of Soviet history" (Brightman 135). Her politics seldom translated into fiction, or at least not in the way those who shared them expected. A reader looking for courageous opposition to Joseph McCarthy, to take one example, will not find it in *The Groves of Academe*, a novel she published in 1952, when anti-Communist hysteria was at its height. Instead of targeting faculty eager to sign loyalty oaths and rid their departments of the politically unreliable, she satirizes a group of liberal professors who rally around an incompetent when he claims to be a victim of right-wing persecution. By the late 1950s, she seemed to lose interest in politics, like many other Americans, and her work turned inward—toward an auto-biography, *Memories of a Catholic Girlhood,* and such autobiographical novels as *The Custom of the Country* and *The Group.*

McCarthy's inconstancy caused Delmore Schwartz, in his notes for "The World Is a Wedding," to observe about her fictional counterpart that she "wants to get married again so that she can once again have someone to whom to be unfaithful" (Brightman 396). As character analysis, the remark may be more cruel than just, though a biographer agrees in finding McCarthy's "Portrait of the Intellectual as a Yale Man," with its devastating picture of the "*ease* with which he slips in and out of his relationship to events, people, ideas," partly a self-portrait (Bright-man 227). "Unfaithful," however, aptly describes a gifted satirist who like many another found permanent unconditional loyalty to most per-sons, groups, and ideologies impossible. Catholics and Stalinists, Trot-skyites and Freudians, all felt the sting of her wit. She might love Philip Rahv yet caricature him mercilessly as the fictional Will Taub; not all of her octogenarian classmates who in 1993 still felt "exposed and vio-lated" by *The Group* were personal enemies (Kiernan 57).

What McCarthy could believe in, for most of her adult life, was a set of liberal intellectual convictions about the moral worth of art and edu-cation and the need for a progressive politics. These remained unques-tioned until her final, most overtly political novel, *Cannibals and Missionaries.* This terrorist fiction by an American woman with no first-hand experience of political violence bleakly interrogates much that she had written before about politics, art, and the role of intellectuals and writers. Terrorism is a pretext for the exploration of the relationship of artists and intellectuals to violence; if the hijackings of the 1970s and several well-publicized terrorist attacks on works of art gave McCarthy her plot, the heart of her last novel lies elsewhere. In its grave reserva-tions about the competence of writers and intellectuals to understand and act in public history, *Cannibals and Missionaries* is the concluding chapter in Mary McCarthy's intellectual autobiography, the sequel to *Seventeenth Parallel,* a collection of her Vietnam journalism. As such, it can only be understood if we contemplate McCarthy's public response to our most unpopular war.

Vietnam drew Mary McCarthy, as it drew many American writers and intellectuals, back into the heat of politics. What is remarkable is not her opposition to the war, soon a fashionable position, but its nature. The satirical impulse, for once, was submerged; she felt moved neither to satirize Johnson and McNamara nor to turn a disabling irony on the war's opponents. More wholeheartedly than she had done in the 1940s, Mary McCarthy embraced the role of witness and public conscience that Emerson urged on American writers: "the good and the wise must learn to act, and carry salvation to the combatants and demagogues in the dusty arena below" (Emerson 103). Her commitments were serious, even courageous, given the personal risk; if one senses in her trips to Saigon (1967) and then Hanoi (1968) something of Emerson's lordly artist swooping down into the dust where ordinary people are scrapping it out, still she did go to see for herself, at a time when the physical risks were real and travelers to Hanoi excoriated. In her Vietnam journalism we see McCarthy faithful to Emerson's notion that intellectuals are morally obliged to save a populace with whom they are never entirely identified. And if we also see his suspicion of politics, the sphere of demagogues, we see a growing suspicion too of intellectuals. In Vietnam McCarthy began by gauging the responsibility of some highly educated people for disastrous public events and ended by losing confidence that intellectuals can still play a positive role in our public life.

As U.S. intervention heated up, McCarthy was living in Paris with her fourth husband, James West, a career diplomat then working for the Organization for Economic Cooperation and Development. She described herself as being in a state of shock as she stood outside a newspaper kiosk on 8 February 1965, reading headlines announcing U.S. bombing of Vietnam; by the summer of 1966 she told Edwin Newman, in a televised interview, that if Americans did not act against the war they would be acting like the good Germans who did nothing to save Jews. Later that year she flew to New York to try, unsuccessfully, to organize a middle-class tax revolt.[1]

Foiled in her first attempt at activism, McCarthy was attracted to the idea of going to Vietnam as a writer. *The Group*—300,000 copies sold within a year of its publication in 1963, a popular film version released in 1966—meant that she was at the height of a fame that she hoped would give her an audience for her political views.[2] Though she had declined an offer to go to Vietnam for the *New York Review of Books* in March 1966 because she feared the impact on her husband's job, nine months later she accepted.

McCarthy went to Saigon as someone with strong convictions about what she would see, "looking for material damaging to the American interest" (63). Restricted from reporting on combat by a promise to

West, she spent her time absorbing atmosphere, attending briefings, interviewing officers, and, probably most valuably, touring refugee camps—this last sometimes in the company of a German Catholic couple. In 1967 the American public, like McCarthy, had many preconceptions about South Vietnam, having read about it daily in the newspaper and having watched combat footage nightly on television. What she could add was the novelist's perspective, the nuances and impressions that escaped the usual coverage.

Her sensitive ear offended by the jargon of war, McCarthy, in reporting her interviews with U.S. officials, offered an Orwellian critique of words designed to conceal meaning, of napalm converted into "Incinder-Jell," a jolly consumer product, rather like Jell-O (63). As used by military officers, *infrastructure,* for example, does not so much point to something out there in the real world as to something the speaker wishes to have believed about himself: "Its primary meaning is that the person using it . . . has an up-to-date scientific grasp of the workings of underground Communism" (121). This last word also proved to McCarthy how far the social sciences taught in American universities had penetrated the military.

Indeed, as she toured South Vietnam, McCarthy was convinced that American intellectuals, particularly social scientists, bore a heavy responsibility for its suffering. Too many had identified themselves with the government; indeed, she saw university political science as a creation of the cold war. Arguing the need to look beyond the quality of refugee camps to our role in creating refugees, she pointed to the "strategic hamlet" program, which burned peasant's houses, poisoned their crops, and moved them to tightly guarded villages where they were expected to observe curfews, wear uniforms, and carry two forms of identification at all times. It was the invention of Stanford's Eugene Staley: "No ordinary desk official in Washington could have imagined the Staley plan," she remarked, wondering if such intellectuals are not worse than the atomic scientists: "conceivably you can outlaw the Bomb, but what about the Brain?" (122).

Social scientists were not the only problem; more disturbingly, she pointed to what she saw as a "modern fusion of intelligence with 'intelligence'" (135). The CIA was the really intractable force in Vietnam: "the Army, like all armies, basically wants to go home, while the CIA wants to stay, discreetly behind the scenes" (135). Behind her attack on the CIA in Vietnam lay her own history with the non-Stalinist (later anti-

Communist) Left, seriously compromised by the CIA in the 1950s and early 1960s, when it funded the Congress for Cultural Freedom and such key journals abroad as *Encounter* and *Preuves*. Far too many books about Vietnam, she claimed, "have been financed, with or without the author's knowledge, by the CIA" (135). But this historical intervention was not the only problem; she believed that the CIA has an affinity for left-wing and former left-wing intellectuals, liking them "because they are walking repositories of information and . . . because the CIA sees itself as a lonely mastermind, the poet and unacknowledged legislator of government" (136).

The adventures of intellectuals in politics had been in her view disastrous, a matter, in a word of those times, of co-optation. Hence McCarthy was driven to define the intellectual's role in stringently moral terms, to see any attempt to recommend policy as a sign of identification with the U.S. administration. This disdain for policy issues aroused Diana Trilling's ire when she read the conclusion to *Vietnam*, "Solutions," in which McCarthy described how the typical hawk, after conceding many of a dove's arguments, would close with the withering question, "Well, what would you do?" Those intellectuals eager to distance themselves from "irresponsible" protesters—Arthur Schlesinger Jr., John Kenneth Galbraith, George Kennan, Senator William Fulbright —had proposed a series of face-saving means by which the United States could extricate itself from Vietnam. The problem with their proposals, McCarthy saw, was that all of them were liable to the accusation, probably justified, that they would not work, in which case the only alternative was to continue the war interminably. Better, she said, for American intellectuals to imitate their French counterparts during the Algerian war: "they confronted their government with an unequivocal moral demand, and far from identifying themselves with that government and thinking helpfully on its behalf, they dissociated themselves from it totally so long as it continued to make war" (152). Thus McCarthy refused to do the what she saw as the government's job, urging only that opponents of the war start "acting so as to provoke intolerance" (165).

Trilling pointed out the constraints McCarthy imposed on the intellectual's political role: "by limiting [it] . . . wholly to that of dissent she deprives them of an historical privilege they have claimed . . . the right to propose and even direct the positive operations of government" (173). Furthermore, she argued, one key issue involved both policy and morality, the fate of the Vietnamese who had helped us in Vietnam. Trilling had no answers either but hoped that "everyone, including intellectuals" would pursue the question, for "without this effort . . . moral intransigence . . . is its own kind of callousness" (174).

McCarthy's response looked more carefully at the compromised Southern Vietnamese. Though a Jesuit priest had assured her that two million would die if the Communists won, she concluded that no one could know for certain that a "bloodbath" would occur. She assumed that the United States would evacuate some Vietnamese, that some would escape on their own, others would reach some form of accommodation with the new government, and still others would have to "face the music" (175). More sympathetically, she acknowledged that massive reprisals had followed some modern civil wars, but not all. She argued that those who worried about possible casualties *after* the war should remember the constant casualties *of* the war; assuming that two million people would be killed after a U.S. withdrawal, would we be "morally obligated to continue fighting until two million and one innocent people had been killed in the war, and then to withdraw because the war was no longer worth it?" (180).[3] Wistfully, McCarthy concluded that no one could find a way to stop Communism and the war on it at the same time: "The power of intellectuals, sadly limited, is to persuade, not to provide against all contingencies. . . . intellectuals and artists, as is well known, are not especially gifted for practical politics. Far from being statesmen with ubiquitous intelligence, they are usually not qualified to be the mayor of a middle-sized city" (186–87).

This sense of moral mission was even more evident when McCarthy traveled to Hanoi. Few well-known Westerners had made the trip; Harrison Salisbury had preceded McCarthy, and, notoriously, Jane Fonda was to follow. Thus, although she was writing about the same war, her subject matter had changed from a terrain that was only too familiar to her audience to one they barely knew at all. But another difference was that McCarthy herself was shaken by her experience in North Vietnam; instead of finding new grounds for her preconceptions, she found her assumptions about herself transformed.

As a guest of the government, McCarthy herself occasionally demonstrates the limitations as well as the strengths of the intellectual as political observer. In the North she was not allowed to be alone, except when sleeping or writing in her room. She often seemed aware of the limitations of not being able to roam around or talk freely to people. She knew, when she saw healthy-looking children in Hanoi, that many others had been evacuated, or that if there were no homeless people sleeping on the streets in front of her hotel, they might have been elsewhere. She was occasionally critical, regretting the decline of the French language and the growth of a political lingo that recalled Stalinism: "the vocabulary repelled me precisely by its familiarity. I had heard this jargon before, and too many lies had been told in it" (272). When an official corrected a museum director for criticizing the Ming dynasty, lest the visitor think she had heard a slur on the People's Republic, she flinched.

Yet at other times McCarthy failed to acknowledge her handicaps. She toured a hospital in Hanoi and found conditions far better than in the South; she did not ask whether they might also be better than in other North Vietnamese hospitals. She quoted approvingly a doctor's statement that Northerners were turning to low-tech solutions, such as water injected instead of plasma or an old folk remedy, a "poultice made of a live young chicken pounded into a paste" for wounds. Anyone who reads Nguyen Ngoc Ngan's description of an uneducated paramedic solemnly "prescribing" a clove of garlic to a doctor suffering from toothache in a postwar re-education center will immediately see the problems of such retreats to the past, even before reaching his gruesome account of a man who committed suicide rather than allow this same paramedic to amputate his leg without anesthesia.

Her intellectual's tendency to approach foreign countries as an anthropologist sometimes seemed to detach her from the very moral issues for which she cared passionately. Among the quaint local customs, she notes that:

> Hospitality requires that tea should be served at the beginning and end of any visit: tea, cigarettes, candies, and long slender little cakes that taste of bananas. The exceptions were the Journalists' Union and the War Crimes Commission, both of which served beer, and the prison where the captured pilots were held, which offered a choice of beer or a soft drink, plus bananas. . . . It was easy to guess why beer was served to journalists . . . while the Writers' and Artists' Union served tea, but why beer at the War Crimes *Commission* and tea at the War Crimes *Museum*? (207–8)

At her best, McCarthy exploits the satirical potential of such incongruous details, but her lack of curiosity about how the POWs were actually being treated prevents her from doing so in this case; she set an academic problem for herself to avoid facing a more troubling issue.

Indeed, McCarthy's limitations are most visible in her description of a
meeting with captured U.S. pilots. It is not that she consciously felt
morally superior to the pilots; on the contrary, she felt that they were
"paying" for U.S. involvement while she was not. What she did feel was
culturally superior. The handwriting on the envelopes of their letters
was childish and unformed, their conversation limited; "the North Vietnamese . . . have been taken aback by [their] low mental attainments."
She described one POW as "gaunt, squirrel-faced" but did not speculate
about his diet. In a postwar footnote she was less kind, quoting notes
that characterized him as "servile" and citing as part of the evidence
his remark, "Oh, gee, bananas too!" (299). By 1974, enough allegations
about tortured prisoners had emerged that one wishes McCarthy had
been less inclined to dismiss them.

McCarthy knew that "a cultural distance so wide that I could see myself reflected in their puzzled, somewhat frightened eyes as a foreigner"
separated her from the captured pilots (300). She grew to feel, too, that
her presence in this Communist nation was "an economic privilege."
More paradoxically, she understood that much of its top leadership was
a product of the same privilege; she and they had studied from the same
textbooks, "Crouzet, Desgranges" (245). If she could barely keep a conversation going with the doltish POWs, she and the "highly intellectual" Pham Van Dong could converse freely for hours, in a feeling of
"happy agreement" (304, 308).

North Vietnam left McCarthy in a "psychic upheaval, a sort of identity crisis" (204), partly because her experiences triggered long-forgotten
memories. The lack of modern plumbing in the countryside, the
kerosene lamps, and old-fashioned school desks, all created a sensation
of traveling back in time and were perhaps responsible for less obvious
associations: "North Vietnam is still pioneer country . . . the ethnic minorities . . . in the mountains of the wild West . . . recall American Indi-
ans" (203). One knows how intensely she disliked the Minnesota
grandmother whose memory the bumpy roads recalled, so perhaps it is
unfair to speak of nostalgia. Yet McCarthy seemed willing to accept
other people's hardships and to overlook symptoms of political repression in a foreign country that she would never have tolerated in her
own. Idealizing the countryside, she never examined the disadvantages
to Vietnamese women of doing laundry without electricity or running
water. When she heard about middle-class "experts" sent from the city,
she understood the repressive potential of that practice but detected a

"tender, Tolstoyan sound, a mild, soft reverent note" in the phrase "learn from the people" as used by her guide (246). Given the subsequent experience of teachers and doctors sent off to re-education camps in the jungle, the allusion seems misplaced.

Still, what redeems McCarthy from such blind spots is that this same identity crisis led to a deeper questioning of her role in Vietnam. However insensitive she seems to the plight of the POWs, the gift of a ring made from a captured U.S. fighter jet led to sleepless nights: "I cannot explain the physical aversion, evidently subliminal, to being touched by this metal. Quite a few of the questions one does not, as an American liberal, want to put in Hanoi are addressed to oneself" (212). Probing such questions in this deeply foreign country, she was forced to admit how typically American she was, how in spite of her "utopian" socialist views she was a "practicing" capitalist: "Everybody knows that you cannot serve God and Mammon, but few can refrain from trying; each counts on being the exception, especially if, as in my case, it is Mammon who seems to be serving *us* gratuitously, with no collusion on our part" (313).

But collusion began to seem inevitable the longer she stayed, and her own ability to go back to America and speak out on the war seemed like only one more privilege: "The illusion of being effective, the sole justification of my presence there, began to waver in North Vietnam the more I called upon it to defend me against the charge of complicity with American ruling circles—a complicity attested by the mirror. . . . if I was nothing but a sample of American society . . . then I had no subjectivity at all" (315). The only way out of this box for McCarthy was to revert to her Catholic upbringing, to a private and not public idea of conscience, the recognition that she had finally gone to Hanoi for her own peace of mind, that for her the greatest benefit of peace would be "to put it as basely as I can . . . [to] be able once again to enjoy my normal pursuits" (317). But even this, she understood, was impossible, for "nothing will be the same again, if only because of the awful self-recognitions, including this one, the war has enforced" (317).

McCarthy's disillusionment with the North Vietnamese and with the intellectual's role in public life slowly unfolded after she left. Stepping off the plane from Hanoi in Laos, she learned that the German Catholics whom she had admired for their refugee work in Hue had been murdered, probably by Communists. Fame as a novelist did not guarantee an audience for her political writing; *Vietnam* and *Hanoi* received few reviews and sold badly. In 1971, when the United States began its infamous Christmas bombing, McCarthy tried to persuade Pope Paul to go to Hanoi as a witness. When he refused, she asked Norman Mailer and Hannah Arendt—an indication that her faith in the moral power of intellectuals was still lively. The North Vietnamese rejected the proposal, saying that their airfields had been too heavily damaged to accommodate civilian travelers. After the war, she continued to send Christmas cards to the charismatic Pham Van Dong, but the flood of refugees, with their stories about harsh conditions in re-education camps and reprisal killings, ended her faith in the regime. In 1979 she told an interviewer, poignantly, that she would have signed a protest letter about human rights in Vietnam organized by Joan Baez, but that she had not been asked.[4] She contemplated a letter to Pham Van Dong asking how it was possible "for men like you to permit what's going on," but she never sent it (McCarthy, "World" 174).

Not only had McCarthy lost faith in the man and his regime, but she had become, in her own words, "skeptical and pessimistic" about "politics in general" (McCarthy, "World" 174). She had reached that terrible point where the world's ignorance and violence no longer seem amenable to the solutions offered by well-meaning intellectuals. For some that point leads to terrorism, to the perception that only direct and violent action can make a difference. For the novelist, it often leads to fiction about terrorism, to an extended meditation on a state of affairs in which words and reason have lost their efficacy. Not surprisingly, 1979 was the year in which McCarthy published *Cannibals and Missionaries*, a novel that satirizes a group of liberals setting off, as she had done in 1967 and 1968, to bear witness to a political wrong. Their plane is hijacked, and their journey, like her own, comes to no good end.

McCarthy's plot comes from the thriller: a committee of high-minded liberals undertakes a fact-finding mission to the shah's Iran. After hijacking their plane, pro-Palestinian terrorists hold them hostage, along with a tour group of rich art collectors, in a farmhouse in Flevoland, the new Dutch province reclaimed from the sea. In time the collectors are exchanged for the masterpieces in their collections; thus in a farmhouse in an obscure corner of Europe, as devoid of European history as Utah, the author assembles people and paintings representing the West's artistic, intellectual, political, and social elites. McCarthy found such "isolation" "crucial" to traditional novels of ideas such as Mann's *The Magic Mountain* or Solzhenitsyn's *The First Circle*, and for the most part *Canni-*

bals and Missionaries (CM) reads like them: highly articulate people spend hours discussing their theories in the shadow of historical catastrophe (McCarthy *Ideas* 20). Indeed, McCarthy's efforts to graft the novel of ideas onto the thriller frustrated reviewers looking for realism; to their complaints that readers do not care about the characters, McCarthy responded haughtily that "You're not meant to . . . the emotional depth of the book is extremely shallow" (Brightman 594).

These characters, more distinguished for the ideas they represent than for their emotional complexity, are, however, drawn from the circle of McCarthy's acquaintances; as she admitted to Rowland Burdon-Mueller, the original for Charles Tennant, "I can't help plagiarizing from real life" (Brightman 586). Brightman duly provides the key: Senator James Carey is a "look-alike" for Eugene McCarthy; Henk Van Vliet de Jonghe is based on both the Dutch liberal deputy Hans van Mierlo and the novelist Cees Nooteboom; the novel's Bishop Hurlbut is based on a retired bishop of St. Louis named Will Scarlett; and Aileen Simmons derives her talkative streak from Elizabeth Hardwick (586–87). Doubtless, McCarthy sees something of herself as well in the successes, failures, and, especially, shallowness of her "anointed band of liberals" (CM 294).

Her portrait is all the more devastating in the end because her liberal intellectuals are allowed many positive characteristics. Detached in the farmhouse from their ordinary lives, they work out a group identity, though some are far more likeable than others. The retired bishop from Missouri is a virtual saint, and the Dutch poet and parliamentary deputy, Henk Van Vliet de Jonghe, is consistently warm and sympathetic; on the other hand, the college president, Aileen Simmons, talks nonstop in kittenish self-preoccupation, and Frank Barber, the foolishly optimistic Episcopal rector, is someone whom, as Mary Gordon remarks, one can hate from the first page. Yet all share the historical situation that puts the liberal American intellectual in a position once occupied by the clergy, a point McCarthy underscores by arranging for the bishop to die early. Their kidnappers believe they represent the national conscience, that violating them will provoke the sense of "sacrilege" essential to terror (220). Engaged on a "mission," the liberals have inherited from their evangelical predecessors an ambivalent identity as potential martyrs and unconscious colonialists, "salesm[e]n for Western democratic merchandise" (5).

McCarthy's liberals are remarkably courageous, partly because they are resourceful enough and able to impose structure and therefore meaning on their captivity. A petulant sense of injustice leads Aileen half-advertently to finger the collectors in the first-class seats; it is the only significant exception to the characters' general decency and courtesy. They impose on degrading conditions the rituals of upper-class life, so that the reader, hearing their witty conversation or watching them play bridge with cleverly decorated cards cut from magazines, forgets how long it has been since they have had a change of underwear.

Yet mental worlds can be frighteningly detached from reality. Early in the novel Senator Carey notices how a trivial misunderstanding spreads through the group until everyone assumes that it is a fact, and he reflects on the "gravity-defying power of ideas to stand unsupported by evidence" (*CM* 68). Unsupported constructions like Henk's fantasy that the Netherlands is an imaginary country have dangerous consequences; this whimsy leads him to ignore two Dutch-speakers on the plane and thus to lose a chance to eavesdrop on its hijackers. When the bishop dies of a stroke and their captors pump his body full of bullets in order to pressure the Dutch government, the committee quickly rationalizes the terrorists' action as a humane alternative to killing one of them, almost as if it ensures their safety.

The intellectuals' capacity for detachment makes them adept at self-criticism: Aileen knows that her motives for going to Iran include a desire to cultivate the eligible senator, Frank suspects that he is running away from his pregnant wife, and Victor Lenz, the CIA stringer sent to watch the others, has no illusions of nobility. Yet self-criticism can paralyze, as Jim Carey knows too well: he "was wary . . . of his brain. . . . It had deterred him, too often, from action by showing him the futility of it" (*CM* 305). Besides, it has its blind spots. Striving for empathy with the Third World, the American intellectuals recast it in their own image as easily as their compatriot Charles Tennant does when he compares a torturing device of SAVAK, the shah's intelligence agency, to a toaster (239).

But the Dutchman Henk, who criticizes Americans for "taking their country for the world" (82), also recasts his captors in his image. During his captivity, the married man falls in love with an American journalist, Sophie Weil, but both circumstance and temperament constrain passion. That both agree they will never consummate their love because they do not want it to be "messy" may help explain why readers find the characters shallow. Yet perhaps the more crucial point is that Henk, who can submit his own passion to rational discipline, believes that the terrorists can also do so. Fatally, he urges their leader, Jeroen, to discontinue the siege because the Dutch government cannot possibly give into the demand that it withdraw from NATO and sever diplomatic ties to Israel. What he cannot feel is the suicidal despair this insight induces.

Perhaps like her own characters McCarthy recasts the terrorist in her image; Brightman may be right to find her portrayal of Jeroen romantic (Brightman 594). But the resemblance is not altogether unconvincing, for terrorists often are well educated (Rubenstein 17). There is an affinity between this man and the committee members; he too is used to thinking in terms of theories and entertaining what may well be delusional notions of changing the world. Jim, at least, thinks so, reflecting on his 1968 challenge to Lyndon Johnson: "He had been as much of a millennialist in his hopes as any 'misguided' terrorist. . . . terror was only the kid brother of minority electoral politics" (*CM* 312). In one Marxist view missionaries and cannibals are much the same species; neither can leave other people alone. However, this rapprochement can only go so far; oddly, we see the critical difference between terrorists and intellectuals in their response to art, rather than in their methods.

We know that a series of physical attacks on artworks in the 1970s, including the *Mona Lisa* and Michelangelo's *Pietà*, as well as the IRA's theft of the "Kenwood House Vermeer" in 1978, led McCarthy to the theme of artworks held hostage by terrorists. McCarthy speculated publicly that press reports about inflated art prices fueled such attacks, underscoring the Marxist perception of artworks as loot. Meditating on whether being surrounded by beautiful objects improves one's character, she concluded that art, unlike music or poetry, induces possessiveness: "the eye is a jealous, concupiscent organ . . . a natural collector, acquisitive, undemocratic, loath to share" ("Living" 111). Our subjective experience of joy when we see beauty makes us imagine that we not only feel good but actually are good (122). Yet McCarthy does not need Hermann Göring to discredit this view; look, she says, at art historians, collectors, and critics; look even at people who live in scenic parts of the United States. "Quite poisonous people . . . are attracted by the visual arts and can become very knowledgeable about them"; the residents of Carmel Valley are "vicious" (120, 123).

Why should art, rather than literature, attract poisonous people? The answer for McCarthy lies in the materiality of art, its embodiment in

unique objects, in originals. No one minds if other people read Jane
Austen; no one expects to be the only person in the audience for Mozart.
Yet, as anyone who has joined the crowds mobbing well-publicized
traveling exhibitions of, say, Monet or Renoir can testify, large crowds
diminish our pleasure in visual art.

One would expect that *Cannibals and Missionaries,* which incorporates
the themes and language of McCarthy's lecture, would be equally negative about art collectors. But from the beginning they are more silly than
despicable and are representatives of "old money" who seem even in
comparison with college presidents and senators to come from a claus-
trophobic world of privilege, where everybody has known everybody
since their undemanding days at Saint Timothy's. Unlike the terrorists
and intellectuals, who focus on the world scene, on food supplies and
prison conditions and foreign elections, the collectors lead intensely private lives, their minds filled with impractical and useless knowledge,
with, for example, the names of dozens of hybrid roses.

If living with their Vermeers and Cézannes has not made them charitable to the poor, their passion for these paintings, which "makes rea-
soning useless," goes deeper than a desire to preserve negotiable assets
(256). Early on it enables them to grasp intuitively that Jeroen will exchange them for their collections, a "nutty example of group-think," to
Henk's mind: "these people had become *possessed* by the notion that
their art treasures were in danger, without . . . considering it aloud as an
objective proposition" (248). It leads Helen Potter, at first glance a
mildly ridiculous woman with a "muffin" head, to beg the terrorists to
take her whole fortune rather than her Vermeer; when she refuses to
comply with their demands, "her dumpy form seem[s] to . . . gain a full
inch and not only in moral stature" (249, 256). Then, too, McCarthy
shows the collectors generally growing throughout the siege: "there was
more to [Lily] mentally than had ever been suspected" (287). Freed from
the time-consuming tasks of the leisure class—dressing, getting their
hair done, having a massage—they finally have the "leisure" to get to
know themselves, "which was like making a new acquaintance" (287).

The collectors, in other words, learn some of the more admirable
qualities of McCarthy's intellectuals. Unfortunately, at the same time,
Jeroen is becoming more like the jealous concupiscent collectors of her
lecture. Before he was a terrorist, Jeroen was an artist, an electrician with
a love of drawing, in whom the masterpieces of the Rijksmuseum inspired "a feeling close to worship" (205). Failing as an artist, he gradu-

ally grew to dislike "art for art's sake" and turned instead to the Communist Party and action. But what he rejected in aesthetics he embraced in politics. Although the text seems to be contradictory, occasionally speaking of the hijacking as though it had a practical goal, much of the time Jeroen sees terrorism as the political equivalent of art for art's sake. The bourgeoisie, in his view, like *"e*volution," but true *r*evolution describes a circle: "the purpose served by the capture of the Boeing was simply the continuance of . . . the original thrust" (226). As committed as any modernist to the autotelic object, he wants nothing from his plot but its perfect embodiment in the world, its "sheer beauty" (227). The hijacking is "a work of art," and he is gratified when the "raw materials of bourgeois life, of their own initiative, spr[i]ng forward to collaborate in a revolutionary design" (215).

What undermines this pure commitment to the revolutionary deed is the presence of real art, which McCarthy finds powerful and distinctive. "You have gone back to your first love," his formidable lover, Greet, warns when he decides to take the collectors hostage (224). In a sense, the greatest masterpiece, Helen's beloved Vermeer *Girl*, corrupts this terrorist and sways him from the purity of his design. He falls in love with it, as the Palestinian Ahmed says, "like a bride," spending hours staring at it obsessively. And when Henk produces his reasonable argument for negotiating with the government, Jeroen chooses to blow himself up with the painting in a classic murder-suicide that Ahmed calls *"le geste sublime d'un grand révolutionnaire"* (358); although he does not mean to, he also kills ten other people.

Ahmed's language tells us what Edmund Burke meant by treating the sublime as an effect of terror: "whatever is fitted in any sort to excite the ideas of pain, and danger . . . or operates in a manner analogous to terror, is a source of the *sublime*; that is, it is productive of the strongest emotion which the mind is capable of feeling." Now in choosing a Vermeer as Jeroen's love object, rather than, say, a Munch or even a Turner, McCarthy deliberately chooses a painter who never strives for the romantic sublime, a painter of domestic tranquillity. Yet she suggests that the aura of this original, its rarity and unobtainability, induces a sublime and terrible gesture in a susceptible man. The Basho poem that Henk, Jim, and Ahmed all know by heart offers a momentary sense of unity, encouraging them to transcend their differences. But the rare original, through no fault of its creator, is a costly object that engenders possessive passion.

Now McCarthy's intellectuals, once the exchange of collectors for paintings takes place, also live in the presence of these beautiful objects. But unlike Helen or Jeroen, they remain singularly unaffected; instead of falling in love, they conduct lengthy disquisitions about the moral effects of art. Frank relativizes its value—an African might not admire a Vermeer—and finds a cult of originals problematic. Sophie and Henk develop a theory of why a Vermeer painting resembles a photograph; Jim cannot appreciate a Cézanne once someone shows him that a figure's arm is "out of drawing" (307). The point is not that McCarthy disagrees; they are parroting ideas she had already set forth in her lecture; but she measures their ineffectuality by the distance separating them from other people's passions.

In the end, the thriller overtakes the novel of ideas, and violence explodes the decorous mental world the characters have created. The "mayhem," as Brightman notes, seems "incongruous in what is essentially a novel of manners" (593). But then, of course, terrorism always changes the tone, turning a day of shopping at Harrods or a cruise on the *Achille Lauro* into a lurid scene from an alien world. But this ending also shocks because the emotional "shallowness" of McCarthy's characters has given them an air of invulnerability.

Liberals, like terrorists, seem in this novel to make nothing happen; Aileen and Frank, the only two to survive unscathed, are also unchanged. In the novel's last paragraph they are flying back to America, entertained by a movie that features David Niven in a tropical helmet, fighting off urban guerrillas. Doubtless this pessimistic ending echoes McCarthy's own disillusionment in the late 1970s. This traveler to Vietnam knew well the missionary impulse that drives her fictional liberals; yet a decade later, disillusioned not only with North Vietnam but with "politics in general," she told Miriam Gross that "America is horribly sad and discouraging"; though she still believed in "socialism with a human face," she was convinced that "nobody will ever give it a chance" to work (McCarthy, "World" 174). After this Götterdämmerung of progressive politics she wrote no more novels; perhaps there was nothing left to be unfaithful to.

4

Doris Lessing's
The Good Terrorist

Like Mary McCarthy, Doris Lessing had a long history of Leftist activism; unlike McCarthy, she joined the Communist Party and remained a member until the Hungarian Revolution of 1956. Like McCarthy, she is a keen satirist of the personal shortcomings of political idealists and the poses and postures of the public meeting. In spite of these considerable strengths, when *The Good Terrorist* appeared in 1985, Denis Donoghue objected to the book's many inaccuracies. The novel's heroine, he argued, is "posthumous," its characters a "libel on hippies": contemporary English protesters do not talk like that, contemporary English class divisions are sharper than Lessing makes them seem (29). Lessing, in the meantime, announced that her novel is "not a book with a political statement" (C. James 3), though even a surface reading would seem to suggest that the problem is more precisely that its political message is far more conservative, both about women and about action, than we might expect from a feminist icon and former Communist. Moreover, the novel seems dependent on literary models of terrorism, though its author, a secondary school dropout, has made much of her independence from literary movements and would doubtless wish to argue that her books are based on direct observation and not on other books. *The Good Terrorist*, in short, is an object lesson in the problematic relationship between realistic novels and terrorism, a relationship grounded in the author's anxiety about the efficacy, the power and clarity, of language. Terrorists, she implies, can teach us a great deal about the failures of novelists.

In *Alchemists of Revolution: Terrorism in the Modern World*, Richard L. Rubenstein argues that terrorism originates in despair about language.

Quoting Lenin's disapproving remark that "terrorism is the violence of intellectuals," Rubenstein argues that most terrorists start out attempting to communicate their programs in speeches and manifestos. Yet when their words go unheeded, they turn to actions meant to speak louder (Rubenstein 8). In *The Good Terrorist*, the fictional Communist Centre Union (CCU) moves from relatively harmless verbal activism— making speeches, heckling politicians, painting slogans on walls—to bombing partly because it senses that its members can no longer communicate with the working class. It is true that when the central character, Alice Mellings, renovates the reeking squat in which one contingent has been living for months she sets off "an explosion of order" (49) in the lives of its inhabitants, and that, as Alison Lurie points out, her "domestic genius" provides a haven for the terrorists, giving them a place where they can stay together long enough to plot the bombing (10). But more importantly, the CCU becomes increasingly alienated from everyone else, increasingly aware that no one listens to its propaganda, that no one understands its fine intentions. If the British working class is dissatisfied with Tory policy in Belfast, it does not say so. Demonstrating a lack of solidarity with the homeless, workers follow Council orders to pour cement into the toilets and rip out the wiring of abandoned houses. Strikers express no gratitude for the group's participation in their rallies: "Crabit, the strikers' representative, said he wished the Trotskyists and the rent-a-picket crowd would keep away. They weren't wanted. The workers could deal with things themselves" (142). When the CCU offers to join forces with the IRA, they are summarily rejected, and although the KGB recruits two of the radicals, its local representative dismisses the rest as "little children playing dangerous games" (279). Police persecution, culminating in an incident in which three off-duty officers toss a bag of excrement into the house, effectively suggests the impossibility of returning to the mainstream. To bomb a London street is to defy not only Margaret Thatcher but also her entrenched opposition: "Who are the IRA to tell us what to do in our own country?" (349)

Rubenstein analyzes such alienation at some length. Although he acknowledges that a long-lived nationalist movement like the IRA becomes proletarianized, he argues that in the first generation, terrorism "is the violence of a new intelligentsia, one that has severed its ties with both the upper classes (masters of the corporate and state bureaucracies) and the lower classes, which the terrorists hope eventually to activate by setting a heroic example and by 'intensifying calamities'" (17). In czarist Russia, as in many contemporary Latin American countries—and, we might add, contemporary England—a generation of working-class and lower-middle-class youth have had access to university educations denied their parents. Yet graduation has left them facing the "disappearance of reform-oriented social management jobs"—those positions in education or social services that might channel their idealism peacefully (79). If they are unwilling to "work exclusively for the repressive state," they have no alternatives but to "work for the people" (79). But when "the more militant working class political parties and trade unions" have either been suppressed or grown conservative, young intellectuals lack a structure to connect them with working-class people whose tastes, habits, and, above all, language are no longer theirs. Such a situation is a formula for disaster: "ambitious idealists without a creative ruling class to follow or a rebellious lower class to lead have . . . often taken upon themselves the burden of representative action" (79).[1]

"Contemporary terrorism," says John Orr, is the "last resort of those who have effectively abandoned the political struggle for mass support . . . [it] is dystopian, arising from the active and at times cynical despair of those who still believe" (5). Lessing's novel follows this model precisely, even adding the point we noted earlier about the alienation of new radicals from established subversives who, like the state, admire middle-class virtues such as common sense and a capacity for hard work.[2]

We have already discussed the critical link between modern terrorism and the invention (1848) and perfection (1881) of the rotary press. The terrorist despairs of "mere words" in an age of mass journalism, arguing that speech can only be heard when it is supplemented with dynamite. More literary figures rejected ordinary language, the socially agreed-upon links between words and things, in large part because it had become the language of journalism. Stéphane Mallarmé, claims Jean-Paul Sartre, practices a "terrorism of politeness": "Since man cannot create, but does have the power to destroy . . . the poem will be a work of destruction" (Sartre 5, 10; my translation). Mallarmé's abstractions, his difficulty, his movement into a private language, correspond in the novel to the experiments of *Finnegans Wake* or *M. Teste*. Yet to a realistic novelist these experiments are, precisely, a work of destruction, exploding assumptions about the power of language to appeal to a large audience, to speak with anything like directness about a shared public life. One can argue that the fascination of so many serious realists with terrorism lies precisely in their too vivid understanding of—and need to defend themselves against—the absolute disillusion with language that terrorists embody.

If terrorists turn to bombs because words do not speak loudly enough, novelists may choose language but secretly share the terrorists' suspicion of it. As we have seen, Conrad's *Under Western Eyes* is riddled with the suspicion that "words . . . are the great foes of reality" (1). In *The Secret Agent,* as William Bysshe Stein has noted, "the flow of action . . . erodes in meaning under the insidious counterflow of language" (523). Every abstract word seems to evoke its opposite: nothing could be more damning in that novel than to be called "loving," "respectable," "scientific," or—worse yet—"genuine."

In Lessing herself this suspicion has come to attach itself to the word *voice,* which has evolving connotations for her. In 1957 Lessing closed an essay celebrating the nineteenth-century realistic novel by paraphrasing Wordsworth—"the novelist talks, as an individual to individuals"—and predicted that in an age of "committee art" people would "feel again a need for the small personal voice" ("Small" 21). A decade later she seems to have changed her mind, and *voice* in her novels became associated with the schizophrenic's paranormal insight. But the schizophrenic's voices relay only impersonal truths; as Elaine Showalter aptly notes, "the feminine ego is merged . . . for Lessing, into a transmitter for the collective consciousness" (311). Thus the narrator in *The Four-Gated City* denies the uniqueness of individual emotions or even historical events: one does not so much hate as "plug into hate," an impersonal force (496); future historians will not speak of particular wars but will say that "war expressed itself" between, say, 1939 and 1945 (132). As small personal voices were replaced with anonymous truth-telling voices, Lessing's style became progressively colorless, abstract, pompous; the bureaucrat Johor's endless summaries of Shikastan history, for example:

> At the top of this structure was the privileged class of technicians and organisers and manipulators, in uniform or out of uniform. An international class of the highly educated in technology, the planners and organisers, were fed, were housed, and interminably travelled, interminably conferred, and formed from country to country a web of experts and administrators whose knowledge of the desperateness of

the Shikastan situation caused ideological and national barriers to mean less than nothing between themselves, while in the strata below them these barriers were always intensifying, strengthening. (234)

The welcomed return to earth in *The Good Terrorist* is accompanied by a renewed sense of speech differences, but also by a heightened sense that the voice in which one speaks may not be a spontaneous authentic expression of a personality but a deception. The most obvious examples of this phenomenon are Comrade Andrew and Comrade O'Leary, who acquired their almost flawless American accents in Soviet spy schools. Her terrorists mostly have acquired voices: Faye, for example, speaks a "pretty cockney" in her calmer moments, but her madness speaks "out of . . . some dreadful deprivation" and is "in no way related to the pretty cockney" (35). Pat has to "work too hard" at "standard middle class" for it to be "how she started off" (32). Roberta has a "made-up" voice, probably "modeled on 'Coronation Street'" (30). Bert and Jasper have genuine middle-class voices, "roughened" to sound working class (311). Alice has a BBC voice that "dated from the days of her girls' school in North London" (30); this the novelist calls Alice's "own voice, unmodified" (32), but she knows enough to address groups in a "meeting voice" (9). The bomb-maker, Jocelin, imitates the IRA gunrunners' Irish accents so perfectly that Alice judges that she may actually be Irish: "Does it matter? Here is another of us with a false voice!" (416).

What matters to Lessing, if not to Alice, is that the terrorists who have chosen action over the word depend on the media—the BBC, *Coronation Street*—both to give them their speaking voices and to give voice to their actions. They reject "mere words," not in favor of "mere action," but in favor of words amplified by violence and its attendant publicity: as we have seen, terrorist activity is notoriously symbolic. As Schmid and de Graaf put it, the "immediate victim . . . is the skin on a drum beaten to achieve a calculated impact" (14). Lessing's terrorists make no such precise calculations, but they do see their violence as requiring mediation. They read the local newspaper's account of their first bombing the way actors check their reviews. If proving themselves to the IRA was a reason to begin a bombing campaign, then the media's failure to recognize their first achievement is the immediate reason for doing more damage the next time: "A paragraph in the local *Advertiser*! They felt it was a snub of them, another in a long series of belittlings of what they really were, of their real capacities, that had begun—like Faye's violences—so long ago they could not remember. They were murderous with the need to impose themselves, prove their power" (386). The decision to escalate to the car bomb that kills five is explicitly a reaction to having received only one "little paragraph in the *Guardian*." "We'll show them" is the unspoken thought "in all their minds" (384). The next bomb must go off during the day, when more people are around: "This way, it'll be front page in all the newspapers tomorrow, and on the news tonight" (426).

Part of the point, of course, is the symbiotic relation between terrorists and the press; bombs sell newspapers. More critically, the blunted language of a debased politics is the language of newspapers and television. Revolutionary graffiti and newspaper headlines have the same style, the same eye-catching slogans designed to fit a small space. The simplistic world view the media promote feeds violence. Thus although the IRA rejects Jason and Bert, the newspapers are willing to accept the IRA as the source of their bomb. Alice's panicky cry that "It's the IRA" is proof enough for the BBC: "This monstrous and callous crime illustrated yet again the total lack of ordinary feeling by the IRA" (444).[3] But if the language of public discourse is debased, Lessing seems to find no consolation in the language of literature and political theory. True, Alice is the image of a person in part created by the mass media who will read nothing but newspapers because she cannot face the "risky equivocal" contents of books, fearing to be "lost without maps" (73). But Pat, who reads Nabokov's *Laughter in the Dark* and then joins the KGB, and Faye, who is "particularly well up on Althusser" and then dies because she mistimes a car bomb, are worse, not better, models (318). Perhaps the point is not that Althusser and Nabokov somehow breed terrorism, but that the small personal voice of printed books is drowned out by the loud impersonal voices of the mass media, with their affiliations to power and consumers' interest in violence. Afloat on a sea of what Lessing calls "undulant rhetoric" in *Documents Relating to the Sentimental Agents,* most of the characters seem prepared to die without understanding that words might point to a reality rather than help structure a fantasy. One of Alice's most sympathetic moments comes when she hears in the single meaningful word *matériel* how far her group has gone in the direction of killing people: "The use of the word *matériel* now, in this context, was not thrilling her at all. In this situation (one she wanted to shake off and be rid of), the word *matériel* was too portentous; it was a word that insisted on being taken seriously" (365).

Thus the exuberant faith in the clarity of language found in Lessing's 1957 essay seems to have been replaced in *The Good Terrorist* by a deep suspicion of public discourse reminiscent of conservative writers such as Flaubert and Conrad. And since, as Dorothy Van Ghent's classic essay on the economic language of *Pride and Prejudice* argues, the good people and the bad, the novelist and the politician, must all use the same language, such a suspicion is incompatible with a romantic commitment to the purity of literature. *The Good Terrorist*, for all its caricaturing of terrorists, seems to understand their impatience with mere words.

If mere words, the language of public discourse, are debased, the writer may well wish to turn to more intuitive models of communication, the discourse of private symbolism and even madness. Madness is a familiar part of the Lessing landscape. In the past thirty years, the attitude we have come to expect is expressed in the fifth volume of the *Canopus in Argos* series, where she explains that on a repressive planet called Sirius "anyone who tries to use language accurately to describe what is in fact happening vanishes into torture rooms and prisons or, diagnosed as mad, into mental hospitals" (*Documents* 81). In *The Four-Gated City* and *Shikasta*, Lynda Coldridge, a diagnosed schizophrenic, is seen as a heroic figure whose voices are really a form of extrasensory perception. Yet in *The Good Terrorist*, certainty that madness is an accurate language expressing the truth that evades logical discourse is gone. Alice has some of Lynda's paranormal powers, though in the more attenuated form of "dreamy knowing states" in which she understands the unstated: that Muriel and Pat are going to spy school (301), that Reggie and Mary have found a flat (343), that Reggie, an industrial chemist, has found a job doing something of which she would disapprove (344). In Alice's case, however, these paranormal powers fail at the critical moment when a British agent comes to the door and she, mistaking him for a Russian, babbles freely about Comrade O'Leary's arms shipment.

Alice's incipient madness, perhaps schizophrenia, becomes more visible as the novel progresses. Her rages and memory lapses are distinctly abnormal; her aversion to sex is total: "She did not like being touched, not ever!" (204). She has nearly uncontrollable rages that belie the image of the "good girl" she can produce on demand for authority figures. When a letter from the Electricity Board explains that her father refuses to guarantee her bill, Alice explodes, "teeth grinding, eyes bulging, fists held as if knives were in them. She stormed around the kitchen, like a big fly shut in a room on a hot afternoon, banging herself against walls, corners of table and stove, not knowing what she did, and making grunting, whining, snarling noises" (150). This private madness explicitly connects to her terrorist impulses: "hot waves of murder beat inside her. I'll blow that house of theirs up . . . I'll kill them" (173). Over an electricity bill. Alice is also frighteningly unable to assimilate or remember unwelcome information: that her mother's house is being sold escapes her even though she telephoned the estate agent herself. "Alice did know that she forgot things," comments the narrator, "but not how badly, or how often" (454).

Alice's disturbances have their roots in a childhood that she has never entirely outgrown and into which she retreats in moments of crisis to dwell "pleasurably on some scene or other that she had smoothed and polished and painted over and over again with fresh colour" (454). Nonetheless, the frequently iterated links between Alice's present behavior and her past do not lead readers to blame her parents for her behavior: as Lurie says, they seem to have been "model liberal parents, warm and affectionate and concerned" (9). Even though Lessing tells her readers, for example, that Alice found giving up her room to her parents' guests unbearably painful, she does not explain why. If a Freudian explanation lurks in her aversion to sleeping on the floor of her parents' bedroom ("she could not cope with it," 263) I do not know why that aversion should be so intense nor why she is compelled to repeat it as an adult; throughout the novel she sleeps on the floor, repelled by the sounds from the next room. Stripped of mantic glamor, such unfathomable and therefore quite possibly incurable madness frightens rather than illuminates.

The link between private madness and terrorist impulses that characterizes Alice also characterizes the other terrorists in the novel, most of whom are also distinctly pathological types who, as we have seen, repel the IRA and the KGB as much as they do the bourgeoisie. Certainly Lessing is successful in making us feel their chilling lack of balance, their rapid transitions from the adolescent pleasures of shouting at policemen and gorging on take-out pizza to deadlier activities, bombmaking and gunrunning. There is Faye, who keeps going, between fits of weeping and raging, on the strength of various anti-psychotic drugs and the motherly attentions of her lover, Roberta; "something [in her] was too dangerous for words, or at least volatile, to be set off like a risky electronic device by an injudicious combination of sounds" (170). Jason, Alice's homosexual companion, respects Alice's aversion to sex while bullying her for money; pale-eyed and vicious, he arouses in almost everyone who meets him "some instinctive warning, or shrinking" (120). Even the other terrorists have trouble looking the bomb-maker, Jocelin, in the face, for "she was angry all the time, as if a generalized anger had taken her over at some point and she had come to believe that this was how one experienced the world" (347). The carpenter Philip's characterization is true of everyone except Alice: "All of you people . . . never lift a finger, never do any work, parasites" (335); a heavy-handed irony about allies of the workers who never work runs through the novel. The CCU's haziness about its political program, which we examine in more detail later, is matched by a corresponding haziness about its members' motives for joining. After Pat, a relatively cheerful and efficient type, goes off to a Soviet spy school without explaining how she became "serious" about revolution, we are left with a collection of sick people whose symptoms have taken a political turn.

Lessing's decision to describe such a fringe group is achieved at the price of rendering a political subject very nearly apolitical. In the real world, discovering why people blow up department stores usually requires asking historical as well as psychological questions. What social conditions, what injustices, or what breakdown of peaceful processes drives people to radical violence and cause significant numbers of their compatriots to tolerate or even support them? By choosing to disable such questions, Lessing follows a well-established literary tradition. One thinks immediately of Dostoevsky's characterization of one such unbalanced terrorist: "The executive line was what was required by this shallow, scant-reasoning character, eternally longing to submit to another's will. . . . little fanatics like Erkel simply cannot understand service to an idea otherwise than by merging it with the very person who . . . expresses this idea" (575). More globally, Conrad sees terrorists feeding on the "sinister impulses which lurk in the blind envy and exasperated vanity of ignorance" (*Secret* 78), while James and his sympathetic terrorist manqué, Hyacinth Robinson, share "a great horror of that kind of invidious jealousy which is at the bottom of the idea of a redistribution" (*Princess* 335).

Moreover, Lessing inserts her novel into a contemporary discourse about terrorism that Edward Said has analyzed perceptively. Speaking of the Reagan administration's response to Middle Eastern terrorism, he notes that since terrorism became "public enemy number one" it has been used to institutionalize "the denial and avoidance of history" (149). If we are terrified enough, the argument goes, we do not ask questions about the public causes of terrorism or about the measures our government adopts for stamping it out.[4] The advantages of seeing terrorists as shiftless, vicious, and delusional are unfortunately clear, for such a view displaces focus from the political and social causes of violence to its private and personal sources.

To be sure, like Conrad, Dostoevsky, and James, Lessing is deeply aware of the flaws of the society in which she lives. As Peter Widdowson notes, the novel suggests that "straight" society has no positive values to "assert against the terrorists" and may even be "the cause of, responsible for terrorism" (15). Alice's rage at the ugliness of public architecture and at the bureaucracy's destruction of livable housing while families are crowded into welfare hotels seems clearly to be Lessing's own. Like Conrad and James, too, she sees an affinity between police and terrorists; references to Greenham Common remind the reader that if the terrorists have time bombs, the government—or the Americans— have *the* bomb. Such implicit criticisms militate against the complacencies of popular fictions in which the villains are the only blot on an ideal scene, but they do not account for the IRA activity with which the CCU seeks to link itself and that Lessing has said compelled her to write the novel[5]. By displacing the action to England and making all of her central characters English, Lessing effectively forecloses any possibility that the reader will enter imaginatively into the experiences that produced and sustain the IRA. Nor does she spell out the political consequences of anti-terrorist legislation, such as the 1988 abolition of the rights of persons accused of terrorist activity to remain silent, or the Prevention of Terrorism Act of 1974, which among other provisions allows for arrest and detention up to seven days without warrant, a provision even the British government's own review found to have had "serious implications in terms of civil liberties" (Jellicoe, 10). A Belfast sequence that included a few old-fashioned Catholics praying for the conversion of Russia would have pointed to contradictions between the traditions of Irish nationalism and Soviet Communism that Lessing's novel effaces.

Lessing instead makes much of the KGB's interest in British radical groups: Comrade Andrew next door not only recruits Pat and Muriel but "organizes" propaganda and "other things," that is, guns, for the IRA (348). Lessing's view again draws on a stereotype much encouraged by conservative politicians and popular novelists: a worldwide network of terrorists trained at "spy schools in Czechoslovakia or Lithuania" (301). Certainly, the Soviet Union and its allies recruited and trained foreign agents; how far the Soviet Union went in supporting the IRA remains debatable. Roberta Goren's highly conservative *The Soviet Union and Terrorism*, which is introduced by Robert Conquest, makes rather searching claims, but these are largely based on what the author takes to be approving references to Irish "freedom fighters" in the Soviet press. Even she concedes that "most of the financial aid to the IRA has come from Irish-Americans sympathetic to the cause" (itself a debatable claim); hard evidence is limited to two interceptions of Czech arms to the Provisional IRA, one in 1971 and one in 1973 (172, 169, 170). Amusingly, a 1990 book coauthored by a former KGB agent says that his employers regarded the Provisional IRA much as Lessing's KGB regards Jasper and Bert:

> On a number of occasions during the 1970s and 1980s, the PIRA made approaches to KGB officers in Dublin and to officers from the London residency visiting Belfast under journalistic cover. The approaches were reported to the Center, which refused permission for them to be followed up. The residency in Dublin was usually reluctant to make contact with any illegal group because of what it regarded as the near-impossibility of keeping secrets in the Irish Republic. KGB officers claimed that merely by listening to conversations in a number of public houses frequented by Sinn Fein supporters they were able to learn a surprising amount. (Andrew and Gordievsky 633)

But whatever further evidence of a Soviet connection one might be able to adduce, the overwhelming majority of experts agree with the British Army Intelligence report that in 1979 found "no indication of any substantial link between the Soviet Union and the IRA" (Maas 33). As Beau Grosscup explains, "the conflict in Northern Ireland, though it has its international components, remains fundamentally Irish, defined by its . . . historical record and by . . . local and regional . . . factors" (213–14). Or as Richard Rubenstein makes the more general case: "It is . . . a myth that terrorist groups can be 'crushed in the egg' by cutting off their external sources of supply. It is the local political base that makes the

terrorist organization or breaks it" (56). Although the 1990s produced a
new power-sharing government for Northern Ireland and a reduction
in the number of casualties, the collapse of the Soviet Union did not
spell the end of Irish terrorism.[6]

One readily sees the point of Denis Donoghue's argument that by
portraying her terrorists as incompetents, Lessing soothes the middle
class: "bourgeois liberalism is safe if these are the only enemies it has to
face" (3). And certainly the consolations of a conspiracy theory that
leaves one free to ignore such apparently intractable problems as Catholic unemployment in Northern Ireland or the threat to civil liberties
even in England are obvious. But, on the whole, Lessing's novel is singularly unconsoling. For one thing, the personal unattractiveness and
clinically significant psychological symptoms of most of its leadership
hardly stood in the way of the Nazi Party; Hitler at the time of the Munich putsch must have been a distinctly unimposing figure. That Jasper,
as Dorothy Mellings predicts, will be minister of culture in the New
Britain is incongruous but hardly impossible for that reason. The novel's
pessimism depends heavily on its attribution of terrorism not to social
conditions—which might, with whatever difficulty, be articulated or improved—but to unapproachable centers of power and unfathomable
madness.

Yet terrorism is premised on a belief in the efficacy, if not of language,
of action. Lessing's novel gives no such reassurances. Her fictional
splinter group of vaguely anarcho-Marxist tendencies, the CCU, is com-
posed largely of young university graduates with working-class origins,
though Alice is upper middle class; Muriel, the radical next door, "was
an upper-class girl and this was why she [Alice] disliked her so much"
(299). The group accepts the line that Britain is "rotten as a bad apple,
and ready for the bulldozers of history" (206), though their analysis
never becomes more specific than the view that unemployment "has to
be exploited," along with "the mass disgust of the British people for the
government's policy over nuclear armaments" and the "budding and
still-unexpressed rejection of the British people for the Tory policy in
Northern Ireland" (274). What form the "full socialism" (275) they advocate would take never becomes clear. As we have seen, the CCU's activities, at the time when the novel begins, have been largely verbal,
occasionally accompanied by symbolic violence such as tomato throwing. Although many of the group's members have been "bound over"

for various protest activities, and all routinely live illegally in condemned buildings and exploit the welfare system, they have avoided violent crime. Unclear about its own political program, its members driven by private madness and paradoxically dependent on the government-controlled media for the very accents of their voices, the CCU can only drift toward irrational action. Their climactic act, setting off a car bomb in front of a London hotel that kills one of their own members and four other people, is a model of senseless violence. Publicity is unfavorable; the IRA threatens to "kneecap those who committed such acts in their name" (449); detection is imminent in the last pages of the novel, where Alice falls into the hands of a "professional," the British agent Peter Cecil.

Well-intentioned liberal attempts to improve social conditions fare no better and are swallowed up by the state and its corporate allies, just as the more effective members of the CCU are swallowed up by the KGB. Mary Williams, for example, takes a job with the Housing Council in order to help the homeless, only to discover that it cooperates with private developers to reduce the amount of affordable housing. Alice's own attempts to help all fail or, as in the case of reviving Faye, who goes on to kill four people, prove worse than useless. As in the last chapters of *The Four-Gated City* and in the Canopus series, power belongs, again as in Foucault, to anonymous forces whose secret will even their critics seem to carry out. In the Canopus books, Lessing invented a master race of benign aliens who look out for humankind; reading *The Good Terrorist*, one certainly sees why she felt the need.

One of the few differences between Lessing's terrorists and those of Conrad and Dostoevsky is that so many more of them are women—as is the prime minister. Yet the novel provides no sense that women temper the violence of public life or even find that political activity empowers them. Just as in *The Secret Agent* Conrad shows how the authoritarian bullying characteristic of the police is replicated in the terrorist network, so Lessing shows women on the left trapped in the patriarchy they despise. *The Good Terrorist*, in the best tradition of *Mansfield Park*, *Jane Eyre*, and *Mrs. Dalloway*, defines a woman in terms of her house. Susan Gubar and Sandra Gilbert's *The Madwoman in the Attic* argues that the spaces that enclose a woman often become a metaphor for her mind. In Brontë's novel, "Thornfield is . . . the house of Jane's life, its floors and walls the architecture of her experience" (347). To be sure, in the more

traditional patriarchal terms suggested by a phrase like "the House of
Atreus," we understand house as a metaphor for a family, tradition, nation; and this sense also operates in Lessing's novel. The first words of
The Good Terrorist describe the sordid squat Alice will transform: "The
house was set back from the noisy main road in what seemed to be a
rubbish tip. A large house. Solid" (3). Alice's first words try to place it: "I
should think 1910" (3). Certainly, throughout the novel, 43 Old Mill
Road is this remnant of Edwardian England, assaulted by land developers who wish to tear it down to build flats, by police who befoul it, by
IRA gunrunners who insist on thrusting their guns through its front
door—but the dry rot in its attic is enough to bring it down. Even more
importantly, one part of the heroine, as Alison Lurie aptly remarks, is
the angel in this house, burying the buckets of excrement that line its
bedrooms, painting its walls, stealing and begging and bullying to get
its electricity and gas hooked up, its water tank replaced, its toilets re-
paired (9). Her happiest moments are those fragile ones ("just one little
thing—puff!—and it would be gone") when, like Woolf's Mrs. Ramsay,
she assembles a group around her well-scrubbed table: "The kitchen
was mellow, alive. The jug on the little stool held tulips and lilacs" (285,
284). A woman who reads no books, who has only the vaguest ideas
even about Lenin or Marx, Alice is extraordinarily attentive to the history of the house, reading the past lives of its occupants in the artifacts
they have left buried in the backyard or stored away in the attic. In the
novels of women, the upper reaches of a house may well conceal what
is essential to the protagonist's soul: one thinks immediately of Bertha
Rochester's rage, but also of Clarissa Dalloway's narrow white bed. If
Brontë's well-trained governess and Woolf's perfect hostess are defined
by the dangerous freedoms of death and madness that the drawing
room does not permit, what does the terrorist find in her attic? Why, a
New Look dress with gold lace: Alice pulls it over her head and then
strips it off angrily, "as if she had been tempted by the forbidden," when
she begins to feel "that the dress was laying a claim on her" (188). To be
not only female but also feminine in the sense of the 1950s is a temptation Alice ruthlessly represses, a perennial source of guilt: "Here I am,
fussing about a house, while they are doing something serious" (88).
Defacing property—painting slogans on walls—is, therefore, Alice's favorite revolutionary activity, scarcely to be distinguished from more private ones, throwing a rock through a window in her father's house or
ripping the curtains out of her mother's.

Alice's long quarrel with her mother is the novel's most vivid conflict, but the reader meets Dorothy Mellings only once, near the end of the novel. The first evocations of the Mellings' past have the flavor of a Margaret Drabble novel. Cedric Mellings, a poor Northerner, comes to London to write books and buys a printing firm, which makes him rich. The sixties are a "golden age. . . times of easy friendships, jobs opportunities, money; people dropping in and out, long family meals around an enormous table" (246). But then the ice age sets in: Cedric and Dorothy divorce, the printing firm loses business, confidence evaporates. Alice's rage is more easily connected to the loss of this Eden than to any public issue: "It had all been rubbish, all of it. What Alice could not forgive herself for was that she had been taken in by it" (248).

But it is more precise to say that she cannot forgive her mother for letting this Eden be lost. Throughout the novel, Alice's thoughts return obsessively to her mother. A family friend calls her a case of "arrested development," and it is difficult to disagree when one notes that at thirty-six Alice still thinks about her mother as a child of ten or thirteen might: "She didn't want to be like her mother—selfish. She used to nag and bitch to have an afternoon to herself: the children had to lump it. Privacy. That lot made such a thing about privacy" (125). Twenty years ago her mother had told Alice that she would shortly begin to menstruate. By doing so, her mother "made it all real. She was angry, not with Nature, but with her mother" (286).

Bearing the burden of being for her daughter a symbol of both Nature and the English bourgeoisie would, indeed, be enough to drive any mother to drink, a fate Dorothy Mellings embraces wholeheartedly. Forced to put her house up for sale because of Jason and Alice's sponging and then to sell it cheaply after Alice steals the curtains a German buyer had insisted on, Dorothy lives alone in a shabby flat. Part of her torment is what Martha Quest would have called the old nightmare Repetition. She sees the irony that has indeed been only too visible to the reader: "it turned out that you spend your life exactly as I did. Cooking and nannying for other people. An all-purpose female drudge" (406). Her voice has real authority: where in *Children of Violence* the daughter took a pitiless look at herself in the mirror of a dreadful mother, now the intelligent mother sees herself in the mirror of an unstable, exploited, and dangerous daughter. The point does not limit itself to the private life, for Dorothy is considerably more lucid about politics than Alice. In Dorothy's eyes the happy progressive sixties led beyond the ice age into the apocalypse. Having come to believe that protests and demonstrations are "fun" for the protesters and "a joke" to the "people who really run this world" (412), she regrets her earlier activism. Her best friend says she is becoming a fascist who sees Reds under every bed: "There are Reds under every bed," said Dorothy seriously. . . . The funny thing was, we *were* the Reds under the beds" (409). Her heresy goes so far as to lead her to consider supporting the policies of Thatcher and Reagan as a case of fighting for the bad against the worse (410).

Whether we should take such statements as proving that Doris Lessing, former Communist Party member and feminist role model, despairs of feminism, votes for Margaret Thatcher, and remains convinced that the most typical mother-daughter relationship damages both, irrevocably, for life, is a matter of debate. Certainly to be isolated, inactive, and alcoholic are grave limitations for a *raisonneur*. Yet the novel offers no other articulated alternative to the demented bomb-throwing politics of the CCU and the terrifying efficiencies of the intelligence services, British and Soviet. Where action always fails, retreat to an empty flat may at least have the spartan virtue of a rigorous honesty. Alison Lurie quite correctly points to affinities between Alice Mellings and her creator that the resemblance between their names reinforces (10), but "Dorothy Mellings" is even closer to "Doris Lessing." One could go so far as to argue that Dorothy defines the novel's point of view, is its hidden narrator. Alice is a radical activist as seen by a woman in late middle age; Alice's obsession with her childhood is less perplexing if the novel's implied narrator is a mother worrying about the roots of her adult daughter's disturbing behavior. For all the novel's surface realism, its bubbling slop buckets and greasy packets of chips, we can never quite believe in Alice's world as we believe in Martha Quest's, but we have no trouble at all accepting Dorothy Mellings's distaste for it. In the novel's last line the tone becomes positively maternal: "Smiling gently, a mug of very strong sweet tea in her hand, looking this morning like a nine-year-old girl who has had, perhaps, a bad dream, the poor baby sat waiting for it to be time to go out and meet the professionals" (456). The perspective from which Alice is a "poor baby" is the one that makes the final judgment on her.

As we have seen, *The Good Terrorist* is an exemplary novel about terrorism. Factually inaccurate or at least radically selective about its facts, despairing about public action, reactionary in its implied politics of quietism and complicity with power, the novel faithfully follows its more prestigious models—*Demons, The Secret Agent, The Princess Casamassima.* Lessing's claim that her novel has no political message, that it is only about a certain type of radical, seems belied by the lack of alternatives to them. Yet the novel's meaning does not really depend on its accuracy about the IRA or contemporary terrorism, about which it in fact seems to care very little. What attracts the novelist to her subject is a fascination with the inaudibility of personal voices, with the fragility of printed books in a world where the electronic media accent our speech and feed our violence. One might argue that we are more endangered by the missiles at Greenham Common than by any number of time bombs assembled by madwomen in their attics, but perhaps the novel does not make that distinction. Secret sharer in the nightmare of a world without the power of speech, *The Good Terrorist* understands only too well why terrorists despair of words.

Part III

Novelist as Terrorist: Terrorism as Fiction

5

J. M. Coetzee's
The Master of Petersburg

n violent times, some novelists abandon literature altogether, taking to the streets or barricades; others, of course, bring the streets and barricades into their fiction, exposing suffering and injustice, arguing, pleading, and persuading. Those who do neither will stand accused of complacency, perhaps collaboration; when bent on justice, many people firmly believe that those who are not for them are against them. In our time South Africa has been one of those places that seem to compel writers into action, and as a professor at the University of Cape Town, J. M. Coetzee has spent much of his adult life in a country where, for many years, guerillas were locked in combat with a repressive state. And though the university was doubtless far more sheltered than some dusty township in Soweto, it was no less vulnerable to the apocalyptic civil war many reasonable people were predicting. In such circumstances, Coetzee's failure to engage politics directly brought him much criticism; Nadine Gordimer, for example, argued that indirection, allegory, and distance in his novels kept Coetzee safe, preventing his work from being banned by the old South African censorship (Gallagher 12).

Yet, of course, Coetzee's novels frequently attend to the cruelest realities. From the bombing and defoliating of *Dusklands* to the labor camps and burning settlements of *The Life and Times of Michael K.* and *The Age of Iron*, history in his novels is marked by violent invasions, by mutilated bodies, by civil war. Standing apart from this history, but somehow engaged and responsible and guilty, is the figure of the writer, perhaps a colonial administrator with a taste for archaeology, perhaps the employee of a think tank, fingering a photo of a sergeant from Texas raping a Vietnamese child. Such figures tell us that Coetzee has always agonized over the question of where writers stand in relationship to public atrocity, what responsibilities they bear for it, and how they might usefully respond.

But the quality of a writer's political engagements, he told an interviewer, should not be measured in the simple way Gordimer suggests; a naive realism only reproduces the injustice it describes, licking wounds rather than offering a critical alternative to the mind-set that produced injustice in the first place. In place of such realism, Coetzee offers a more sophisticated, ironic narrative, one capable of "demythologizing history" (Attwell 15). Such narratives, he says, are not "supplementary" to history; that is, they cannot be checked against it, as a teacher might check a child's homework against the answer book; rather, they are a rival, sometimes even an enemy, discourse. Thus the point of an ironic narrative is not so much that it substitutes a more accurate version of history and politics for the received one as that it lays bare the unacknowledged assumptions that shape both stories.

Coetzee's impulse to assess the relationship between writers and public violence becomes even more evident in *The Master of Petersburg*, where he turns to the theme of terrorism. This time, however, the fictional figure of the writer is played not by an obscure bureaucrat or a cancer-ridden professor writing her last letters to a daughter in America, but by Fyodor Dostoevsky, whose *Demons* is the master narrative of the writer's vexed relation to terrorism. The historical Dostoevsky had transformed the notorious Sergei Nechaev into the sociopath Peter Verkhovensky; Coetzee invents an encounter between a fictional Dostoevsky and Nechaev that thoroughly destabilizes the relationship between the novelist, by middle age a staunch czarist, and his subject. Although never simply doubles for each other, Dostoevsky and Nechaev, in Coetzee's version, are drawn into a dialogue that points to their disturbing similarities.

To understand how Coetzee reimagines the relationship between a semi-fictionalized Dostoevsky and Nechaev requires us to consider their relationship in real life and in Dostoevsky's *Demons*. Sergei Nechaev was the author of the "Catechism of the Revolutionist," a 1869 manifesto setting forth a program of systematic terrorism. The catechism calls for total dedication to overthrowing the existing system, to doing anything, however cruel and treacherous, that furthers the cause; "he is not a revolutionary if he feels pity for anything in this world" (70). Hazy about specific historical circumstances, free of concrete alternatives to czarism, the catechism reads like a document produced by some desperate contemporary movement, the Khmer Rouge or the Shining Path.

Although, as far as we know, Nechaev and Dostoevsky never met, both spent some time in the Russian quarter of Geneva, where in September 1869 a Nechaev supporter, Nikolai Ogarev, encouraged the novelist to sit through a session of a congress sponsored by the League of Peace and Freedom. Nechaev himself was in Russia at the time, and Dostoevsky apparently missed the two most famous speakers at the congress, Garibaldi and Bakunin; as he retailed the event to his favorite niece, the posturing revolutionaries seemed more comical than horrifying. However, later in the year, when newspapers linked the self-proclaimed terrorist with the murder of a Petersburg student, Ivan Ivanov, Nechaev came to embody for Dostoevsky everything that was most sinister in the radical politics of his day. He began a pamphlet denouncing the terrorists; *Demons* represents a fusion of this pamphlet with a very different project, a novel about Stavrogin called *The Great Sinner*. As Dostoevsky compiled notebooks and then drafts of *Demons*, he consistently referred to the terrorist who finally became Peter Verkhovensky as "Nechaev." At the end of *Demons*, Peter attempts to consolidate his revolutionary cell by accusing the innocent Shatov of being an informer and cons its members into assisting him in murdering Shatov, an act that closely follows newspaper descriptions of the Ivanov murder. On the other hand, Dostoevsky freely acknowledged to friends the element of invention in his Nechaev figure. Peter Verkhovensky is the archetypal terrorist as sociopath; every element in his portrayal, from the wolfish greed with which he attacks his beefsteak to his compulsive toadying up to Stavrogin, repels sympathy and suggests that his politics mask personal derangement.

Where Dostoevsky had pathologized Nechaev, Coetzee restores his connections to the Russian people and suggests the social and not primarily private sources of his politics. In *The Master of Petersburg*, fictionalizing Dostoevsky and Nechaev equally allows Coetzee to bring the argument between writer and revolutionary into his own text and address it more explicitly than he has done elsewhere. In order to do so, he pulls the biographical Dostoevsky, who in *Demons* so artfully conceals himself behind Anton G——v, into the center of the stage; and if he does not exactly pathologize Dostoevsky, he certainly explores the private and psychological sources of the novelist's art and politics.

The highly conservative politics of *Demons,* coupled with its great authority, challenge any reader with progressive views. A good deal of this
authority is, of course, that of any highly successful realistic novel with
vivid characters. Dostoevsky does not lecture about the perfidies of expatriate intellectuals; he shows us Karmazinov's fussy preparations for
his public reading and lets us hear the drunken audience booing him off
the stage. A clever narrative strategy, in which many of the apocalyptic
events of the novel are seen through the eyes of the colorless, pedantic
Anton G——v, who spends quite a bit of time sorting out his sources
and offering alternative interpretations of motive, tends to persuade
readers that they are getting the accurate account of a nearly disinter-
ested man. When G——v is further effaced, so that the narrative slips
into the omniscient mode for chapters at a time, the reality effect only
further intensifies. But the authority of the novel also derives from the
author's well-known personal history: his imprisonment in Saint Peter
and Paul's Fortress, the mock execution, the years in Siberia. It is easier
to dismiss the conservative politics of a sheltered writer like Henry
James. Moreover, the course of Soviet history added a note of authenticity to the bloodthirsty plans of old revolutionaries like Dostoevsky's
Shigalov, who regretfully tabulates the millions of Russians who will
have to die for the new order. For good reason, Dostoevsky is one of our
most visible images of the romantic writer as tormented prophet in
whose works can be found a truthful vision of the coming apocalypse.

But Dostoevsky offers further problems for a novelist: his most political novel strongly questions the authority of writers to understand the
consequences of ideas embraced in the library or drawing room.
Demons is full of idle thinkers, university dropouts debating Fourier and
Proudhon over vodka and then, ashamed of their own ineffectualness,
murdering a harmless man. The sillier or the more pretentious a man is,
the more likely it is that he has an unpublished manuscript he wants
you to read; even the ridiculous governor, von Lembke, is a novelist.
Karmazinov, the Europeanized novelist modeled on Turgenev, fawns
over Peter Verkhovensky even as he declares his intention to move back
to Germany as soon as possible. The liberal intellectual not only offers
aid and comfort to terrorists; he actually breeds them. Stepan Verkhovensky, that classic liberal of the 1840s, farms his son out to distant
relatives and produces in Peter a disrespect for fathers—for authority,
tradition, common sense—that leads inexorably from bad manners to
blackmail, arson, and murder.

Challenging Dostoevsky is, in short, no easy task, but it takes Coetzee right to the heart of pressing questions about the authority of writers to speak out on public issues. As Coetzee conceives Dostoevsky as character rather than author, object rather than subject of a discourse, he both humanizes the man and subtly defamiliarizes his world. His Dostoevsky returns to Petersburg from Dresden to investigate the suspicious circumstances under which his stepson Pavel fell to his death from a disused tower on Stolyarny Quay. The fictional Dostoevsky's grief is movingly depicted as he visits the cemetery and becomes involved with a police investigation of the death and then with Pavel's radical friends. But Coetzee also refers liberally to deflating details, true enough to the biographical facts: his Dostoevsky worries about his indigestion and his hemorrhoids quite as much as about the famous epilepsy; he evinces mild anti-Semitism, needs a bath and clean underwear, is improvident, writes begging letters to his long-suffering friend Apollon Maikov. Unlike *Foe*, Coetzee's rewriting of the Robinson Crusoe story, *The Master of Petersburg* is written in late-twentieth-century language that also defamiliarizes Dostoevsky's world; Coetzee takes advantage, for example, of late-twentieth-century freedoms to spell out details of sexual relationships. Familiar features, samovars and tenements, philosophical policemen and saintly beggars, share the pages with apparently deliberate anachronisms such as Anna Sergeyevna's tendency to sound like a talk-show therapist: "what struck me when you told the story was how angry . . . you still seemed to be" (27).

Coetzee keeps visible the tension between his Dostoevsky as character and the famous author through alienation effects reminiscent of Brecht's. His allusions to Dostoevsky's work remind readers that they are not really at Dostoevsky's side in 1869. Dostoevsky's plaint early in the novel, "I am behaving like a character in a book," (27) is totally self-conscious. The reader recognizes the source of a joke that puzzles Dostoevsky; when Anna Sergeyevna, his landlady, urges him to move on so that he will not become "the eternal lodger," she asks, "Isn't that the name of a book?" "No, not that I know of," remarks Dostoevsky, whose real life counterpart was writing *The Eternal Husband* late in 1869. A similar effect occurs when Coetzee describes a golden-hearted young woman who supports her family by prostitution and then limits her pathos by having her introduced to Dostoevsky as "Sonya," which naturally gives the author of *Crime and Punishment* pause—"can her name really be Sonya?" (197).[1] The play between such alienation effects and the emphasis on humanizing a writer whose reality has been swallowed up in image reconfigures the relations between Dostoevsky and his characters. In *Demons* foreign residence equals deracination; it is at the heart of Karmazinov's irrelevance and one source of Stavrogin's pathology; Coetzee keeps reminding us of Dostoevsky's own long residence abroad. In suggesting that the motherless Pavel might have felt abandoned by his stepfather, who left him to the care of servants and sent him to boarding schools, Coetzee's Anna Sergeyevna links the author and Stepan Verkhovensky and invites us to remember that the youthful Dostoevsky shared Stepan's enthusiasm for Belinsky, Herzen, and the liberalization of Russia.

Maintaining an unsettled relationship throughout *The Master of Petersburg* between biography and fiction, history and plot, Coetzee develops the relationship between Nechaev and Dostoevsky against the backdrop of another disturbing relationship, that between the author and the central character in *Demons,* Stavrogin. Dostoevsky's basic strategy for linking his anti-revolutionary pamphlet with *The Great Sinner* was to create a friendship between Stavrogin and Peter Verkhovensky, who dreams of making this charismatic figure into a revolutionary hero. Coetzee, on the other hand, collapses Stavrogin into Dostoevsky—thus stripping the great sinner of all of his Romantic trappings, from his noble birth and his duels to his secret marriage to a holy madwoman and his Byronic appearance, so fatal to so many women. Then, through the invented medium of Pavel Isaev's suspicious death, he makes Dostoevsky himself the link to Nechaev and thus narrows the distance between the author and the radical politics of the late sixties.

Russian censors insisted that Dostoevsky rewrite the scandalous chapter in which Stavrogin gives the monk Tikhon a written confession accusing himself of having seduced a twelve-year-old girl and having failed to intervene in the suicide to which he had driven her. Although the exact nature of Stavrogin's crime is more ambiguous in the revision, it was still too shocking for the censor and remained unpublished in Dostoevsky's lifetime. Dostoevsky went around reading the suppressed chapter, which of course was narrated in the first person, to almost anyone who would listen, with the probably inevitable result of starting rumors that he too was a child molester.[2]

Coetzee stops short of actual accusation, but he portrays his Dostoevsky's growing obsession with his landlady's daughter, who is named Matryona after Stavrogin's victim. Seducing mother instead of child, a point that does not escape Anna's psychotherapeutic eye, Dostoevsky contents himself with occasionally patting the child while she sits on his bed. One result, evident in early reviews, is that some readers see Coetzee reinforcing a stereotyped view of Dostoevsky or at least a facile notion of the correspondence between authors and characters. Where the only context for Stavrogin's crime is Dostoevsky's putative desire for Matryona, the great sinner surely seems inseparable from his creator. But the nature of this inseparability, the degree of the writer's guilt, is Coetzee's more interesting subject.

In Coetzee's novel, Pavel Isaev, son of Dostoevsky's long-dead first wife, and not Stavrogin, is the link between Dostoevsky and Nechaev. The Pavel we see in *The Master of Petersburg* and his relationship with his stepfather contain large amounts of invention. In real life, Pavel outlived the author, whose second wife and children disliked him heartily, by almost twenty years. Drawing heavily on Aimée Dostoevsky's biography of her father and on Anna Dostoevsky's diary, biographers tend to use adjectives like "lazy," "ugly," "ridiculous," and "stupid" freely whenever his name comes up. Most cite approvingly Anna Dostoevsky's story about how she turned Pavel away from his stepfather's deathbed, believing that the author finally deserved some relief from a man who had sponged off him for years. The near universality of this reaction is somewhat strange, given the unintended sympathy we might expect Aimée Dostoevsky's harsh view of Pavel to create. He was, she says, a "mulatto" whose dark coloring compared unfavorably with the "blond Slavo-Norman heads" of the Dostoevsky children; his "African blood" explains why he had so many children.[3] She sneers at his habit of calling the famous author "papa," noting that her mother taught the children never to use the familiar pronoun with Pavel; she accuses him of trading on the Dostoevsky name to get jobs he could never keep and of giving his children "our names—Fyodor, Alexey, and Aimée"—to "make them as it were the grandchildren of Dostoevsky" (196, 197). Whatever Pavel's faults, we can easily imagine the unwanted boy's misery, his longing for acceptance. Coetzee articulates this pain, but in giving Pavel substance and a point of view relies heavily on pure invention: Pavel as a beloved son, Pavel as an aspiring writer with radical political views, Pavel as an associate of Nechaev, Pavel, finally, as his stepfather's alter ego.[4]

Slipping across the border with a passport bearing the name "Isaev," Coetzee's Dostoevsky almost immediately begins to absorb some of

Pavel's identity; "at moments . . . he cannot distinguish Pavel from himself" (21). He visits the cemetery, lies down on Pavel's grave, returns
with its mud in his hair; he moves into Pavel's room, dresses in Pavel's
suit, reads Pavel's stories, sleeps with Pavel's landlady, meets Pavel's
friend Nechaev, visits the scene of his death. Reliving Pavel's fall from
the tower, he imagines that time must have seemed to stop, just as it
does in the auras preceding his own seizures: " We live most intensely
when we are falling, a truth that wrings the heart!" (121). The drive to
understand Pavel, to get to the bottom of the facts surrounding his
death, becomes obsessive, an appropriation of Pavel's lost life marked
by strong evidence of rivalry; Coetzee's Dostoevsky, in other words, behaves like a Dostoevskyan double, Golyadkin or Velchaninov.

Pavel's youth and Matryona's obvious affection for him feed the rivalry, but more crucially the judicial counselor in charge of investigating
Pavel's death, Maximov, gives Dostoevsky a manuscript found among
Pavel's belongings. Learning that the young man had ambitions to
write touches his stepfather, who immediately starts to appropriate his
story, mentally editing out the clichés in a naive but powerful account of
the murder of a lecherous old landowner, Karamzin, by an escaped political prisoner. Maximov reads the story as a confession of Pavel's revolutionary sympathies. Dostoevsky protests that a "fantasy, written in the
privacy of his room" (42), should never be taken as evidence against its
writer, but nonetheless he sets out on a painful exploration of Petersburg's underground and the criminal connections between writers and
terrorists.

When Finnish Katri appears on his doorstep, ostensibly looking for
those incriminating documents that have already fallen into police
hands, Dostoevsky allows himself to be drawn in by her assertion that
Pavel was murdered by the police. The next day she takes him to meet
a tall woman who turns out to be Nechaev in disguise. Coetzee's
Nechaev, like Dostoevsky's Peter Verkhovensky, accurately reflects the
desperate politics of the "Catechism of a Revolutionist." Coetzee leaves
a few reminders of Peter, Nechaev's unpleasant habit of "wolfing" his
food, for example, and the diversion of the nineteenth-century pathological homosexuality suggested in Peter's obsession with Stavrogin
into Nechaev's almost frivolous pleasure in cross-dressing. But Coetzee's Nechaev appears only in dialogues with his Dostoevsky; there's
nothing in the book to replicate the subplots of *Demons*, which show

Peter manipulating and betraying everyone from his father and the provincial governor to the members of his own cell. No longer the fully embodied villain of a realistic novel, Coetzee's Nechaev can argue for his ideas without being automatically disqualified by his behavior.

In one reading, then, Nechaev is a spokesperson for Russian revolution, offering a credible alternative to Dostoevsky, whose novels, he claims, reproduce the suffering of the people but do nothing to end it. You, he says to Dostoevsky, lead a "bourgeois" life; you're "appalled" by hunger, but you don't understand it, or any of the other brutal impersonal forces that determine the course of history. In their wretched rooms Nechaev and his group "share" the life of the poor (186); they know that "history is made in the streets" and not in books (200). Yet there's a contradiction in this simple contrast between the activist and the writer; Nechaev claims to have been inspired by Raskolnikov (177), for one thing, and believes that a writer can serve the cause. If only, he urges Dostoevsky, you will give us a statement blaming the police for Pavel's death, the People's Vengeance will publish and distribute it, and the students of Petersburg will rise up against their oppressors.

That Coetzee allows Nechaev a degree of idealism and permits him to make serious proposals does not mean that his portrait of the terrorist is finally sympathetic. Dostoevsky comes to believe that Nechaev's group, and not the police, killed the son in order to lure his famous father to Petersburg. Further, when he tries to outwit Nechaev by making him promise to print a statement acknowledging responsibility for murdering Pavel, Dostoevsky is horrified to discover that his words mean nothing to the terrorist, who is only interested in using his name. "What is truth?" howls this killer, showing the advantages of a good Christian upbringing, and orders his associates to start up the presses. With his single-minded devotion to the cause, Nechaev never hesitates over methods, using little Matryona as a courier, supplying her with poison to pass on to Katri after her arrest.

Coetzee's Dostoevsky cannot, however, judge Nechaev dispassionately. Confronting Nechaev's guilt, he has to confront his stepson's association with the People's Vengeance and the possibility that he bears some responsibility for it; even more fundamentally, he has to confront the striking resemblances between himself and Nechaev, and perhaps between all writers and terrorists. From the beginning of the novel, Dostoevsky recognizes the violence of his dreams and desires and fears writing because what comes out of his pen may be "vileness, obscenity, page after page of it, untamable" (18). Councillor Maximov notes that Dostoevsky unconsciously uses the same metaphor for literary activity that he had used for revolution: "You speak of reading as though it were demon-possession" (47). Dostoevsky himself makes the link between his "vocation" and his childhood habit of spying on visitors; he knows that writers use everyone as material, a "perversion" and "betrayal of love" (235); "[I] sold Pavel alive and will now sell the Pavel inside me, if I can find a way. Hope to find a way of selling Sergei Nechaev too" (222). It is more than his youthful involvement with the Petrashevsky Circle that leads Dostoevsky to admit that Nechaev "is like me, I was like him . . . only I did not have the courage" (193).

Nor can Coetzee's Dostoevsky console himself by reflecting that his emotional violence is less consequential than Nechaev's physical violence. Language is not transparent; writers cannot trust their words "to travel from heart to heart" (195); Raskolnikov inspires Nechaev, and Nechaev tricks Dostoevsky into signing his name to a document published by revolutionaries who a few days later have succeeded in setting part of the city on fire. Writers themselves can use their words as weapons. Dostoevsky does not just soil Matryona with his thoughts or use her as material; at the end of the novel, when he departs for Dresden he leaves behind two preliminary sketches for *Demons*. One is a story about a man who makes love to his mistress knowing that they are being watched, through a crack in the door, by a child whom he wishes to corrupt; the story ends with the man ruffling the child's hair as Dostoevsky had ruffled Matryona's. The other revises a story he had told Matryona earlier about a madwoman named Maria Lebyatkin and Pavel, who, on hearing that she imagined him her suitor, put on his white suit and went calling on her. In the oral version Pavel's motives were generous and noble; in the written version, however, he admits to a child that he had acted out of boredom, as a joke, and urges her to lie about his whereabouts if Maria comes looking for him.

One story is intended to undermine Matryona's faith in her dead hero and the other to create a sense of sexual shame; leaving them where she will almost surely read them is "an assault upon the innocence of a child" (249). This assault, like the suicides he had once explained to her, is his challenge to God. As Nechaev killed Pavel to trap Dostoevsky, so Dostoevsky has "corrupt[ed] a child" to make "a trap to catch God"

(249). As a writer, he sets himself up as God's adversary; he watches while "he and God circle each other" (249). As the novel ends, Dostoevsky goes off into the night, reflecting darkly that he may be paid well for his books, but the price of writing them is to "give up his soul" (250).

As we have seen, one Leftist objection to *Demons* is that Dostoevsky privatizes public history, locating the sources of revolutionary violence in pathologies like Peter's rather than in Russian social conditions. Coetzee's Nechaev, a much less fully realized character than Peter, gives a voice to the revolutionary movement to which his Dostoevsky attends, though finally without assent. But *The Master of Petersburg* is no more a conventional political novel than *Demons*, and its Nechaev also plays a part in a larger psychological drama. It is not just that he embodies some "demon" (44) of the times; "the Nechaev phenomenon," as Maximov points out in a sly allusion to Turgenev, may be "just the old matter of fathers and sons" (45). It is Dostoevsky, in that early scene, who insists on Nechaev's particularity, his historicity; nonetheless, within minutes of leaving the police station he has already begun to conflate the terrorist with his son (49). Much later, remembering meeting Pavel in Semipalatinsk when the boy was seven, he imagines him accompanied by a troll with Nechaev's features "haunting the beginnings of his son!" (143).

Dostoevsky has to ask himself whether his life seems empty because it had been grounded in "the contest with his son," and he wonders whether that eternal struggle, in which sons scheme to steal their fathers' money and fathers "envy their sons their women," is what "underlies revolution," so that the "People's Vengeance" might more accurately be named "the Vengeance of the Sons" (108). Recalling a fellow prisoner in Siberia who had raped and then murdered his daughter, Dostoevsky has a vision of "fathers devouring their children" in comparison with which Nechaev's complaint about the "greed" of fathers (158) seems quite mild. Dostoevsky's anxieties about sons surface when he remarks twice that parents can seem like copies of which their children are the originals (13, 67). Separated from a wife only a few months younger than his stepson, Dostoevsky analyzes his affair with a woman of his own age in generational terms, as an alliance of "those who are not children" against those who are (63). Nechaev represents "what we do not even dare to imagine about our sons" (112), a perspective from which Nechaev's remark to Dostoevsky that the two of them look like a "father and son out for a walk" seems less than reassuring. Renouncing his "faith in Pavel's innocence," Dostoevsky finally acknowledges that his son had freely followed Nechaev, not only in the "adventures of conspiracy" but in the "ecstasies of death dealing," his "implacable war" on the fathers (239, 240). To allow Pavel this fury is to feel his own and to understand "fathers and sons" as "foes to the death" (239).

Pavel mediates between Dostoevsky and Nechaev, the writer and the terrorist, as an unpublished writer of fiction intended to support the revolution. Within the world Coetzee creates, this mediation is a failure; Pavel is the one who dies young while Dostoevsky and Nechaev seem to grow stronger at his expense: Nechaev's murder of Pavel being nearly matched by Dostoevsky's appropriation of his stepson's fiction. We know that Karamzin will become old Karamazov without so much as a footnote, and for Pavel's politics, the revolutionary who justifiably kills a rapacious landlord, Dostoevsky will silently substitute the tortured family dynamics that cause Dmitri, on trial for his father's murder, to speculate that every son wishes to kill his father. We can watch, at the end of Coetzee's novel, the process by which Dostoevsky will ransack Nechaev and Pavel, as well as himself, to produce Stavrogin, a character who is identical to neither but who bodies forth everything his creator envies and fears in the new generation, to which "everything is permitted" (200).

The relationship of terrorist to writer, of violent public history to fiction, emerges in *The Master of Petersburg* with all the unresolved complexity of an urgent contemporary dilemma. Coetzee's Dostoevsky considers the old arguments for the writer's superiority to time, listens as Anna tells him in the familiar romantic—and Christian—vocabulary that he is "an artist, a master" who can "bring" Pavel "back to life" in his work. But the image for his relationship to Pavel that haunts Dostoevsky, a goddess-fiend "ecstatically" riding the Indian god Shiva, drawing the seed from his dead body and "saving it" (76, 241), neither consoles nor forgives. Reimagining Dostoevsky, Coetzee reconstructs the origins of *Demons* and *The Brothers Karamazov* in the swamp of its author's least noble impulses and under the pressures of history. This history is understood, not as some grand force, but in terms of daily encounters with a repressive bureaucracy and a hectoring radical youth, both of which can be lethal but are ordinarily experienced as tedious barriers to getting on with one's life. Coetzee's Dostoevsky recognizes that he is "required to live a Russian life" (221) but does not imagine himself either able to resurrect his son or save Russia from the coming apocalypse, to which his work may even contribute.

The violence Coetzee's Dostoevsky recognizes in himself, and in terms of which he understands the process of artistic creation as plagiarism, appropriation, and perversion, is always visible in this novel, not least in the contrast between this fictional character and what we know about his historical counterpart. In real life, Pavel Isaev did not die young, and his stepfather's generosity to him through his own years of poverty is one of his most redeeming qualities. There is, apparently, little reason to believe the old gossip about Dostoevsky and child prostitutes, and it is patently unfair to conflate an author with his own characters, as Coetzee does when, omitting references to Dostoevsky's career as the editor of an influential journal or to his numerous family members, he makes Dostoevsky out to be as febrile and isolated as Raskolnikov. But this unfairness, this incompatibility between the text of history and the text of fiction, is, of course, Coetzee's point. He is not out to "correct" the historical record, replacing it with a more accurate version; in the best postmodern way, he shows us the gaps and distortions in the received version without trying to conceal the problems of his own. But Coetzee shares little of the often alleged playfulness of the deconstructive view. His Dostoevsky slinks off in the night, meditating on the silence of God, which persists in spite of the betrayals by which he had tried to end it. He is more than a little stagy and melodramatic, this guilt-ridden genius, but he is also a powerful image of the failure of a romantic view of literature, a great writer who can finally neither transcend history nor shape it to his liking.

6

Friedrich Dürrenmatt's
The Assignment

Throughout the twentieth century, most terrorist fiction, even that critical of popular beliefs about terrorism, continued to follow the conventions of nineteenth-century realism. For their part, government officials and the press still construct terrorism much as popular fiction does, and terrorists continue to stage their spectacles with an eye to what is now a global stage. Recognizing how often revolutionaries, politicians, and journalists draw on the familiar terrorist story inevitably leads to wondering how it might be disrupted, and Friedrich Dürrenmatt's *The Assignment* offers an extended response to that question. In this 1986 novella, Dürrenmatt links the inadequacy of familiar representations to the limitations of realism itself, blending an absurdist critique of contemporary politics with a postmodern conception of terrorism.

Before turning to Dürrenmatt, we need to look at the public conceptions of terrorism his novel implicitly criticizes and at some of the alternatives to them. In popular representations, the terrorist is always the other, an outsider who—if not a representative of a once-colonized people, a swarthy Islamic archfiend, say, or a grubby chain-smoking product of the Shankill Road—is at the very least a drug-crazed adolescent from a subculture that defies everything the middle class values. Clever enough to elude the police, terrorists, as we see in Lessing, are often assumed to be mad bombers, motivated more by their traumatic childhoods and personal failures than by the causes they publicly adopt. It is their deviance from mainstream values and solutions, rather than their connection to a familiar social setting or recognizable political problems, that defines them.

In this familiar representation, the plot of the terrorist story, whether we find it within the embossed covers of a paperback novel or in the headlines of the *Washington Post,* is almost reassuringly familiar; "terrorist acts are never really news" (Spurr 94). Paradoxically, "as the actual practice of terrorism is dissolved into the numbing repetitions of terror's mediated images . . . theatre and terrorism become . . . emptied of terror" (Kubiak 4). We know about bombings and hijackings, about SWAT teams and exhausted negotiators, about communiqués issued in halting English by dark-eyed men in ski masks, and we are reasonably sure, most of the time, that in the end the security forces, the orderly state, will triumph.

Mick Taussig argues that this terrorist myth props up the unstable and violence-ridden regimes of much of the Third World, where "terror in . . . disruption is no less than that of the order it is bent on eliminating" (4). The state's attempt to brainwash the population into accepting its violence as orderly seems even more futile when one recognizes that the state itself is disappearing under the pressures of modern corporations and technologies of knowledge: "might not the very concept of the social, itself a relatively modern idea, be outdated in so far as it rests on assumptions of stability and structure? In which case what is all the talk about order about?" (Taussig 7). Terrorists, half-creations of the unstable state, serve to legitimate its own violence: "there may even arise in the political economy of news a certain 'demand' for publicized terrorist activity in order, paradoxically, to continually reaffirm the principle that the use of force rightly belongs only with the state" (Spurr 95).[1]

Like Taussig, Edward Said and Noam Chomsky conclude that the word *terrorism* itself is hopelessly polemic, useless in serious political analysis. "Terrorism," says Jenny Hocking, "takes its place alongside such euphemisms as 'subversion,'' 'national security,' 'stability,' and 'pacification' in the typically self-legitimating language of ideological hegemony" (3). The anthropologists Joseba Zulaika and William A. Douglass agree: what *terrorism* chiefly denotes, they argue, is a "terrorism discourse" created and sustained by Western governments, journalists, and, too often, terrorist experts. This discourse, they argue, pays enormous attention to bombings by revolutionary groups, while slighting the much larger incidence of domestic violence or, in the United States, deaths from firearms.[2] Disproportionate emphasis on the dangers of terrorism discourages citizens of the democracies from criticizing their governments' stockpiling of nuclear and biological weapons, which, the discourse tells us, are to be feared mainly because terrorists might get hold of them (Zulaika and Douglass 230). At the same time, this emphasis on terrorism encourages us to accept serious curtailments in our civil liberties as measures necessary to keep terrorists at bay.[3] Moreover, say Zulaika and Douglass, such outcomes play into the hands of tiny militant groups who have much to gain if every threat is taken at face value. Hence, while not discounting the reality of hijackings and bombings, or the need for security forces that assess threats soberly and respond effectively to actual incidents, they worry that the usual "terrorist discourse . . . furthers the very thing it abominates" (Zulaika and Douglass 22).[4]

Dürrenmatt shares with these political commentators a wish to expose the myths and explore the realities of terrorism. An experimental fiction, *The Assignment* points to the complex reality that lies behind the too-familiar story and suggests as well the actual experience of human beings caught up in terrorist activities. Fragmentation of identity in the novel's unstable world leads to a longing for order that asserts itself in totalitarian politics, fundamentalist religion, and documentary realism, all disciplines, in Foucault's sense, that depend on observation. Suggesting the difficulty of distinguishing between the victims and practitioners of terror, Dürrenmatt undermines the usual story of sinister Islamic terrorists. Terrorism, in this novel, proves impossible to locate; it is dispersed through state and society, felt in the psychiatrist's case study and the realistic painting. Yet Dürrenmatt stops short of identifying literacy itself with terror, implicitly arguing that an experimental novel about terrorism can liberate us to see what is otherwise "unrepresentable." His manipulations of the myth present terror both as an understandable private response to the conditions of late-twentieth-century life and as a public practice that intensifies and conditions panic.

Although *The Assignment* begins like a standard thriller, with the funeral of a European woman found "dead and violated at the foot of the Al-Hakim ruin," the briefest survey of its bizarre plot demonstrates how Dürrenmatt borrows from, but quickly revises, the familiar story in order to deny the reader the comfortable satisfaction of identifying the usual culprits and bringing them to an unexamined justice (3). After Tina von Lambert's funeral, her husband, a psychiatrist, engages another woman, the filmmaker "F.," to find her murderer. F. goes to an unnamed location in North Africa, where she interviews two officials, a police chief resembling Göring and a mild-mannered "investigating magistrate" who is actually the head of the secret service. She films the murder site and the execution of an obviously innocent man condemned for the crime; then F. allows the head of the secret service to persuade her to help him track down the real murderer by impersonating the victim, wearing Tina's red fur coat while another woman plays F.'s part, touring the country with her film crew. On a tip from Björn Olsen, a Danish journalist who is almost immediately murdered, F. discovers that Tina is still alive, and that the real victim was another journalist, Jytte Sörensen. Wandering down the road on which she discovered Olsen's body, F. is picked up by a Vietnam veteran who mans a giant observatory intended to keep track of the country's war with its next-door neighbor. This veteran and his brain-damaged friend are the real murderers of Jytte Sörensen and Björn Olsen, and F. is saved from their fate only in the eleventh hour.

The filmmaker F. and, very likely, the reader look for some sinister Arab as Tina von Lambert's killer because her body was found not only in an Islamic country but at a shrine sacred to Shi'ite Moslems, a group consistently demonized in the Western press for its role in the Iranian revolution. Dürrenmatt, however, immediately complicates the case by presenting Tina's husband as "a man who had defended the Arab resistance movement and hadn't called it a terrorist organization" (39). Although nothing in the book suggests empathy for Islamic culture or political causes—Dürrenmatt's point, indeed, is that nationalist causes have become meaningless—*The Assignment* refuses the stereotype of the "Arab terrorist." The Shi'ite "saints" may be fanatics, starving to death as they wait for their caliph to emerge from his stone cube, but they are dangerous only to themselves. The westernized head of the secret service, lecturing F. about Khomeini and the finer features of Islamic fundamentalism as he sips an Alsatian white wine, is a considerably more sinister figure because he is more European, more powerfully interested in weaving F. into his plots, which include turning his country's war into an "international scandal" (94). Two of the novel's three victims (Sörensen and Olsen; the third victim was the Scandinavian prisoner executed for von Lambert's murder) are killed not by the infidel but by Americans, Vietnam veterans with names taken from Homer.

At its simplest level, the novel complicates the terrorist myth by making the identities of the victims as problematic as those of the killers. Nothing is what it seems: Jytte Sörensen, not Tina von Lambert, is the first murder victim of Polypheme and Achilles; F., the once-detached filmmaker, nearly becomes the third. Surely few readers can have the moral certainty to decide whether a brain-damaged Vietnam veteran-turned-rapist is a victim or a terrorizer. Identity also remains problematic in part because few characters, including the protagonist, have names. The second subtitle of the original text (omitted from the translation), *Novelle in vierundzwanzig Sätzen*, calls the reader's attention to the artifice of constructing a short novel in twenty-four chapters, each consisting of a single long sentence or — to draw on another connotation of the German word — philosophical proposition. And this device, too, by departing from the conventions of realistic fiction and documentary journalism and by at least suggesting an allusion to the twenty-four books of the *Iliad*, reminds us that the text does not correspond neatly to some external reality. Dürrenmatt's mock omniscient narration, presenting everything as summary, refusing to render dialogue directly, to give the protagonist a personal history, to name the country in which the novel is set, and so on, frustrates the reader's desire to master the whole story. If it is true that "the [criminal] underworld is the phantasmagoric paranoid construction of the ruling class," surely the desire for a solid external reality, for the identities and oppositions that contemporary thought and events refuse to give us, drives that construction (Taussig 13).

Terrorism in the novel deviates, then, from the story we already know to become what Taussig calls "terror as usual," a dispersed and decentered phenomenon of the postcolonial world. His phrase provides a pale suggestion of the nightmarish confusion of the apparently normative and social with terror that Dürrenmatt's novel develops. In the streets of his fictional North African country one finds "a multiracial thicket of travelers all busily photographing and filming each other and forming an unreal contrast to the secret life inside the compound of the police ministry, like two interlocking realities, one of them cruel and demonic, the other as banal as tourism itself" (47–48). Yet the presence of a Grand Hotel Maréchal Lyautey, with its large portrait of that quintessential empire builder, suggests that tourism is colonialism by other means and as such is not only banal but cruel in its indifference to the "secret life" of local people.[5] The state is unstable: the mild bespectacled investigating magistrate turns out to be the head of the secret service, locked in a power struggle with the chief of police, "who didn't even know who the head of the secret service was" (55).

One of the accomplishments of *The Assignment* is to depict "terror as usual" as more than a political phenomenon and to communicate to the reader an anxiety corresponding to the symptoms of postmodernism as Jean-François Lyotard diagnoses them. In a world incommensurable with our desires and conceptions, something unrepresentable always remains outside art, and though we long for the consolations of form and order, we must make up the rules as we go along. Such views are not, of course, an invention of the twentieth century—Lyotard himself refers to Montaigne's essays as possessing some of these qualities—and in *The Assignment* they are represented by a passage from Kierkegaard and enacted in the fate of the three Europeans killed in North Africa (Lyotard 81). When F. discovers the quotation from Kierkegaard, it is in Jytte Sörensen's handwriting and in her native Danish, which F. parses out, believing that she has discovered a code. The fuller quotation forms the novel's epigraph: "What will come? What will the future bring? I do not know. I have no presentiment. When a spider plunges from a fixed point to its consequences, it always sees before it an empty space where it can never set foot, no matter how it wriggles. It is that way with me: before me always an empty space; what drives me forward is a consequence that lies behind me. This life is perverse and frightful, it is unbearable." The quotation, of course, evokes the conditions of life lived in a period of frequent terrorist attacks, a radical insecurity conditioned by a historical past, as well as the familiar existential angst felt by the human moving forward into a future at once unknowable and deeply determined. The now-dated slogans of "alienation" become fresh in the experience of Europeans encountering in North Africa not Oriental romance but the cruelties of a world in which they have lost all familiar points of reference and every benign expectation is crushed. Reducing the human being to a short-lived pest is not only unwelcome but Kafkaesque.

More precisely, like Jytte Sörensen, who came to North Africa to track down a story, and F., who came to find the killer of a still living woman, the spider is a weaver of traps, in popular lore a plotter, in Swift the very image of the "modern" scholar with his dictionaries and footnotes, ready to strip a rich traditional culture of its living grace. It would be hard to construct a better metaphor for a documentary realism that seeks to "capture" the real in its nets, at the risk of destroying its mysterious, unpresentable life. And when F., almost as if the message were in code, begins to identify with Jytte Sörensen, walking off "helpless as a

spider" along the road that leads to Polypheme's cave, "a consequence
of her whole life," she does so as the representative of a certain kind of
art, of a documentary realism whose premises began to explode for her
the day she filmed the burial of Tina von Lambert (77).

"I am being watched," writes Tina in her journal, and the problem of
being watched and its relation to identity enters a political and philosophical context when the logician "D." ruminates on these matters (12).
D., apparently a disciple of Derrida, for whom he may even have been
named, lectures F. about the impossibility of self-identity, for "everyone
was subject to time and was therefore, strictly speaking, a different
person at every moment" (14).[6] Given this insight, portrayal becomes
impossible; the human self is a fiction, an "accumulation of shreds of experience and memory, comparable to a mound of leaves" (25). The
novel then presents the process by which late-twentieth-century human
beings struggle to understand each other, the world outside the ego,
with no certainty of achieving more than "reconstruction, raking together scattered leaves to build up the subject of [a] portrait, never being
sure, all the while, whether the leaves . . . actually belonged together, or
whether, in fact, [one] wasn't ultimately making a self-portrait" (26).[7]

Therefore, although no novelists stalk Dürrenmatt's pages, although
no one ever reads or quotes from a novel or play, *The Assignment* repeatedly demonstrates a concern with the problematics, and especially with
the political implications, of literary realism. The novel's first subtitle,
Or on the Observing of the Observer of the Observers, recalls a Shake-
spearean phrase that had, by the late nineteenth century, become ominous; given "the depersonalized relations of the information society . . .
the condition of being 'the observed of all observers' [is] no longer a
compliment, as it was intended for Hamlet, but a threat of exposure"
(Welsh 340).

As we saw in our discussion of James, the critique of realism offered
by neo-Marxist critics suggests its repressive potential as a "fantasy of
surveillance" corresponding to nineteenth-century developments in
psychiatry and urban sociology, a form of policing, enforcing social
norms and denying aberrations (Mehlman 124; Seltzer 52). Yet in spite
of the frequency with which recent critics cite Bakhtin's argument that
the realistic novel's dialogism brings about "a destruction of any absolute bonding of ideological meaning to language, which is *the* defining
factor of mythological and magical thought," the critique of realism as

allied with official views of reality remains a key point in the postmodernist program (Bakhtin 369). Dürrenmatt obviously takes it seriously, especially as Lyotard presents the critique in *The Postmodern Condition: A Report on Knowledge*. Lyotard argues that "terror" is "the efficiency gained by eliminating, or threatening to eliminate, a player from the language game one shares with him" (63). In his peroration he argues eloquently for an experimental, postmodern art that preserves the living contradictions and incompletion of the world:

> it is our business not to supply reality but to invent allusions to the conceivable which cannot be presented. And it is not to be expected that this task will effect the last reconciliation between language games (which, under the name of faculties, Kant knew to be separated by a chasm), and that only the transcendental illusion (that of Hegel) can hope to totalize them into a real unity. But Kant also knew that the price to pay for such an illusion is terror. The nineteenth and twentieth centuries have given us as much terror as we can take. We have paid a high enough price for the nostalgia of the whole and the one, for the reconciliation of the concept and the sensible, of the transparent and the communicable experience. Under the general demand for slackening and for appeasement, we can hear the mutterings of the desire for a return of terror, for the realization of the fantasy to seize reality. (81–82)

Lyotard's theory goes some way toward explaining the significance of the paired themes of terrorism and literary realism in *The Assignment*. The holes in Dürrenmatt's plot, the unanswered questions about unnamed characters, the fragmentary glimpses of landscapes, interiors, motives, and political contexts are as so many refusals of "the transparent and communicable." The effect is perhaps not so anti-mimetic as it might seem; refusing transcendent illusions, the novelist suggests an elusive dimension of personality or experience that withers under the harsh floodlights of documentary realism.

For many years F. has wished to create a documentary, "a total portrait . . . of our planet," a goal that leads her to film Tina von Lambert's funeral and then to agree to the psychiatrist Otto von Lambert's request that she find his wife's killers (5). But even before F. leaves Europe, her faith in representation is shaken by her reading of Tina von Lambert's journal, in which Tina has recorded her husband's every minute action with Balzacian intensity. Yet her descriptions have not re-created her

husband's identity but rather have destroyed it, putting into question
the old humanistic idea of the unique person: "reading this journal was
like being immersed in a cloud of pure observations gradually condens-
ing into a lump of hate and revulsion, or like reading a film script for a
documentary of every human being, as if every person, if he or she were
filmed in this manner, would turn into a von Lambert as he was described by this woman, all individuality crushed out by such ruthless
observation" (11). This terroristic "ruthless observation" that ends by
destroying the identity it seeks to establish, what Lyotard might call the
"unpresentable" in the person, resembles the medical jargon that turns
us into unflattering synecdoches of ourselves, the ruptured appendix in
412 B, the morbidly enlarged liver in 413 A.

In von Lambert's notes on his wife, whom he fears having seen as a
case, we find such observations carried to the point where they are no
longer "observations at all but literally an abstracting of her humanity,
defining depression as a psychosomatic phenomenon resulting from insight into the meaninglessness of existence, which is inherent in existence itself, since the meaning of existence *is* existence, which insight,
once accepted and affirmed, makes existence unbearable, so that Tina's
insight into that insight *was* the depression, and so forth, this sort of id-
iocy page after page" (12). Neither journal nor case notes—both like
documentary film allotropes of literary realism and the faith in commu-
nicating observation—provide F. with insight into Tina's motives for
running off to North Africa, and she is left feeling like some adjunct of
the contemporary information system, "one of those probes they shoot
out into space in the hope that they will transmit back to the earth information about its still unknown composition" (13).

Because its representations are closest to a commonsense, consensus
notion of reality, Dürrenmatt sees a realistic art as potentially dangerous. Its illusions appear graphically when F., having found the address
of a famous, but recently deceased, painter in Tina's journal, goes to his
studio. Its floors and walls are lined with paintings that recall F.'s own
project of creating a "total portrait . . . of our planet" (5): a whole gallery
of the city's more disreputable citizens. "At the feet of these figures who
were no longer present except on canvas stood smaller pictures, representing a streetcar, toilets, pans, wrecked cars, bicycles, umbrellas, traf-
fic policemen, Cinzano bottles, there was nothing the painter had not
depicted, the disorder was tremendous" (29).

As in the von Lamberts' writings, but here presumably only because of the riotous juxtaposition of the paintings, a representational art suggests what its critics say it is intended to repress, the underlying chaos and disorder of the world. F., turning to let in light from a window, sees a portrait of a woman in a red fur coat that she "at first took for a portrait of Tina von Lambert, but which turned out not to be Tina after all, it could just as well be a portrait of a woman who looked like Tina, and then, with a shock, it seemed to her that this woman standing before her defiantly with wide-open eyes was herself" (29–30). Yet when she returns later in the day the "portrait" is gone, and the apparently real studio turns out to be a "reconstruction" made for a film crew intended to "give an impression . . . of how the studio had looked when the artist was using it" (30). And indeed, at the end of the novel, F., who has barely escaped rape and murder in North Africa, realizes that the woman in the portrait must have been Jytte Sörensen and the one standing in front of her Tina von Lambert; "no doubt the director was her lover" (121).

The dangerous illusions of realism have more specifically political implications. F.'s "total portrait . . . of our planet" (5) would indeed be that kind of totalizing, totalitarian art that Lyotard deplores.[8] In *The Assignment*, the political terrors of realism are seen at their simplest in North Africa when the police chief steals F.'s film of the execution of the Scandinavian prisoner and replaces it with an official "documentary," complete with shots of cheerful cadets at a police training academy, which might be equally convincing to a European audience. Such documentaries seem to carry out the logical implications of nineteenth-century realism: "Photography did not appear as a challenge to painting from the outside, any more than industrial cinema did to narrative literature. . . . The challenge lay essentially in that photographic and cinematographic processes can accomplish better, faster, and with a circulation a hundred thousand times larger than narrative or pictorial realism, the task which academicism had assigned to realism: to preserve various consciousnesses from doubt" (Lyotard 74). Indeed film, while clearly an art form for F., often associates itself directly with the police and with surveillance in *The Assignment*. F., to take one example, rides to Al-Hakim in a convoy of "policemen and television people" (35).

More nakedly still, the complex technology on which F.'s art depends can be separated almost entirely from human agency. The ultimate surveillance of the novel's last chapter, for example, depends on a series of cameras, each operated by a computer, watching each other observe the world. Achilles spoke of that nightmare in Vietnam, where he flew a computerized bomber: "their plane was a flying computer, programmed to start, fly to the target, drop its bombs, all automatic, their only function was to observe" (115). Discipline, in short, becomes the *only* human function, reducing a person to an observer of machines made *pour surveiller et punir.*

Dürrenmatt clearly agrees with Foucault that such observation is a fundamental condition of twentieth-century life: his Arab jail is positively Benthamite, with its courtyard that looks like a shaft and its series of peepholes. As D. puts it, "a very suitable definition of contemporary man might be that he is man under observation—observed by the state, for one" (16). Yet D. argues that such a Foucauldian discipline is not only necessary but deeply desired. Fundamentalism, both religious and political, has revived because "many, indeed most, people could not stand themselves if they were not observed by someone" (21). Nuclear weaponry, requiring spy satellites and at best eventuating in mutually agreed-upon onsite inspections, enacts the same need, "which was why they basically hoped to be able to keep up the arms race forever, so that they would have to observe one another forever, since without an arms race, the contending powers would sink into insignificance" (20).

If the novel could have a center, then, it would be the terrifying underground observatory, equipped with the latest cameras, from which the half-crazed Vietnam veteran nicknamed Polypheme observes the desert border war that is the mainstay of this unnamed country's economy. It is the ultimate panoptical war, Undershaft-gone-mad, existing only to be observed for the benefit of the people who really run things, that is, the sellers of weapons: "the war effort was constantly seeking out new battlefields, quite logically, since the stability of the market depended on weapons exports" (93). Polypheme himself, the camera his one eye, links the most ancient violence with the problematics of modern identity: "Nobody injured me." His original purpose had been to provide such close documentation of the weapons that he could make "espionage obsolete" (98), but "he really wasn't needed anymore, he had been replaced by fully automated video cameras, then a satellite had been launched to a permanent position above the observation center" (104).

Polypheme exists at a disquieting nexus between immemorial violence and its contemporary manifestations. During the Vietnam War, his life was saved by his closest friend, a classics professor and bomber pilot nicknamed Achilles. In a world of automatic weapons, where computers do most of the work, Achilles had complained that "the idea of a human being was an illusion, man either became a soulless machine, a camera, a computer, or a beast," and he "sometimes wished he could be a real criminal, do something inhuman, be a beast, rape and strangle a woman" (115). Horribly brain damaged in the war, Achilles is locked in a VA hospital, from which he occasionally escapes to rape and murder women, and since it is the only pleasure he is able to feel, Polypheme feels obliged to procure it for him after he liberates his friend and installs him at the observation center. In his case, "terror as usual" takes the form suggested by Robin Morgan, who argues for a direct link between the old classical heroes and modern terrorism, the "sexuality of violence," the capture and rape of women that is, in fact, taken for granted in the *Iliad* (50). By suggesting that terrorism has affinity with beautiful and durable monuments of Western, not Islamic, culture, Dürrenmatt reminds us of Walter Benjamin's famous observation that there is "no document of civilization which is not at the same time a document of barbarism" (256).

Better than any political analyst, Dürrenmatt draws us close to understanding the emotional and intellectual costs of living in the late twentieth century, when even terrorism cannot be counted on to correspond to our conceptions of it. Otto von Lambert's insight that "Auschwitz . . . was not the work of terrorists but of state employees" (58) is well supported in this novel. Terrorists serve the need to believe that there are centers of resistance against a well-established order, yet as the novel amply demonstrates, the very notion of a center is illusory. The new physical terror of computerized bombing and the old one of rape correspond to a condition in which contemporary human beings live and move, their identity fragmented by new philosophical conceptions of memory and the self but also by new technologies that violate their privacy or reduce their importance in traditional roles, such as that of the warrior. Surveillance and observation, intended to reduce the likelihood of nuclear war or successful terrorist attacks, are oppressive but desired. F., ironically, is at last saved from Achilles because a camera crew rises up in the desert to film her. (Similarly, Taussig explains how a friend in

Bogotá warned him to "Always make sure that if anything happens to you there will be publicity. Make sure there are journalists who know where you are going" [17].) Fear of nuclear holocaust feeds the conventional weapons industry; the barbarous high-tech warfare of Vietnam turns a highly civilized man into a primitive rapist; computerized satellites observing other computerized satellites make a mockery of human observers and of the idea of God; "the world [is] spinning back to its origin," that is, to chaos (110).

Part IV

Is Terrorism Dead?

7

Philip Roth's and Robert Stone's Jerusalem Novels

D ürrenmatt's suspicion of realism takes to one extreme that loss of confidence that we have already seen: a failure of belief in the power of art, and in particular of the realistic novel, to bring about meaningful change in the world. But is terrorism really more effective? Mary McCarthy and Don DeLillo do not seem hopeful for literary art, but their terrorists still throw their bombs in a world where independent political action still makes sense. However crude or uncontrolled its devastations, one cannot doubt that terrorism makes a mark in McNamee's Belfast, just as it does in Coetzee's version of czarist Russia. But some recent novels, strangely enough, are even more despairing; they see art and terrorism as equally illusory and politically ineffective. Perhaps we should not be surprised that novels about the Israeli-Palestinian conflict have been among the most pessimistic. Philip Roth's *Operation Shylock* and Robert Stone's *Damascus Gate,* in the main realistic novels, make Jerusalem the highly suggestive setting for exploring the last days of the old belief that marginalized people can change the world.

Whether Russian anarchists seeking to "intensify calamities" or Weathermen wishing to demonstrate that the university cannot carry on "business as usual," revolutionaries often image their struggle as an Armageddon from which a new reign of justice will emerge. In 1999, as fear of the Y2K apocalypse took hold in America, Israeli security forces braced for an invasion of doomsday cultists, the people to whom an enterprising hotelier sent a letter asking, "How would you like to be staying at the Mount of Olives Hotel the day that Jesus returns?" ("Israel's"). Indeed, the association of political violence with the three great monotheistic religions is nowhere stronger than in Jerusalem, a reason perhaps for the evolution, in England and America, of the Jerusalem novel as a small but thriving subgenre. Effacing daily life in Israel to focus on the activities of English-speaking diplomats, expatriates, intelligence agents, and the occasional displaced Palestinian, the Jerusalem novel borrows from the colonial thrillers of Agatha Christie and Eric Ambler. Espionage, kidnapping, disguises, and mistaken identities abound.

For a writer actually born there, like A. B. Yehoshua, Jerusalem is as real as Newark. But visitors often feel torn between biblical images and urban reality: part John the Divine's "bride come down from heaven," part contemporary city, it is home alike to the Hasidic rabbi and the video technician. Past and present coexist there as they do nowhere else, claims Robert Stone: "its crumbling stones . . . do not represent a time that has vanished from relevance, but ongoing history . . . the stuff of present struggle" (*Damascus Gate,* "Author's Note" 501). This same city even provokes its own form of madness. During his years as director of the Kfar Shaul Psychiatric Hospital, Dr. Yair Bar-El studied dozens of tourists, both Christian and Jewish, who experienced what he came to call the Jerusalem syndrome. Perhaps overcome by the "cognitive dissonance" between the "earthly Jerusalem" and their idealized image of it, Bar-El speculates, these tourists developed religious delusions that helped them "bridge the reality with the dream city" (Abramowitz 4). His 1987 sample of eighty-nine such patients found twenty-four messiahs, three Satans, and four people convinced they were God (Bar-El 240). Some become a public nuisance, dressing themselves in biblical robes, singing hymns, and preaching loudly at holy sites, a behavior with which Roth and Stone seem to empathize.[1] Both writers refer explicitly to the "Jerusalem syndrome" (Roth 90; Stone 45–46).

Although Muriel Spark wrote *The Mandelbaum Gate* before this syndrome was named, she also depicts Jerusalem as a place that overwhelms, even deranges, the British visitor. This 1965 work makes an instructive introduction to the contemporary Jerusalem novel. A witty and not quite doctrinally correct Catholic novel, *The Mandelbaum Gate* shows real insight into the effect of Israeli and Palestinian history on the English outsider. Like Spark, the novel's central character, Barbara Vaughan, is half-Jewish, a convert to Catholicism; while she tours Israel, her fiancé, Harry, an archaeologist, works at Qumran, in 1961 still part of Jordan. Thinking of herself as a pilgrim, she insists on seeing only ancient Israel, but her guide goes on about Beersheba's new Scotch tape factory and badgers her about her conversion. To his questions she can only reply, "I am what I am," a grandiose and unsatisfactory response, since it is what the voice in the burning bush said to Moses (29, 26). She becomes exhausted and panicky, startled by her own image in the mirror wearing the "disguise" of "an English spinster" (42).

Barbara's identity crisis peaks when she attends the Eichmann trial. Eichmann's belief system recognizes no human agency, no choice to be made beyond answering to the requirements of "the system" (213). The accused war criminal answers questions, one after the other, "with the meticulous undiscriminating reflex of a computing machine" (210). The bureaucrat who represented the "banality of evil" for Hannah Arendt makes real for Barbara a nihilism she has known only in art, in Beckett and the *anti-roman:* "repetition, boredom, despair, going nowhere for nothing" (210).

Through Freddy Hamilton, a minor British diplomat, Spark introduces the themes of Palestinian dispossession and revenge, the spies and secret plots that we expect to find in terrorist fiction. Yet since the novel is set in 1961, three years before the founding of the Palestine Liberation Organization (PLO), no one uses the word *terrorism;* the Egyptian government, not a revolutionary underground, runs the spy network. If the bitterness of Barbara's once-Czech guide and the spectacle of Eichmann's trial prevent the reader from ignoring the role of the Holocaust in shaping Israel, Freddy's circle of Palestinian shop owners, travel agents, and brothel keepers keeps visible "the bewildered homeless souls" who live on dreams of recovered houses and orange groves (116). Ignoring the Zionist pieties of Leon Uris's *Exodus* (1958; film, 1960) that dominated popular conceptions of Israel when she wrote this novel, Spark presents Jerusalem as a site of moral ambiguity, a place that awakens, but does not satisfy, her visitors' desire for revelation and clarity.

The Mandelbaum Gate appears enlightened and thoughtful in comparison with the *Black Sunday* genre of terrorist fiction that became commonplace in the 1970s. History provides some explanations. After the defeat of Egypt, Jordan, and Syria in the 1967 war, the PLO replaced Arab states as the most visible agent of armed Palestinian resistance. School buses were bombed and jetliners skyjacked; the killings of eleven Israeli athletes and five of their Black September captors at the Munich Olympics ended, as we have noted, the world's first global telecast of a terrorist act. These were, of course, very real events, but as popular fiction, movies, and television shows endlessly reenacted them, *Palestinian* all but became a synonym for *terrorist*. It is true that by 1992, when Philip Roth was writing *Operation Shylock,* more moderate Palestinian voices, Edward Said's in particular, spoke to readers of the *Nation* and the *London Review of Books.* Nonetheless, popular response to such provocations as the ayatollah's *fatwa* of 1989 and the Iraqi invasion of Kuwait late in 1990 indicated how easily the British and American publics could return to virulent anti-Arab sentiment.

Roth's Jerusalem novel thus lies in the shadow of the "international thriller" that provides one of its models (Updike 109). But like *The Mandelbaum Gate, Operation Shylock* offers the simple binaries of the Palestinian-Israeli conflict, but ties them to its own pervasive interest in the ambiguities and instabilities of agency and identity. Among its characters are spies and policemen; a Mossad agent recruits a novelist to write a preface to the diaries of Leon Klinghoffer, the Jewish American shot in his wheelchair during the 1985 hijacking of the *Achille Lauro* by members of the Abu Abbas faction of the Palestinian Liberation Front.[2] Later, this same novelist heads off to Athens on a mission to identify Jewish supporters of the PLO. Though Roth uses the word *terrorist* sparingly, *Operation Shylock* returns to the familiar dyad of writer and terrorist.

If literary terrorists represent the writer's suppressed violence, in Philip Roth's version the terrorist is first a reader, then an importunate admirer who claims the writer as coconspirator.[3] Roth's anxieties that there are only remnants of a reading public, "176 in Nashville" and "3,017 in Los Angeles," are well known (Roth, "Philip Roth" 3). Even so, in *Operation Shylock,* readers tend to menace authors; an especially importunate one is a central character. "He's my terrorist for life!" exclaims the bewildered novelist, his public persona stolen by a detective from Chicago, who also calls himself Philip Roth and who publicly advocates the return of Israeli citizens to the European countries from which their families emigrated (281).[4] Though he finds the detective's version of Diasporism risible, this double, the man of action, "THE YOU THAT IS NOT WORDS," embodies a fantasy the writer knows too well (87). Reflecting on the irony that his bedtime story puts his double to sleep, he wistfully recalls those lectures about endangering Jews: "would that I could! A narrative as deadly as a gun!" (186).

At the beginning of *Operation Shylock*, "Philip Roth" is recovering from a major breakdown triggered by Halcion prescribed after failed knee surgery. "Depersonalization and derealization," according to the *Lancet*, are among its side-effects; for "Roth" they manifest themselves as constant panic, a sense of being physically ripped apart (25). "Where's Philip? Where's Philip Roth?" he asks his wife, so profoundly dissociated from his own body that he hardly believes the fingers fumbling in his pill box are his own (22). Still convalescent, he moves to London, where he and his wife become "refugees," living "as though aground on the dividing line between past and future" (19). "Roth" learns that his double is touring Israel just as he is packing to fly to Jerusalem to interview the novelist and Holocaust survivor Aharon Appelfeld.

For the already uprooted "Roth" to meet this imposter, this seemingly objective correlative of his drug-induced disintegration, strikes his wife as dangerously liable to trigger a relapse, but after one phone call to his double the writer is hooked. After all, for years his novels have featured autobiographical figures, and he can hardly resist the notion that "if it isn't Halcion . . . it's got to be literature" (34). His *Doppelgänger*, whom he dubs "Moishe Pipik," proves capable, like anyone's private thoughts, of ludicrously overrating and then ruthlessly hectoring the author. If the only way to prevent a second, Middle Eastern holocaust is to get the Jews out of Israel, then it is his, Moishe Pipik's, moral obligation to use the public persona of "Roth" to make the case. This persona is wasted on the original, as he sees it, because the writer is reclusive and apolitical. The problem with you writers, he lectures "Roth," is that you think "it's *all* make-believe" (200). But as "Roth" realizes, Pipik's argument assumes that novels themselves have no political influence; what Pipik covets is the writer's celebrity:

> Eminent Jewish writer shows up in Jerusalem espousing a massive transfer of Israel's Ashkenazi population back to their European countries of origin. The idea may appear as grossly unrealistic to a Palestinian militant as to Menachem Begin, but that an eminent writer should come up with such an idea might not seem unrealistic to either. . . . Of course, politically speaking, the eminent writer is a joke; of course nothing the man thinks moves anyone in Israel or anywhere else to act one way or another, but he's a cultural celebrity, he commands column inches all over the world, and consequently

the eminent writer who thinks that the Jews should get the hell out of Palestine is not to be ignored or ridiculed but to be encouraged and exploited. (288)

As the Holocaust colors Israeli politics, it colors "Roth's" encounters with his old friend from graduate school, George Ziad, a Palestinian-American who returned to his father's homeland consumed with grief and rage. Ziad—the name manages to suggest "Said," "Zionism," and "Zuckerman" all at once—assumes that Pipik's Diasporism speaks for "Roth," who does not disabuse him. Like Pipik, he assumes that a writer's celebrity outweighs any ideas he might have. Ziad proposes introducing "Roth" to Yassir Arafat, not to discuss politics, but to have their picture taken together: "in the public-relations battle with the Jews, which well might decide more . . . than all of the terrorism would, a photograph in *Time* with a celebrity Jew might . . . be worth ten seconds of the leader's . . . time" (164).

Ziad's diatribes, or the ones "Roth" makes up for him, are, like Pipik's Diasporism, too comically excessive to be mistaken for the author's political views. Nonetheless, he is a device for putting a Palestinian perspective into play in the novel and not simply for satirizing it. Ziad's remark, for example, about the "terrorist Begin" recalls Irgun and the Stern Gang, as do references to the King David Hotel, where Pipik has a room (132). This historical reminder is more deeply ironic, again in Ziad's view, because Israeli fund-raisers include *terrorism* with *Holocaust* and *anti-Semitism* on the short list of words guaranteed to get generous donations from American Jews. But just as no amount of exploitation can cancel out the reality of the Holocaust, not even Americans are immune from the bombings, hijackings, and hostage-taking incidents for which some radical Palestinians are responsible. When Mossad's David Supposnik supplies "Roth" with Leon Klinghoffer's diaries, he makes it impossible for the American writer to pretend that anti-Semitism ended with the Nazis. Klinghoffer's death, like Anne Frank's, is an intractable reality, however much "Roth" may distrust people who sentimentalize it or use it to justify their own violence.

Through Supposnik, "Roth," previously a "spy on the Jews" only in his fiction and found "guilty of the crime of 'informing'" only by critics, enters the actual world of espionage (395, 377). If his celebrity is still his main attraction, as it was for Pipik and Ziad, the job they have in mind for him requires writing. In Supposnik's view, the diaries of Anne Frank acquired their special status only after their publication in the United States, with an introduction by Eleanor Roosevelt. If Roth writes an introduction to Leon Klinghoffer's travel diaries, then they too will become the moving testimony of a martyr; without it, presumably, they will remain dull lists of sights: "Wailing Wall. Jesus tomb. David's. . . . The goings on in front of the W.W. were interesting. The constant praying. Bar Mitzvahs. Weddings. Etc." (326).[5] Not blind to the demands of the "Roth" ego, Supposnik claims he is the only man for the job, since Klinghoffer is virtually one of his own characters: "No other writer writes about these Jewish men in the way you do" (279). Thus when Mossad agents kidnap him, he assumes that it is because they want that introduction, and he obediently sits down to write it: "The alphabet is all there is to protect me; it's what I was given instead of a gun" (323).

"Roth" wants to see writing as a refuge, an answer to violence—"I looked to print to subjugate my fears and keep the world from coming apart"—but readers, critics, and interrogators keep pressuring him to reflect on writing as action, to tailor his work to the needs of the Jewish community or the Israeli state (321). Because "Roth" resists Jewish religious observances and Zionist pieties, he cannot define himself simply in terms of a community as, say, early kibbutzniks tried to do. On the other hand, no matter how divided and problematic his identity, no matter how hard put he would be to define what being Jewish means, he cannot imagine himself as not-Jewish. He can argue that he is not responsible for Pipik's plan to kidnap Demjanjuk's son, he can even head to the airport, but when a flash of memory brings back a British newspaper caricature of Menachem Begin, he orders the cab driver to take him back to the city. The cartoon, "a perfectly realistic, unequivocal depiction of a kike as classically represented in the Nazi press," suggests just how eager the world press will be to judge Pipik's crazed plot as a representative Jewish action, proof that no Ukrainian could get a fair trial in Israel (248). This recognition produces a gunslinger's vow "to face down this bastard once and for all" (249).

His recognition that *"everything"* came out of that experience, "out of the inscrutable words . . . on this blackboard had evolved every English word I had ever written" is not an exercise in nostalgia (312). With those first Hebrew lessons, "Roth" went through the mirror to a world that was implausible, unintelligible, unreasonable, but for all that no less real than his childish conception of America. Hebrew lessons gave him

double vision, the satirist's eye for incongruity, the outsider's sense that
in any situation two people may have not only different opinions but a
different sense of what the fundamental issues are, what is real. And it
gave him as well his first premonition of the terrible world that Aharon
Appelfeld met in a concentration camp and rediscovered in Kafka.
Doubtless this sense of self-division, of guilt and helplessness, of the
enormous power of the invisible and irrational over what we can see
and reason about, is by no means exclusively Jewish. For "Roth," however, it will always bear the indelible marks of Jacob's struggle: "thy
name shall be called no more Jacob, but Israel."

This recognition that his Jewishness and his writing are tied together,
not just in other people's minds, but in his own, seems to influence
"Roth's" capitulation. For the rest, he professes not to know himself
why he finally agreed to exercise his instinct for "impersonation" outside the relatively safe world of fiction. But naturally, having gone to
Athens to finger Jewish supporters of the PLO for Mossad, he writes a
novel about his experience. Fearing that the passage of five years has
left some of the details vague, he sends the completed manuscript to
Louis Smilesburger, expecting his old Mossad handler to serve as fact-
checker and to fill in the gaps in his memory. "Roth" professes to be
amazed, since he has no contract with Mossad, when Smilesburger calls
up from Kennedy Airport to plead with him not to publish the Athens
chapter. His reasons are those we would find in any thriller—danger of
compromising agents in the field, the secret agent's inability to understand the Big Picture, the power of the organization to punish those
who disobey. The twist is in the way Mossad plans to go after Roth; no
"barbaric *fatwa*," just the traditional *loshon hora*—malicious rumors, un-
attributable stories, a ruined reputation. "There is . . . no evil speech,"
says Smilesburger, "that is unutterable to a Jew with an unguarded
tongue" (397). With a postmodern touch, after telling us that it is all
true, Roth appends a note: "This confession is false." Which confession,
we may well wonder (Safer 161).

Terrorized by readers and interrogated by critics, "Roth" plays at
being a secret agent but seems, for all his egotism, to lack a real sense of
agency as a writer. The stuff from which novels are made—words, images, plots—all operates, and powerfully so, in the social world. Television has even given the prize-winning novelist a certain celebrity that a
man of action might wish to exploit. But no one, not even he, thinks that

he can forge in the iron smithy of his soul the uncreated conscience of his race, or even change minds about one or two key social policies. If the suppressed chapter of his *Operation Shylock* might be dangerous to someone, he did not intend it to be so and cannot be told why. Better, for the first time in his life, to accede to censorship. Better, too, not to inquire too closely about whether George Ziad, a revolutionary and associate of terrorists, is also a Mossad agent, as much under the state's control as any foot soldier.

In *Operation Shylock,* then, the writer's power derives largely from the celebrity that attends literary success in a world where few people actually read the books whose authors they see interviewed on morning television. "Roth" apparently can act heroically, but only outside the novel; even after the fact, the chapter that would show him as agent of history, or even of Mossad, goes missing.[6] In *Damascus Gate,* Christopher Lucas, inevitably a writer, follows in the old heroic footsteps; it is he and the beautiful woman he loves who, just in the nick of time, discover the bomb hidden in a centuries-old maze under the Temple Mount. But the bomb is a fake; the terrorists are all under the state's control, and the writer's agency, like theirs, is only an illusion. Robert Stone's Jerusalem is not only the divided and disorienting city that we see in Spark and Roth; it also marks a temporal border between history and the end of time: the place where Jews expect the true messiah to reveal himself and where Christians await the Last Judgment. In this millenarian novel, Stone both critiques and engages in the task of ending history, and in doing so he writes one conclusion to the romantic myth of the writer and terrorist.

As in Roth and Spark, Jerusalem is a city of outsiders, spies and travelers and expatriates. To these Stone adds the mix of schizophrenics, drug addicts, and cultists that his readers have come to expect, making enough factual errors to cause an Israeli reviewer to complain that the author "ends up writing about the wrong country" and an American to suggest that he was still writing about New Orleans (Halkin 4).[7] Like Spark's heroine, Christopher Lucas is half-Jewish; like her, he barely knew his Jewish parent and neither identifies as a religious Jew nor feels at home culturally, as "Roth" does, with secular Jews. Jerusalem, where some people still see Jewishness as a racial identity, a life-and-death matter, forces him to examine the meaning and consequences of an inheritance his father, a refugee from Hitler, left behind.

Over and over, people ask him if he is Jewish, and over and over he
invents new ways to temporize. When he is distressed by a local
gypsy's remark that those who have been wronged always seek revenge, the man asks, "You are sad? You are a Jew?" Lucas concedes, "I
am sad" (335). Many people, like the mob in Gaza that chases him,
screaming "Kill the Jew," simply impose their definitions on him. Whatever he says is likely to be wrong; when he tells the woman he loves that
he is already half-converted to Judaism, she tells him he will be a Catholic until his dying day, "whatever you say . . . or think you believe"
(492). Even the author mocks him for his hesitations; trapped again by
an angry crowd, Lucas wonders whether he will deny being Jewish and
hears—of course—a rooster crowing (448).

Like some figure out of Flannery O'Connor, Lucas has an enormous
drive to believe but struggles against his rage at the God he associates
with the brutalities of his working-class parochial school and the violence of the godly in the Middle East. Lucas is an investigative journalist, author of a book about the U.S. invasion of Grenada. Childless,
unmarried, he comes to Israel to freelance after quitting a job with a
major newspaper; as a writer he "represents no one," an uncongenial
position, given his precarious sense of identity (16). Casting about for a
story, he talks to a self-described former KGB man who offers him a
choice between politics and religion: either probe the dismissal of an Israeli cabinet minister, Avram Lind, or collaborate with a local psychiatrist on a book about the Jerusalem syndrome. Not surprisingly, almost
as soon as Lucas opts for religion, he agrees with one of the doctor's
more troubled patients that he too is afflicted with the syndrome, that a
"consecrated buffoon" lurks within him. He shares Stone's sense of Jerusalem as a place where antiquities remain contemporary. Moreover,
he wants to think of Israel as essential, a place of origins where "there
are no metaphors. . . . where things themselves resided and the only
symbols were the holy letters of a book" (409).

Lucas's dependence on someone else to find a story and his willingness to collaborate would underscore his distance from the romantic
writer bent on powerful self-expression even if the psychiatrist in question were not named Dr. Obermann. In a 1989 essay on the political
novel, Stone expressed aversion to what he characterized as the "romantic antinomian tendency" of Nietzsche and Oscar Wilde, of Shaw's
Major Barbara and Joyce's Stephen Dedalus:

In this antinomian vision, morality and art are independent and even in opposition. On the right squats morality. . . . Its self-satisfaction, lack of imagination and philistine sentimentality are advertised in its every plane and line. Architecturally, it resembles the Mormon Tabernacle. . . . And on the left—art. Art is nothing but beautiful. Art is like a black panther. It has the glamour of the desperado. Art is radical, the appealing cousin of crime. Never a dull moment with art. Morality . . . is not only its opposite but its enemy. ("We Are Not Excused" 20)

Stone, in short, explicitly rejects the romantic conception of the artist as desperado or, we might say, terrorist, and *Damascus Gate* reveals no desire to revive it. Neither the terrorist's alter ego or rival, neither secret agent nor informer, Christopher Lucas is the man of good will and agonized conscience caught up in other people's plots, desperately trying to get the story right. It never occurs to him that he might impose his vision on the world; struggling to avoid being the hostage of less scrupulous people takes all his energy. After escaping from a Palestinian mob, Lucas is beaten up by right-wing Israeli settlers who threaten him with unspecified consequences if he does not agree to become their mouthpiece, to print any story they send him under his byline, without alterations.

In addition to millennial Christians and Jews, Stone's Jerusalem is full of displaced Marxists—émigrés from the former Soviet Union, former KGB men, "red diaper babies," true believers soldiering on with only faith to guide them. Just as Christians and Jews in their different ways can wait for the arrival of a Messiah who will bring the tribulations of history to an end, orthodox Marxists look to the Communist state to end the tribulations of the class struggle. Once this struggle has ended, nothing and no one will need to be "held in subjection"; in Engels's famous words, "state interference in social relations becomes superfluous. . . . The state . . . . withers away" (306–7).[8] As the twentieth century wore on, this millennial, end-of-history-as-we-know-it side of Marxism lost much of its credibility, and by 1992, the year in which *Damascus Gate* is set, the Communist Party in the West was in remnants.

Lucas is drawn to see the relation between a Marxist and Jewish millennialism through Sonia Barnes, the talented American with whom he falls in love almost as soon as he hears her singing like Sarah Vaughan. As her Jewish mother and black father were ardent Communists, Sonia spent much of her childhood on the lam from the FBI. After college, she worked ten years in Cuba, and being a person who "required the proximity of faith," she became a Sufi on returning to New York (108). She is in Israel because her New York friends "somehow passed her on" to Berger al-Tariq, a Sufi teacher, who in 1992 is dying of cancer. Where Lucas's reaction to his mixed parentage is to feel perennially divided, "half in, half out," Sonia inclines to synthesis, the sense of being "double in" (108). "A new world is coming," she tells Lucas and agrees when he says that her parents thought so, too; she needs "the same revolution" (167). When Janusz Zimmer, a former Soviet agent, approaches her with vague allusions to helping his spy network, the "Jewish orchestra," she is touched that he still believes in "the perfect world" and reminds him that "the truth is one" (158). Such millennial impulses make her vulnerable, after Berger's death, to the Messianic Judaism her former lover, Ralph Melker, now Raziel, espouses.

The new Messiah, Adam De Kuff, is an elderly Jewish cellist, the son of a prominent New Orleans family. A bipolar depressive inclined to mysticism and ashamed of having once converted to Catholicism, he is a pilgrim of sorts in Jerusalem even before Raziel spots him in Dr. Obermann's waiting room. Raziel himself, who is much younger and an American congressman's son, is being treated for heroin addiction; like De Kuff, he is a talented musician living on family money. Raziel has been a "Zen monk, a yeshiva student, a member of a Hebrew-Christian commune" and is often taken for a "Mormon or a Jew for Jesus" (61, 65). Raziel tells De Kuff that he is the "Son of David brought back," and once De Kuff stops taking his lithium, his own delusions do the rest. Soon he is preaching to disciples at the Pool of Bethesda that the "old world will disappear and things will become the word of God incarnate" (161).

Stone develops De Kuff sympathetically, as a gentle, tormented man preaching a message of love and forgiveness. "Everything is Torah," he proclaims in his oddly Emersonian way, and for about the first third of the novel the reader may well suspect that Stone intends to vindicate him. It is entirely plausible that Sonia adopts him as a guru, and even as Lucas insists that De Kuff is quite mad, he reads and rereads the Kabbalist texts Raziel and De Kuff favor. Searching out a Catholic priest whose Jewish parents died in the Holocaust, Lucas tells him that the Kabbala offers "the greatest interpretations of life and truth" he has ever encountered (262). Trekking to the river Jordan with De Kuff and Sonia,

Lucas understands that he "would give anything to believe it all" (401). As Flannery O'Connor might put it, Stone takes great care that his readers should be able to "believe in the beliefs" of his characters.

Although Stone analyzes the psychology of the true believer, he seems much less interested in those traditional subjects of the realistic novel, middle-class people who live in families and go to work. As a result, the novel's politics are also skewed toward extremism. Stone's evocations of the *infitada*, of frightened teenagers barricading themselves behind piles of burning tires, are extraordinarily vivid. What goes missing is any sense of day-to-day Israeli politics, of negotiations, say, between leftists willing to exchange land for peace and conservatives who argue for the strategic importance of the Golan Heights. Indeed, as Israelis are mostly represented as belligerent settlers and soldiers guarding checkpoints, Stone's Israel itself seems more of an idea, or a system, than a country where real people live.

This derealization of so much of Israel makes it rather too easy for the novel to espouse a conspiratorial view of Israeli politics. In *The Mandelbaum Gate*, the discovery of a spy is still a major plot development; our inability, in *Operation Shylock*, to be sure of having penetrated the spy's last disguise, is still a source of mystery. But *Damascus Gate* starts out with the assumption that Mossad routinely encourages Palestinian terrorist factions; even Hamas is an Israeli operation that got out of control. It is an easy assumption that "Palestinians" beating up informers are really Israeli soldiers beating up their more effective opponents, or that the government encourages gunrunning and drug running in the Occupied Territories. On the political plane, distinctions between legitimate and illegitimate force are not just obscured—they have ceased to exist. The novel suggests that believing in an apocalyptic cult or a revolutionary underground is quite understandable but hardly imagines anyone delusional enough to take electoral politics seriously.

Having lived with Watergate, the Iran-Contra scandal, and Monica Lewinsky, a contemporary American can hardly find this cynicism strange. But it is more troubling that, lacking an equivalent to the Eichmann or Demjanjuk trials, or to "Roth's" interview with Aharon Appelfeld, *Damascus Gate* turns the Holocaust into a distant idea. Lucas gestures toward the Holocaust; he visits Yad Vashem immediately before he heads out to the Gaza strip for the first time, and "although he understood . . . it was a cheap equivalence," he thinks that "the chain of circumstance connecting the two shaped the underlying [Israeli] reality" (221). But this point, so vividly felt in "Roth's" exchanges with Ziad, remains only notional here. Stripped of Jewish history, Jerusalem becomes what Lucas says it is, "Belfast without the Guinness" (459).

As he grows closer to Jerusalem's cults, Lucas picks up rumors about a plot to bomb the Temple Mount. Now covered by the Islamic Dome of the Rock and the Al-Aksa mosque, the Mount is the site of the First and Second Temples. Reconstructing the Temple at its original site is important for some Jewish and Christian fundamentalists, who regard the Islamic holy places as a blasphemous intrusion on their sacred space. Since some also believe that removing the impediments to reconstruction would hasten the Second Coming of Christ or the appearance of the true Messiah, threats to bomb it are a recurrent concern for Israeli police.[9] Naturally enough, almost everyone Lucas interviews for his Jerusalem syndrome book seems a likely suspect: the House of the Galilean has hired its own archaeologist to research the original dimensions of the Temple, the right-wing settlers welcome any excuse to provoke a massacre, and everybody uses doomsday rhetoric. More troubling to Lucas is the possibility that someone is trying to implicate Sonia in the plot.

The first third of the novel permits the reader to speculate that Raziel's interest in De Kuff is entirely innocent, a possibility abruptly cut off in the brief twenty-fifth chapter, where we find Raziel at the Wailing Wall, costumed as an Orthodox Jew with *tzitzit* (fringes of a prayer shawl) showing under his black coat. Next to him stands Janusz Zimmer, the former Polish Communist secret agent, talking about smuggling explosives and alluding to a plan for Raziel and his associates to "take the fall" when some unspecified catastrophe occurs. From this point on, the novel, which has been heavy on exposition and long on theology, becomes plot driven, at times almost a parody of a thriller. Nuala is running guns and drugs; she is a Communist; she is protected by Shin Bet; she is murdered by unidentified men with Russian accents. Palestinians, settlers, and people with ties to the House of the Galilean chase, beat, threaten Lucas. On the banks of the Jordan, De Kuff proclaims himself the "Lamb of God," and the river reverses its course to signal the "end of illusions" (402). But no, it's the Ecstasy that Raziel put in the tea; besides, he has gone back on heroin supplied by one Fotheringill, who was supposed to be a hotel cook but is really an SAS man. No wonder Raziel forgets that he left a clearly labeled blueprint of the Temple Mount in his van for Lucas to find. Lucas rushes about the Old Quarter trying to figure out the details as glaring Palestinians, their emotions stirred up by agents provocateurs, shout insults and throw stones. Meanwhile, Sonia, having discovered more diagrams in Raziel's van, pushes him to reveal the bomb plot. It turns out that he had cooperated with Zimmer because he believed that the bomb would usher in the end of time and that no one would really be killed; recent doubts have driven him back to drugs, which offer some simulacrum of the beatific vision. Will Sonia be able to crawl through the ancient labyrinth under the Temple Mount in time to stop the bomb? Yes, but Janusz Zimmer and Fotheringill are waiting for her; but then again not to worry — Lucas will be there with the police in a minute. Order will be restored in the city, but not before a mob of screaming Palestinians kills Adam De Kuff, who was indiscreet enough to admit to being Christ. As for his companion, Raziel is still in a coma at the novel's end.

As we have seen, popular thrillers offer us the satisfaction of a world to which order has been restored and the pleasures of clearing away mystery and understanding the hidden links between events. The revelations at the end of *Damascus Gate*, however, are more disturbing. The issue has never been, as we might have assumed, a clash of ideological extremes, religious or political. Raziel, the House of the Galilean, the militant settlers of Kfar Gottlieb, all are pawns in a sting operation; even Janusz Zimmer and Fotheringill are only agents. Its real mastermind is Avram Lind, the cabinet minister whose story was originally proposed to Lucas by his former KGB source; its chief goal is forcing his replacement, Yossi Zhidov, to resign and persuading the prime minister to reinstate Lind. Lind's contacts in Mossad set up the operation in order to expose Zhidov's involvement in drug smuggling; as additional benefits, the project is thought to have set the Jewish underground back two years, hurt those who were cooperating with the American religious right, flushed out the most violent elements of Hamas, and helped the government find reasons to legislate against cults and Christian missionaries.

Not only does Lucas the writer have limited agency, then, but the terrorists he tried to identify turn out to be equally powerless, and every story line traces back to the same story about a power struggle in a bureaucracy. "And it will all stop," Lucas said. "The end of history" (367).

If the millenarian enthusiasms of its characters are disappointed, *Damascus Gate* does, after all, suggest something like Francis Fukuyama's end of history.

Fukuyama's argument, first made as the cold war ended in 1989, is that communism, fascism, and hereditary monarchy no longer offer serious competition to the ideal of Western, liberal democracy. These systems of government continue, of course, in the Third World and are even sometimes displaced by more primitive models, such as the military dictatorship or the theocracy. But the flaws in these systems have become so obvious that no one seriously proposes them as an ideal. The persistence of inequality in liberal democracies, on the other hand, is not a failure inherent in the model, as Karl Marx argued, but simply a failure to apply the model rigorously. The cure for incomplete democracy is more democracy. Since everyone who matters pretty much concedes that we have evolved an ideal of government that "cannot be improved on," we have reached the end of serious ideological conflict and hence of history (xi).

There is something of the complacent Victorian, even of Dr. Pangloss, in Fukuyama, yet he helps us diagnose the ideological stalemate at the end of *Damascus Gate*. Any model that identifies history as conflict—the Marxist class struggle, the Christian fundamentalist idea of a struggle between Satan and God for human souls—must see history ending when one of its defining terms wins. But history, in this grand sense of a vision of history, also ends when its defining terms collapse, blur together, seem only different manifestations of the same force. For a long time, in politics and literature, it was plausible to believe in the rebel, the creative genius, the powerful individual imposing a personal vision on the collective. But when the terrorist plot is conceived in the government office, when the prophet is as useful to the bureaucrat as the soldier, we cannot be surprised that the writer's heroics lead only to the end of a maze where a bogus bomb goes up in chemical smoke. The private imagination, the solitary brooding of DeLillo's "men in small rooms," does not drive public events. For the terrorist as for the novelist, there is only the austere consolation of renunciation: "losing . . . is the same as having" (499).

8

Volodine's
Lisbonne dernière marge

Throughout this study, we have noted variations on the terrorist as
the writer's rival, double, and secret sharer, tracing their origins
from the romantic conviction of the writer's originality and power
through a century of political, social, and technological developments
that undermine that belief. But it seems safe to say that Antoine Volodine's *Lisbonne dernière marge* takes this theme to its logical extreme.[1] In
this 1990 novel, the terrorist *is* a novelist. Volodine reconstructs the
whole romantic literary scene as a scene of subversion against a violent
state and then deconstructs it, suggesting that not only the novel, but
more fundamentally the revolutionary impulse, might be dead.

When it first appeared, Adrian Tahourdin described *Lisbonne dernière
marge* in the *Times Literary Supplement* as "impossibly oblique" (28);
quoting its heroine's boast that her novel would be "uninterprétable"
[impenetrable], *La Quinzaine Littéraire*'s Pascale Casanova advised that
his audience read the book "pour le plaisir de se perdre et devenir une
victime consentante" [for the pleasure of getting lost and becoming a
consenting victim] (13). Perhaps the reader need not be a victim, though
Casanova's metaphor is apt for a novel that constantly juxtaposes violence and writing; certainly the reader cannot hope to *master* the book. A
brief description will help.

Lisbonne dernière marge does not so much resemble a traditional novel-
within-a-novel as hypertext, "writing where there is a dynamic link between two or more texts: clicking on a word in one text transports you
immediately to another text, from which you click on another word and
arrive at yet a third text" (Bennahum 31). The print text, of course, has a
limited ability to emulate an electronic one, but Volodine's medium

seems remarkably fluid. Texts generate texts, a story about a serious writer leading to a copy of her stories, followed by critical commentary and examples of the popular writing of the same period; at any moment a concealed narrator seems to click us back to a previous story. Characterization is equally fluid, the text itself introducing the concept of the *heteronym*, a term invented by the Portuguese poet Fernando Pessoa. Like a patient suffering from a multiple personality disorder, Pessoa had a series of distinct personas, or heteronyms, each with its own history and style—"Alexander Search," for example, wrote only in English—and published his work under their names. The identities of Volodine's characters merge and blur as they assume new names or create stories whose characters appear to act out their own dilemmas, disguises assumed and then dropped; to further complicate matters, a name such as "Verena Goergens" may refer to one person or to the writers' cell to which she belongs.

The framing story seems simple enough, reproducing many of the familiar moves of the thriller. Ingrid Vogel, formerly an active member of a West German terrorist cell, has escaped to Lisbon under a false identity with the help of her lover, a policeman named Kurt Wellenkind; he plans to put her on a ship for some remote destination, possibly in Asia. Although Volodine does not mention the Red Army Faction (RAF) by name, some association is inevitable: Ingrid's organization staged demonstrations in the 1970s, at least eight characters or communes share their surnames with RAF members, and an early reference to the suicide of Ingrid's favorite philosophy professor evokes the troubled relationship between the RAF and the Frankfurt School.[2] Ingrid is obsessed with writing a novel, Kurt with stopping her from setting down a story that he is convinced will "puera . . . le terrorisme" [will stink of terrorism], will betray them both no matter how ingeniously she disguises it (18). Though the frame suggests that Ingrid never commits a single word to paper, most of the book consists of that novel, *Einige Einzelheiten über die Seele der Fälscher* [Some particulars of the forger's mind], replete with all the conventions of print including footnotes.

Volodine began as a science fiction writer—he won the Grand Prix de la science-fiction française in 1986—and Ingrid's novel borrows from that genre, creating an alternative society, the Second Century Renaissance. Vaguely German, the Renaissance's distinguishing characteristic is its total suppression of history. Most older languages have been lost (though for some reason, the Peruvian Indian language Quechua has survived and is used in some experimental poetry); no one knows what happened before the Black War, itself remembered only by name. Collective memory, in fact, is so brief that no one can remember his or her childhood, no one knows even in theory where babies come from. Children are separated from adults, growing up in *ruches* [hives] run by the state; these are presumably located somewhere in the vast tracts of land that adults have been unable to enter since the war. Evidently the society is a dictatorship administered by "une construction politique de pure façade" (127). Its real leaders are invisible, occasionally issuing orders with signatures like "Ruche 807" through newspapers; hence the common tendency to refer to those in power as "les ruches." The only visible arm of real power is the police, usually assumed to obey the invisible leadership.

On one level, explicitly evoked midway through the novel, the Renaissance is an allegory for the Federal Republic, the amnesiac Germany where parents conceal their Nazi past from children, and the schoolbooks minimize its crimes. Like Second Century adults, Ingrid and Kurt feel like orphans who cannot remember their parents because a father's denial of having been in the Hitler Youth, of having shouted Nazi slogans, of having known about death camps, or even of having heard the word *extermination* amounts to "la négation de son existence" (78). Yet clearly the text is open-ended, the Renaissance not so much the German Economic Miracle as a Foucauldian conception of late capitalist society, where the workings of power are impossible to specify and history seems lost.

In the Second Century Renaissance, writers come to have a status, at once peculiar and familiar, as the acknowledged opponents of the *ruches*. To be sure, the state recognizes and regulates literature: books must be registered at a central office, a prominent cultural organ, *Coeur du IIe Siècle* [Heart of the Second Century], publishes critical reviews and even photographs of approved writers. The complex literary system includes a host of other "supports de la pensée (journaux officiels, revues fondées ou encouragées en sous-main par la sociale-démocratie, revues manipulées par la police, revues indépendantes, feuilles confidentielles d'avant-garde ou même éditions clandestines)" [apparatus of thought (official journals, reviews founded or encouraged behind the scenes by the social democracy, reviews manipulated by the police,

independent reviews, confidential avant-garde papers, or even clan-
destine publications)] (148). One romantic conception, that of writing
as personal expression, seems to have disappeared; writers and intellectuals live in communes or cells with RAF-style names, "le bataillon
Silke Proll," "le commandement unifié Siegfried Schulz," "le groupe
d'assaut Uwe Heissler." While the text continually refers generically to
"l'homme de la Renaissance," virtually all of the writers, for reasons
never made entirely clear, are female; the police, at least those mentioned by name, are male. Some of these groups produce scholarship,
others romances, psalmody, or experimental poetry; somewhere outside
this literary system a "littérature des poubelles," vulgar and violent
trash, is written and circulated, its precise origins a mystery. Because the
ruches are liable at any moment to launch brutal attacks, the groups operate like subversive cells, dodging police watchers, elaborately dividing up and concealing manuscripts.

One of the dangers the state anticipates from its writers and intellectuals is their curiosity about the past and their skill in reconstructing it
from texts. Every generation or so, the *ruches* issue anthologies of children's literature, and since these are the only visible traces of childhood,
the communes scrutinize them closely. Katalina Raspe, in her introduction to an otherwise banal paraphrase of previous anthologies called *Le
monde Moô-Moô* [The world of Moô-Moô] explains the stakes: the oral
stories children tell are the sole form of cultural transmission uninter-
rupted by the war and thus contain "les plus anciennes images de l'in-
conscient collectif" [the oldest images of the collective unconscious]
(75). Although Katalina's work largely slips into obscurity for twenty
years, *le commandement unifié Siegfried Schulz* picks up the hint, arguing
that since scholars cannot interview the children directly, they must
work with filtered and censored texts (85). This pedantic-seeming observation, expressed with "virulence," has revolutionary implications; in
demanding access to children, Siegfried Schultz is inveighing against
the most basic arrangements of its society. Shortly after *L'Authenticité de
l'oeuvre orale* [The authenticity of the oral work] appears, all fourteen of
its members are savagely beaten to death.

The state would seem to have even more to fear from *la compagnie
Inge Albrecht,* which clamors for freedom of the press, arguing that even
"les vérités détestables" [hateful truths] should be published. Its own
contribution to the debate over children's literature questions one of the
Renaissance's founding assumptions, that all adults were once children.

In *Brèves conclusions sur le monde de l'enfance* [Brief conclusions on the world of childhood], Inge Albrecht raises the key points: if we all once were children yet cannot remember our childhood, then our memories must have migrated into some area of our unconscious minds; the point of access to this collective unconscious ought to be literary texts produced by adults in the first century of the Renaissance. Yet for all its efforts, Inge Albrecht fails to reconstruct the bridge between adulthood and childhood, reluctantly concluding that it never existed: "Nous n'avons pas été enfants" [We have never been children] (89). In their "vision chaotique et énigmatique" the world is still divided into two inhabited territories, one for children and one for adults, but these exist *"sans relation organique entre les deux groupes"* [without organic relation to each other] (89). Not surprisingly, the dismembered bodies of Inge Albrecht are found packed in watertight trunks, floating in the river; a fire meanwhile has "caramelized" all but one of the copies of *Brèves conclusions*, along with the editor of a journal that had undertaken to publish it, its press, and every member of the *commando Verena Goergens,* which had collaborated in the project.

Inge Albrecht, Verena Goergens, Siegfried Schultz; these are all collective entities, allotropes for the writer-intellectual as the state's opponent. Katalina Raspe, martyred after them, is more sharply delineated as a woman and not a collective; she emerges as Ingrid Vogel's alter ego, or heteronym. Having begun the exploration of children's literature with her pallid *Le monde Moô-Moô,* Katalina has gone on to become a successful critic; twenty years later, after the extermination of the other scholars of children's literature, she returns to her original interest, picking up where Inge Albrecht left off. She agrees that it is pointless to search through the texts of children's literature for clues about children but draws an even more radical conclusion. The samples of children's literature offered to scholars are fabrications, offering insight into nothing but the minds and souls of the fabricators, valuable only as they reveal the logic of the society's shadowy ruling class and a startling fact: "l'absence totale d'enfants sur les territoires gigantesques qu'ils colonisent" [the total absence of children in the vast territories they colonized] (91).

Katalina Raspe is thus the ultimate enemy of the state, challenging its cosmology, threatening one of its most vital secrets, laying down a plan of study for other rebels. The most romantic and certainly the most sympathetic character in the novel, she is also its first image of the writer. In the strikingly cinematic scene that begins Ingrid's novel, she is walking at night through deserted streets, clutching *Clarté des secrets* [Secrets brought to light] every sense alert for signs that she is being followed. Like a character trapped behind the Berlin Wall in a John le Carré novel, she struggles to stay calm, to reassure herself that the plans are working, that the network is still intact; then, in a dreadful moment, she realizes what the darkened car in the shadows really is, and understands, when she hears its engine turning over, that she is about to die.

Katalina is not only a martyr but also a love object for the policeman charged with exterminating writers and intellectuals, Konrad Etzelkind. It is apparently he who narrates the story of her death in the second person, giving it an immediacy that the rest of the novel lacks; "Tu t'appelles Katalina Raspe . . . . tu serres contre ton ventre, ta poitrine, contre ton corps privé de respiration . . . tu protèges l'introduction de *Clarté des secrets*" [You are Katalina Raspe . . . you press against your stomach, your chest, your breathless body . . . you protect the introduction of *Clarté des secrets*] (43). Later scholars speculate that Etzelkind, in his day a symbol of "la froideur calculatrice, l'intelligence associée à la violence (implacable) d'un exterminateur" [calculating coldness, the implacably violent intelligence of an exterminator] (54), felt every bit as much an orphan of the Second Century as the writers he persecuted did. Evidently, in the course of investigating Katalina and her history he became fascinated with her in spite of himself, to the point where he too began to write.

Etzelkind's text, "Une rencontre magique des parallèles" [A magical encounter with parallels], has obvious affinities with the Kurt-Ingrid frame. Narrated in the first person, it is the story of a boy who follows his father through the streets of some nameless city, evidently in the Far East, where a woman he loves is hiding, in peril of her life. The father is a policeman, a man with "une tête rude de beater, de hunter, de stalker" [the rugged head of a beater, a hunter, a stalker] (58), all phrases that recall Ingrid's habit of referring to Kurt as "mon dogue" [my big dog] and the woman is Katalina Raspe, now the keeper of a small import-export shop. While the couple make love in a nearby room, the boy tends the cash register, where he sometimes yields to the temptation to smoke the opium pipe left lying on the counter.

Etzelkind—the name blends *Nibelungenleid* German for "Attila" with "child"—and his text are the counterpart of Katalina and her *Clarté des secrets*, an apparent affirmation of the romantic conception of writing. Katalina the rebellious writer is so powerful that even in her martyrdom she transforms her persecutor, brings him into contact with his re-pressed longings. His skillfully overwritten evocation of Katalina's shop produces the novel's only sensually rich moment, with a Baude-lairean *volupté* that makes even more visible the severity and inhuman-ity of the Second Century. The literary text is thus not only subversive, a place where alternatives to the grimly utilitarian state can be contem-plated, but is at least potentially therapeutic. In a literary text Katalina can be saved, and Etzelkind can have what no one in his society has, a father.

Yet, of course, the deep attraction of the policeman to the writer al-ready compromises and tends to deconstruct the opposition between the two, much as those old staples of popular fiction, the renegade cop and the outlaw detective, deconstruct the opposition between the law-ful and the criminal. If Etzelkind so readily becomes a writer, is it pos-sible that writers are also on the side of the police? Certainly most of the writers in Ingrid's novel have also been critics, publishing in the official journal that disciplines, or "polices," high culture. In the romantic con-struction, the critic is always the enemy of genius, and in a totalitarian society reviewers who ferret out the deviant tendencies of a text are vir-tually indistinguishable from, say, cryptographers for the state intelli-gence service. When the police erroneously announce that *la commune Elise Dellwo* has been "vaporized," *la section du combat Irene Schelm* re-joices on the pages of *Coeur du IIe Siècle*, quoting previous virulent at-tacks on Elise Dellwo by, among others, Inge Albrecht and Katalina Raspe. Indeed, guilt over her critical role follows Katalina to the end; she goes to her death meditating on a difficult, highly abstract text she had once denounced for its "injustifiable démence" [wrong-headed lu-nacy] and now finds entirely accurate (39).

The title of Ingrid Schmitz's *Leurre des bergers* [The shepherd's trap] puns on *l'heure du berger* [the lover's opportune moment]. Its central fig-ure crouches in the dark, nearly catatonic, prey to a crippling anxiety; in such moments of extraordinary isolation, "l'homme . . . supplie la police qui est en lui; il l'invoque, il la somme d'apparaître" [man supplicates the policeman within himself; he invokes him, he summons him to ap-pear] (29). Although the succeeding fragments of the text suggest that the anonymous man in question is also, like Katalina, trying to evade an external policeman hidden in the shadows, they continue to gloss the familiar spy-novel scene in philosophical terms. If the police are de-sired, if only as a real face on an undefinable existential anguish, they are also, like that anguish, finally as unknowable as they are inevitable. In a book much given to textual metaphors, they are compared to language itself.

Schmitz's man sees a tattered notice posted on a wooden fence and meditates on the steps he would have to take in order to read it—learning the alphabet, learning the appropriate language; these would not guarantee, however, that he would be able to understand what he read. Such notices are sometimes posted by the police, sometimes not:

> Derrière le langage, en tout cas, il y a les mots, et derrière les mots, parfois il y a un code, parfois il y a une culture, parfois il y a un hurlement, et parfois il n'y a rien. Tout texte obéit à des forces, mais pour un homme accroupi dans la poussière, terrifié, il n'est pas simple de définir ces forces. (38)

> [Behind language, nevertheless, there are words; and behind words, sometimes there is a code, sometimes a culture, sometimes a howl, and sometimes there is nothing. Every text obeys forces, but for a man crouched in the dust, terrified, it isn't easy to define these forces.]

Leurre des bergers uses the same terms to describe the police themselves; they obey forces, if not laws, but "il est malaisé de définir ces forces" [it is hard to define these forces] (37). It also contemplates a further possibility, which it scarcely finds more reassuring, that "derrière la police, il n'y a rien" [behind the police, there is nothing] (33).

In the dystopian Second Century, which denies everyone the most basic knowledge of his or her origins, the most terrifying possibility is a Derridean one, that no point of origin exists: no childhood, no invisible masters on whose behalf the police act, no meaning concealed beneath the indecipherable text. Even the sense of personal identity is threatened; during the Renaissance, human beings must fear that they are at present "le reflet, et non l'original" (116). If this is the case, the writer's act loses its definition and something of its heroism. While most of Ingrid's novel resists this grimmest conclusion of Katalina's work, assuming indeed that *someone* gives Etzelkind his orders, it certainly suggests, most notably in the case of *la brigade Eva Rollnik*, that the writer/terrorist is to some extent a creation of the state.

Eva Rollnik appears in the third part of Ingrid's novel, where Etzelkind again takes up the narrative, this time to talk about an investigation that began when his father the stalker was ordered to find the creators of a new experimental genre. A Shaggå is a sequence of seven short tableaus, each of identical length; its abstract, symbolic language, its baffling, oneiric scenes that appear to lack all dramatic progression, even, in one of the two extended examples, its use of Quechua words and a pseudo-Quechuan mythology, all serve to disorient the reader. As if in acknowledgment of its indecipherability, the authors append a lengthy commentary to each sequence.

An example of high imaginative literature, the Shaggå might seem less of a threat to a totalitarian state than *Clarté des secrets* or *Brèves conclusions sur le monde d'enfance*. But Etzelkind's father takes the broader view that an experimental text inculcates "des habitudes de révolte" (102). The "Shaggå of Abdallah," for example, describes a mythical pirate who slowly comes back to life centuries after his shipwreck. It does not say that the state has suppressed history, but it suggests that what people regard as the natural, commonsense categories of time might be subject to change. The whole genre, as Etzelkind *père* sees it, introduces the idea of gulfs in memory, of a general falsification of the real world, of manipulated doubles and all-powerful fabricators who alone understand essential truths (106). Eva Rollnik must surely be plotting to undermine "les valeurs fondamentales sur lesquelles la Renaissance faisait reposer son sense du réel" [the fundamental values on which the Renaissance based its sense of reality] (102).

This idea, that a postmodern fiction offers an effective form of political resistance because it undermines categories through which we experience official views of reality as reality itself, is but the most recent expression of the old romantic idea of writer as rebel. It is one obviously close to Volodine, who in his 1991 novel *Alto Solo* describes a writer suspiciously like himself, a man whose anguish over the real world leads him to write about alternative societies, even though he longs to denounce the dominant ideology directly. Iakoub Khadjbakiro obsesses over the real twenty-four hours a day, "et . . . pourtant s'exprime de manière ésotérique, sibylline, en logeant ses héros dans des sociétés nébuleuses, à des époques irreconnaissables" [and nonetheless expresses himself in an esoteric, sibylline manner, placing his heroes in nebulous societies in unrecognizable times] (34). Certainly, *Lisbonne dernière marge* takes the political claims of postmodernism seriously, yet in the end they too prove dubious.

As Etzelkind *père* moves in to arrest *la brigade Eva Rollnik* at the gas
works where they are employed as a security and maintenance crew, he
is suddenly beset with doubts about the provenance of the texts attributed to them. His stalker's instincts tell him the young technicians are
not reacting the way they would if they had ever heard of the debate
over the Shaggå. He recognizes how fundamentally improbable the idea
of an oppositional cell is in a society where saboteurs and subversives
belong to no other reality than that of the journalists "dont la complai-
sance facilitait les opérations . . . de la police" [whose cooperative attitude made police operations smoother] (118). Social democrats are too
corrupt to intrigue against the state; the literary milieu is too effete; one
has only to compare the impetuous *élan* of Eva Rollnik's texts to the elegant, ideologically empty productions of their literary imitators.

"Eva Rollnik" can only be a pseudonym employed by agents of *les
ruches,* who launched the Shaggå for their own purposes, to produce
some modification in the public consciousness, and have now decided
that the genre has taken an unwanted aesthetic direction. The real
deaths of these young workers, their nonfictional bodies, must cement
the fiction that the texts originated with them; if future scholars detect
differences between their texts and those of their literary imitators, they
will attribute them to "sociocultural differences" and not to the hand of
the state. The powerful, Volodine suggests, are likely to remain the fabricators of reality, and a difficult experimental form quickly degenerates
into aesthetic game-playing.

If high literature fails to offer genuine resistance, romantic mythology
suggests that the culture of the people might do so. For this reason *la
commune Elise Dellwo,* which opposes the state more directly and suc-
cessfully than the others, producing belligerent manifestoes and surviving an attempted police assassination, issues samples of *la littérature des
poubelles* under one of its heteronyms. Irene Schelm sees Elise Dellwo's
enthusiasm for this "trash" as related to their absurd idealization of
the "non-intellectual population," though properly speaking no one
knows precisely how it is produced: a later historian concludes that its
authors were a race apart from "l'homme de la Renaissance" (131, 150).
La littérature des poubelles is significant not so much because it is perverse
and indecent, or because it violates the recognized aesthetic canons, but
because it is *autre chose* [a thing apart], something outside the boundaries of the official culture that reveals the survival of obsessions long
thought extinct (147–48, 159).

The revolutionary potential of *Le montreur des cochons* [The exhibitor of pigs], an example preserved and transmitted by Elise Dellwo, lies partly in its themes. Nearly as static as a Shaggâ, it is a beast fable consisting entirely of a monologue by a character named "Gueule de lune" [Moon Face] that one of Ingrid's critics accurately describes as interminable.[3] Once a monk, he has escaped a massacre only to end up as valet to a pig trainer and spends most of his time praying to a nightmarish goddess named "Madame la gauche mort" [Madame Crude Death (a pun with *cauchemar* 'nightmare')] for vengeance on all of his enemies, in remarkably elaborate terms, such as, "let him swing for 73,000 days over a red hot grill" (163). Persuaded by a vision of chanting demons that it is up to him to conduct the vengeance, he begins a massacre that goes on, also interminably and shapelessly, pausing only to attend a magic show to which the original manuscript is said to have devoted thirty-five pages; eventually he is horribly wounded and immobilized, all of his body except his face covered with stagnant water.

According to later critics of the Second Century, this debased text also kept forbidden questions alive in the guise of allegory. Gueule de lune stops his mechanical butchering for a moment and forces his way into the hovel of Babouli, "la femelle commune" [common female] where he witnesses a magic show. In the highly sexualized atmosphere of this place, an otherwise tedious description of a magician conjuring a living pig out of a cookstove seems to reveal the culture's hunger to understand the origins of human life and its need to have a place where mystery and doubt are acceptable. The text contemplates the irrational and symbolically plays out the process of reproduction and the link between human beings and animals it inevitably suggests. Doing so, it provides a bridge between the masses and the educated "l'homme de la Renaissance."

Aside from raising these issues, the story seems to take to one extreme the theme of verbal violence we first noted in Conrad. Gueule de lune's invectives at least aspire to be a form of flyting, or performative cursing, on the printed page more horrible than the various physical atrocities that follow in their wake. Placed near the end of Ingrid's novel, his story gradually blends in with the frame story, rather in the manner of a cinematic dream episode gradually resolving into reality. In one sense this fantastic and horrible bestiary seems totally removed from contemporary Lisbon; in another, the valet is yet another heteronym for Ingrid, who announces on the first page her desire to write a novel that will begin "par une phrase qui les gifle" [with a sentence like a slap in the face]. For her, too, words and bludgeons, scarcely distinguishable, are weapons for expressing a corrosive rage; her enemies list is equally inclusive, she and her fellow revolutionaries having taken up arms: "contre la chiennerie humaine, contre l'absurdité du monde, contre toutes les armées non rouges, contre le ventre insolemment repu de l'Amérique, contre le ventre insolemment repu de l'Europe, contre la vacherie humaine, contre le patron des patrons, contre l'argent totalitaire" [against human meanness, against the absurdity of the world, against all the armies that are not Red, against the insolently swollen belly of America, against the insolently swollen belly of Europe, against filthy tricks, against the boss's boss, against totalitarian money] (240).

This almost incoherent raving, this impotent verbal violence unable to distinguish its objects, becomes something like the last breath of the old romantic alliance between literature and revolution. Although most of the transitions in *Lisbonne dernière marge* are abrupt, an imaginary electronic click, the scholarly gloss that follows *Le montreur des cochons* acts, perhaps appropriately, like an Aesopian moral spelling out the connection between the imaginary and the real. After arguing that the fable illustrates the Second Century's ignorance of the origins of human life, the commentator explains that it also reveals "un autre abîme de non-savoir" [another abyss of not knowing] (190). No one in that world—not the characters in the story, nor Elise Dellwo, nor the publicists who insulted them, nor the public who read it—understood the most basic facts about the physiology of life, or of death, or of nondeath: "En d'autres mots, ils ne savaient pas ce qui se passe après la mort" [In other words, they did not know what happens after death]. And the chapter ends with heavy irony: "L'ignorance et la peur, à cet époque, étaient épaisses . . ." [Ignorance and fear, in that epoch, were gross . . .] (191).

Out of ignorance and fear, the beast world erupts into genocidal violence. Yet the commentator points out that what is truly frightening about its wars is that the participants are indistinguishable: "un univers de boue, de solitude et de sang, et ces quatre groupes entre lesquels il faut la rumination délirante de Gueule de lune pour noter des différences" [a universe of mud, of solitude and blood, and these four groups it would take the delirious ruminations of Guele de lune to tell apart] (171). In Ingrid's world, a similar "uniformité répugnante" comes to characterize terrorists and the states and corporations against which they struggle. In the end, she sees no meaningful difference between "justiciers anarchistes" [anarchist judges] and "justiciers en uniforme" [judges in uniform]; both are "créatures du fumier militaro-industriel" [creatures of the military-industrial dung-heap] (174). Disgusted with the "cochonnerie de la violence" [obscenity of violence], she wants her novel above all else to make readers feel the absurd and scandalous character of all combatants and the hypocrisy of the official reasons they give for their conflicts. Among us, she says, there were people who had clear ideas about the society they wanted to destroy and who could formulate coldly all the political, historical, and ideological circumstances that had made the West so loathsome. Yet reasoned violence is impossible; once they took up arms they found themselves following a bloody interior path into a landscape where lucidity and rationality were simply phantoms: "C'était le sentier de l'élite, déjà piétiné mille fois par l'élite des cochons occidentaux, et qui cheminait d'une guerre à une autre" [It was the path of the elite, already trampled a thousand times by the elite of the Western swine, and which led from one war to another] (174). A revolution will inevitably fail because those who rebel can only do so in terms already laid down by the powerful, who are themselves taking a direction already overdetermined by history and, apparently, biology.

This blurring of the fantastic and the realistic, and the state and its opponents, has its parallel, as we have seen, in the heteronyms that prevent us from imagining that any character in this novel has a unique identity. Toward the end, the policemen—Etzelkind *père*, Etzelkind, Kurt—collapse into a single character. Heading up a team assigned to burn down a building occupied by social democrats, the son not only carries on the family calling but is described as his father had been, with "ses lèvres closes de stalker" [sealed lips of a stalker] (226). When he seizes an untitled gramophone disk on which he believes that Katalina Raspe's voice has been recorded, the words he expects to hear are Ingrid's at the beginning of the novel, "Rue de l'Arsenal, à Lisbonne, les potences abondent" [On Arsenal Street, in Lisbon, gallows abound]. Or, remarks the narrator, he might hear a voice describing the Sicherheitsgruppe's attacks on terrorist cells and Kurt Wellenkind's fascination with a file photo of Ingrid Vogel. In the next chapter, when Kurt emerges from his shower, the person he sees on the bed is Katalina

Raspe; although his face retains its vaguely Asiatic cast, the shower water glistens on the body of Konrad Etzelkind. Finally, to complete the merger of the characters, in the last five pages of the novel, the usual third-person narrative is interrupted four times so that Kurt can take up a first-person narration, a form previously used only by Konrad Etzelkind.

Konrad Etzelkind's last appearance as a police incendiary who cannot bear to destroy Katalina Raspe's voice is already charged with contradictions, but its deepest irony lies in his attitude toward audio recordings themselves. This assassin of writers is a deep-dyed cultural conservative who believes, as apparently his masters do, that paper is a more "natural" support for the human voice than a wax disk (230). What Elizabeth Eisenstein called "print fixity" is as meaningful to a totalitarian state as it has been to most novelists: books can be stored in the Archives Frankhauser; they can be endlessly scrutinized and analyzed "un mois, cinq siècles ou trente mille ans plus tard" [a month, five centuries or thirty thousand years later] (225). The recording, on the other hand, is an ephemeral document that does not speak to the intelligence as a text does and that must be transcribed anyway if it is to be studied (226). Less fixed and bounded, too, the electronic medium escapes the state's control. The social democrats who have amassed this collection of disks have for all practical purposes given themselves the right to "des archives privées, incontrôlées et incontrôlables," forgetting that they are only the state's valets (226).

Puzzling over the wax disk in his hands, trying to read its grooves like the bookman he is, Konrad Etzelkind may or may not survive the conflagration of the Ministry of Information. An account of his death after an overeager colleague tosses a match into the gasoline-soaked office in which his boss remains transfixed is couched in the conditional tense, and in the last chapter Ingrid asks Kurt whether Etzelkind should be allowed to live. "'Sujet de dissertation,' she adds, 'Métamorphosé en torche vivante, l'incendiaire peut-il cesser d'être incendiare?'" ["Subject for a dissertation," she adds, "If he turns himself into a living torch, can the incendiary cease to be incendiary?"] (244). One cannot answer, of course, except to say that in his world the distinctions between killer and victim that make such questions possible are deeply problematic. Nor do we know with any certainty whether Ingrid herself will survive. Kurt, who is gradually taking over the narrative, likes her suggestion that they go drown themselves: "'Sujet de dissertation: Le suicide peut-il sauver l'individu de la noyade?' dis-je, approuvant de tout coeur son projet" ["Subject for a dissertation: Can suicide save the individual from drowning?" I said, approving her plan wholeheartedly] (245).

At the end of this novel, then, we sense not only that Ingrid/Katalina and Kurt/Etzelkind are doomed, but that a whole system that defined them is also dying. In portraying the police incendiaries as driven by fear that the social democrats' record collection is uncontrollable, Volodine avoids the suggestion that the electronic media are inevitably enemies of culture and freedom. Still, he offers little evidence that this particular collection is subversive. The titles pencilled on their stark black and white covers suggest the futile bureaucratic preoccupations of their owners—for example, *Werner Frankhauser et le problème des jardins en communauté urbaine* [Werner Frankhauser and the problem of gardens in an urban community]; even the more promising *Willy Frankhauser: Toujours plus loin vers l'égalité entre les hommes* [Willy Frankhauser: Always further toward equality among men] seems not to offer any fundamental resistance to *les ruches* (230, 231). The key point perhaps is that a print system that long seemed to enable and sustain an opposition between writers and the state has been replaced by a system in which the putative means of resistance are in the hands of people who are themselves entirely tools of the repressive state. As we have been told often enough, even the police are contemptuous of the social democrats as puppets whose occasional mild "velléités d'indépendance" [inclinations toward independence] can easily be corrected (220).

As we have seen, while its early reviewers complained of the obscurity of *Lisbonne dernière marge*, one of its characters perversely fears that it is only too readable; Kurt initially argues that every text betrays its author's secrets. At the end he admits that Ingrid's novel is an exception, that the most avid decoder could extract from it only a few universal givens: "l'opacité de l'état, sa violence illimitée, son rôle de paravent pour des activités inconcevables, la solitude tragique du chercheur de vérité, la médiocrité congénitale des marionnettes au pouvoir, le mutisme de leurs manipulateurs" [the opacity of the state, its unlimited violence, its role as a screen for inconceivable activities, the tragic solitude of the truth seeker, the congenital mediocrity of the puppets in power, the muteness of those who pull their strings] (242–43). These givens, as he says, are "peu instructives"; by no means a program for action, they are hardly even a call to revolution. If anything, the text increasingly persuades the reader of the futility of resistance, of its identity with that which it opposes: the revolutionary's identification with the state, the writer's with the police. The text finally fails not because it is too readable or because it is unreadable or subject to misreading, but because it cannot occupy an uncontaminated pure space from which to offer a critique of power. Writer and critic, terrorist and police officer, are not only at the last margins of Europe but also at the last margins of the printed text, in a novel that suggests that a revolutionary impulse that has driven Western art and politics for two centuries has, at last, perished.

Epilogue

Conrad and the Unabomber

I n an apocryphal story, taught as fact to American schoolchildren for a century, Abraham Lincoln is introduced to Harriet Beecher Stowe. "Ah," remarks the melancholy president, "so this is the little woman who made the great war." Tiresomely, Stowe's biographer points out that Lincoln never met the author of *Uncle Tom's Cabin*, but we can recognize folkloric truth when we see it. It was once possible to believe that an American president attributed the terrible war over which he presided to the power of a pen wielded by a person who never was allowed to vote in a United States election.

For perhaps two generations after the French Revolution, writers were the half-acknowledged legislators of mankind, claiming real power, the kind that changes human institutions forever, and real moral authority. Though it is hard to imagine that the average mill hand in Manchester or Lowell took them as seriously as they took themselves, the reading public seems to have faithfully acknowledged their claims. The vision of the writer as revolutionary, Byron in Greece or Lamartine on the barricades in 1848, is too compelling to be abandoned easily, even or especially when it is accompanied by the expectation that the writer in old age will be a hoary sage, a Victor Hugo living in the comfort a grateful nation bestows on its benefactors.

Such grand and hopeful views of the writer's authority are the lighted backdrop that accentuates the dark outlines of terrorist fiction, that most pessimistic of genres, and supplies it with its deeper ironies. From James to Coetzee, novelists who imagine a bond between terrorist and writer assume that both are isolated and marginal, incapable of gaining a hearing in the ordinary language of civic life. Estranged from those they hope to represent, they plot to revolutionize society from its shadows. Our fictional terrorists, to a man (and the occasional woman) are failures: betrayed like Stone's Hamas, inept like Lessing's IRA rejects, hopelessly torn, like McCarthy's Jeroen, between the claims of high culture and the needs of the proletariat. Only those writers, such as Dostoevsky and DeLillo, who imagine terrorists more as rivals than secret sharers, are willing to concede them some success.

With few exceptions, the serious terrorist novel portrays writers as petty and pretentious, their occasionally noble speeches masking an innate violence or a surly jealousy of more active and powerful people. As early as Henry James, the genre has considered the view, so often attributed to poststructural theory, that the author's conscious intentions count for nothing and that works of literature always end by supporting the dominant ideology—that is, if they are heeded at all. Meanwhile, the social world moves further and further away from the model of organized society that underlies both eighteenth-century notions of social contract and nineteenth-century visions of organic community. As it does so, the very notion of the writer addressing humanity, Wordsworth's "man speaking to other men," loses credibility. A mass culture sustained by a global electronic media does not listen to the single voice; perhaps, suggests Volodine, we are seeing the death of revolution along with the death of the novel.

Having watched so many of our major novelists come to these grim conclusions, we can take particular interest in a series of newspaper and television stories that began running in the United States after the bombing of the Murrah Federal Building in Oklahoma City on 19 April 1995. True to form, the major networks first broadcast the story that a man of "Islamic appearance" had been seen lurking in the vicinity of the explosion. The arrest of Timothy McVeigh a few hours later forced Americans to confront the reality of a homegrown terrorism that could be blamed neither on the international Communist conspiracy, by 1995 safely dead, nor the ferocious Arabs. The quest to discover what could trigger violence in clean-shaven former GIs such as McVeigh and his coconspirator, Terry Nichols, led quickly to—a novel. "Evidence of McVeigh's admiration for a novel called *The Turner Diaries*," *Time* magazine reported solemnly, "will aid the prosecution's effort to portray him as a hate-filled radical" ("McVeigh"). A photocopy of a page from the novel turned up, along with a passage from John Locke, in the trunk of the car McVeigh was driving when he was arrested after the bombing.

"An eager evangelist" for *The Turner Diaries*, McVeigh had "handed it out to friends and sold it at gun shows—often for a loss" ("McVeigh").[1] Indeed, when McVeigh actually was brought to trial, a copy of *The Turner Diaries* that he had given his cousin as a Christmas gift in 1991 became Government Exhibit Number One (Serrano 51).

One may object to *Time*'s simplicities, but media claims that *The Turner Diaries* furnished a "blueprint" for the Oklahoma City bombing have some credibility. Its author is William Pierce, a former professor of physics and leader of the National Alliance, a neo-Nazi organization based in Hillsboro, West Virginia. Pierce is editor of the National Vanguard, the press that published *The Turner Diaries* and its successor, *Hunter*, under his pseudonym, Andrew Macdonald.[2] The National Alliance hydra includes a Web site, a short-wave radio program, a "New World Order Comix" series targeted to white teenagers, and a Cosmotheist Church that preaches that whites are the chosen people and Jews and blacks are children of Satan.[3] In all of these activities Pierce exhibits remarkable canniness about his First Amendment Rights; indeed, until 1983, when he was taken to court by the NAACP and others, Pierce claimed that the National Alliance was an "educational organization" and therefore deserving of tax-exempt status (Shinbaum 2). Pierce's decision to found a church and write novels probably says more about the special legal protection extended to religious and artistic expression than about his own spiritual and aesthetic impulses.

The Turner Diaries, first published in 1975, is set in the future, beginning in 1989; it details a revolutionary takeover of the United States by a right-wing organization called the Organization. By 1999, after an apocalyptic "Day of the Rope," when tens of thousands of race traitors—among whom UCLA faculty figure prominently—are hanged from lampposts all over Southern California, the Organization launches nuclear attacks on New York, Miami Beach, and Tel Aviv. Newspaper articles urging the "blueprint" theory tend to concentrate on an early scene in the novel in which the Organization blows up the FBI Building in Washington, D.C., using a truck loaded with a fertilizer bomb (Macdonald 36). The Oklahoma City bombing took place on 19 April, the anniversary of the Battle of Lexington and more recently of the FBI storming of the Branch Davidian compound at Waco, Texas; the same commemorative impulse leads the fictional Organization to blow up the Israeli Embassy on 20 April, Hitler's birthday.[4] Throughout, the book

perpetuates, revives really, the crudest racist and anti-Semitic stereotypes; its narrator, a hero who will die in a suicide mission to bomb the
Pentagon, has only the mildest and most occasional of qualms about the
most horrendous violence. He speaks approvingly of the genocide of
not just African Americans but all Africans; by the end of the book, not
only are they and "Satan's spawn," the Jews, dead, but all of Asia has
been destroyed by a "combination of chemical, biological, and radiolog-
ical means, on an enormous scale" (210).

One has no difficulty in discovering why Timothy McVeigh admired
The Turner Diaries. Here is a book to feed every revenge fantasy an ill-
educated young white man, drifting around the margins of his prosper-
ous society, might invent to assuage his resentment of the visible
successes of others—the minorities and their white liberal advocates.
Would his 168 victims still be alive if he had never found this book?
William Pierce certainly thinks not; indeed, since the bombing he has argued for an almost Joycean distance between fiction and history. The
novel, he says, merely predicted what would happen if the liberal
trends of the 1970s continued; when asked who should make "the
life/death decisions on a 'Day of the Rope,'" he rejected this "hypothet-
ical question about a fictional scenario" (*"Turner"*). When a questioner
characterized as "disingenuous" his argument "that people attack the
government for what it does (or did) not because of what they read in a
book of fiction," Pierce agreed that people are "inspired to act by the
written word every day." Nonetheless, he insisted that what the "government is and . . . does" outweighs "some book . . . written twenty
years ago" (*"Turner"*).[5]

Pierce's fling with modernist aesthetics aside, we can agree that drawing a straight line from his book to the worst domestic terrorist incident
in U.S. history is impossible. Something in mainstream American culture, or in Timothy McVeigh's psyche, must have predisposed him to
act out the fantasies of *The Turner Diaries* as other young men act out the
fantasies of the made-for-TV movie. The hatred preached in the novel is
freely available in dozens of other publications; clearer directions for
building a fertilizer bomb can be found on the Internet or, for that matter, in *Homemade C-4: A Recipe for Survival*, which McVeigh ordered from
a Colorado firm in 1993 (Serrano 57). Yet a novel that snickers over a
reenactment of Babi Yar, this time in California and with African and
Asian American victims as well as Jews, is no more neutral politically
than it is morally.[6] Pierce has added his voice to those of others sum-

moning us to brutal racial violence; he has found an audience to listen; he has lived to see a scenario described in the pages of his novel acted out by an admiring reader; he need not fear, as Henry James did in the wake of *The Bostonians,* that his book has disappeared without an echo.

Ironically, then, while our serious novelists tell us that their books have no lively political influence, in large part because mass journalism and the electronic media have displaced them, these same media insist that *The Turner Diaries* incited Timothy McVeigh to bomb the Murrah Federal Building. Nor did the media stop with Pierce's crude polemic; when Theodore Kaczynski was arrested in April 1996, a year after the Oklahoma City bombing, the search was on for another novelist to implicate. This time they were after richer game. News stories explicitly made the parallel between McVeigh and Kaczynski, and between *The Turner Diaries* and, remarkably, Joseph Conrad's *The Secret Agent.* The NBC news magazine *Dateline* introduced its story, "Heart of Darkness," with a graphic juxtaposing the front covers of *The Turner Diaries* and *The Secret Agent.*[7]

Evidence for Conrad's culpability was found, as Pierce's had been, in parallels between his text and recent events. The *Washington Post* noted that in the course of their investigation, "federal agents were struck by the similarity between Conrad's themes of anarchy, alienation and dehumanization and the written justifications the Unabomber gave for his deeds" (Kovaleski 2). It went on to quote Frederick Karl's statement that throughout *The Secret Agent* "science, pseudo-science, and technology are perverted forms, false idols," a view thought to line up rather smartly with the Unabomber's Luddite diatribes. Stevie, the "troubled boy" blown up by the Greenwich bomb, is "strikingly similar to the youthful Kaczynski as described by his family" — all the more so, presumably, if we have not noticed that Stevie is mentally retarded. But the main parallel was between Kaczynski and the Professor, both brilliant, isolated, ascetic bomb-makers. *Dateline* adduced a further textual parallel: a character in *The Secret Agent* says "you are perfectly determined to make a clean sweep of the whole social creation," which is tantamount to the Unabomber's statement that "A revolutionary movement offers to solve all problems at one stroke and create a whole new world" ("Heart," p. 12 of transcript]).

Now Timothy McVeigh, we remember, had been caught with the goods, some photocopied pages of *The Turner Diaries.* Kaczynski, according to the FBI, had used the name "Conrad" or "Konrad" when checking into hotels. But was there any evidence that the Unabomber had actually read *The Secret Agent*? Terry Teachout, in an op-ed piece in the *New York Times,* quotes Anthony Bisceglie, a lawyer for the Unabomber's mother and brother: "in 1984 the suspect reportedly told his family he was reading Conrad's novels for 'about the dozenth time'" (19). The *Dateline* story, however, failed to cite this claim, focusing instead on evidence that in the 1970s his brother, David, had checked "even obscure Conrad novels" out of a library in Cedar Rapids, Iowa. For expert testimony, they turned to a distinguished professor of English, George Stade, who testified that this same brother had read *The Secret Agent* in his course at Columbia University in the spring of 1969. Stade went further, agreeing with his interviewer that Conrad's Professor "sounds like what I know" of the Unabomber and suggesting that an extremely "resentful" person might see the Professor "as a kind of revolutionary saint" ("Heart" 12). In the end, no smoking gun emerged, but the program left the viewer with a question: "Is it a literary parlor game, or was the man who may have checked into cheap hotels using the name Konrad with [a] K leaving his pursuers with a highbrow literary clue about how he'd stumbled into his own heart of darkness?" (13).

It is with real relief that we find National Public Radio interviewing Frederick Karl, the Conrad scholar quoted by the *Washington Post.* Asked what he would say about the Unabomber's "link to Conrad," if called to testify in court by the FBI, Karl replied sharply, "I would say that he completely misunderstood Conrad." The great novelist, said Karl, "saw . . . all these people like the . . . Unabomber . . . as scum." Conrad's portrayal of the anarchists, Karl added, "is deep in sarcasm and irony and cynicism" ("FBI Suspects," p. 10 of transcript). Terry Teachout makes the same point, adding that Conrad would not have been surprised to learn that a terrorist had mistaken his "ferocious satires" of the "revolutionary mind-set" for "a plan of revolutionary action." After all, a Russian revolutionary in Conrad's *Under Western Eyes* declares that "women, children, and revolutionists hate irony, which is the negation . . . of all action" (19).

To other scholars at least, Karl's and Teachout's arguments will seem unassailable: Conrad cannot be taken at face value; the opinions expressed by his characters are not those of the author. A great realistic novel re-creates the complexity of the world; it will always be the antithesis of a blueprint. Pierce's unambiguous message can be translated into unambiguous action; Conrad's irony creates interpretive difficulties and leaves his work subject to endless misreadings. Even where Conrad seems least ambiguous, in condemning violent revolution, for example, it is difficult to imagine how we would measure his influence. When Pierce's readers blow up daycare centers or torture and murder a randomly chosen African American, we may feel we have some hard evidence of his impact. We can imagine men and women who become disillusioned with revolution after reading Conrad, but we will never be able to count them.

But if all of these points instinctively feel right to a professor of English, they may simply show how far we have accepted as fact what for James and Conrad was a nightmarish possibility, that the serious novel has no power in the social world. It is true that media stories about Timothy McVeigh and Theodore Kaczynski and their reading suggest that the romantic view of literature as dangerous remains alive in some attenuated form: the popular press is willing to pay that much tribute to art. The strange case of Conrad and the Unabomber, however, in giving us a rare opportunity to see network television reading a serious terrorist novel, points to their radical incompatibility. Television, a "hot" medium, demands, as Browning might have put it, that everything mean, and mean intensely; it does not tolerate, and indeed has trouble representing, irony. For the producers of *Dateline* there was no real difference between a crude polemicist like Pierce and a high artist like Conrad. *Dateline* could pay Conrad the dubious compliment of attributing to him something of television's own direct influence on society only at the cost of ignoring everything about *The Secret Agent* that mattered to its author. It is cold comfort, indeed, for those who care about serious fiction to realize that it can be said to have social influence only when it is seriously misunderstood.

As the quick sound bites, glossy images, scandals, and explosions of television programming increasingly define our reality, a popular fiction that emulates such qualities, that does not make too many demands on its readers, may continue to play some part in our collective life. But a fiction that requires readers to proceed slowly, that requires them to tolerate ambiguity and difference, to attend to subtleties of tone and diction, is at odds with the dominant media of the time. As such, it appears further and further marginalized, speaking to ever smaller audiences. One of the successes of serious terrorist fiction has been to trace this marginalization, often by suggesting the strange affinities of the writer and the terrorist. If we want an image for the once dangerous writer left with a diminished audience, we can do no better than to turn back to *The Secret Agent*. In a fly-spotted room at the back of Mr. Verloc's pornography store, three of his revolutionary friends gather to argue and reminisce. One of them, Karl Yundt, "the old terrorist," a man of "worn-out passion" and "impotent fierceness," staggers to his feet. His "dried throat and toothless gums" make every word a struggle, but still he rasps out the slogans of his youth: "discard all scruples," "no pity," "death enlisted for good," "strong enough to give themselves frankly the name of destroyers." It is all very fiery talk, but no one outside the circle will ever hear it: "His enunciation would have been almost totally unintelligible to a stranger (47)."

Notes

Introduction

1. The invention of dynamite in 1867 was also strategically crucial because the "infernal engine" could be easily concealed, even planted in advance, improving the odds that the user could escape undetected.

2. One might argue, however, that in the nuclear age warfare has become increasingly "symbolic." Since regular wide-scale use of nuclear weapons is a practical impossibility, the cold war strategies of deterrence quickly developed into what anthropologists call ritual combat: "Setting aside obvious differences in scale and technology, as well as the fact that intimidation through nuclear deterrence is thought to be based on retaliatory anticipation alone, whereas the intimidation of terrorism springs from concrete acts of terror, it is the presence of similar premises in both kinds of terror (threat, simulation, bluffing, symbolic posturing) that is most instructive" (Zulaika and Douglass 80).

3. See Representative Thomas Luken's charge in 1985 that "TV becom[es] . . . a coproducer of hostage drama, coproducer with the terrorists" (quoted in Weimann and Winn 264).

4. Miller notes that the term *disorganization* was initially intended to denote a more limited program of violence than was advocated by Nechaev's "Catechism for Revolutionaries." However, the more violent elements in the Land and Freedom movement rapidly took control.

5. Christopher Hitchens once publicly challenged Terrell E. Arnold, director of the Institute on Terrorism and Subnational Conflict, to produce a definition that was not "tautological or vacuous," "a cliché . . . employed by all warring states . . . in denouncing their enemies," or a "synonym . . . for 'swarthy opponent of United States foreign policy.'" Arnold was unable to do so, perhaps because, as Alex Schmid discovered in 1983, experts use at least 109 definitions of terrorism (Zulaika and Douglass 97).

6. Several critics, readers of Foucault, remind us that literary realism arose at the same time as urban sociology and psychiatry, disciplines that also enact a "fantasy of surveillance" and stigmatize aberrations (Mehlman 124; Seltzer 52). See also the introduction to Armstrong and Tennenhouse, in which the editors claim that about half of the contributors to the volume accept the view that "writing is not so much about violence as a form of violence in its own right" (2). In their brief analysis of *Jane Eyre* the editors demonstrate how Jane's power as a writer, reader, and speaker enables her to "build around herself a community that excludes those who do not think and feel and read and write as she does. . . . [Thus] the violence of an earlier political order maintained by overt forms of social control gives way to a more subtle kind of power that . . . works through the printed word upon mind and emotions rather than body and soul" (4). One might infer that the violence of writing might be used as a revolutionary tool, but Armstrong and Tennenhouse draw the familiar Foucauldian conclusion: "Successive phases of imperialism . . . have turned the violence of representation into the ubiquitous form of power that is the ultimate though elusive topic and target of this book" (9). For a passionate and reasoned critique of this tendency to collapse "what goes on in the interrogation cells of South Korea and South Africa with what happens . . . on a SoHo stage," see Kubiak. "For no matter how irrational they may seem, terror and terrorism have their meanings, and those meanings, which become intelligible *as* difference, must be read before resistance can become possible. . . . Though certain kinds of theory may be violent *as* theory, to equate *theory* with shrapnel in the belly is to forget the real pain of the bodies upon which the theatrical performances of culture— whether as 'art' or as political violence—are founded" (157–59).

7. Crelinsten analyzed *The New York Times Index, The London Times Index,* the *Reader's Guide to Periodical Literature,* and the *British Humanities Index.*

1. Don DeLillo's *Mao II* and the Rushdie Affair

1. In a telephone interview with Lorrie Moore, DeLillo confirmed "a connection between [*Mao II*] and the silencing" of Rushdie. "Mr. DeLillo said his planning and notes on the book preceded the Rushdie affair by a short time. He was one of the writers who read from Mr. Rushdie's works in the tumultuous days just after Feb. 14, 1989. . . . By March 8, Mr. DeLillo had begun putting his own words on paper."

2. For a fuller discussion of the Hawkes Bay incident see Ruthven, 45–47. Hawkes Bay is in Karachi; Fatima is the name of Muhammed's daughter, the mother of the Shi'ites' "arch martyr," Husain, who was killed at Kerbala (Schimmel 21). To a Western reader, therefore, Rushdie's use of the name of Muhammed's favorite wife, Ayesha, for a fictional character based on Naseem Fatima seems like business as usual, but it was deeply offensive to some Muslims.

3. The term *satanic verses* was not invented by Rushdie but was long used to describe the story he incorporates into his novel: that Muhammed, prompted by Satan, briefly accepted as revelation two verses that gave three pagan goddesses the status of intermediaries between human beings and Allah; subsequently, after an admonition from Allah, Muhammed removed the verses, but only after the false verses had led to the conversion of the pagan Qurayshites. Maxime Rodinson describes the satanic verses episode (106, 113) and argues that "it may reasonably be accepted as true because the makers of Muslim tradition would never have invented a story with such damaging implications" (106). While this eminent French scholar is widely regarded in the West as having produced the standard biography of Muhammed, for Ziauddin Sardar he belongs in the ranks of the "aggressively anti-Islamic Orientalists" (302). Rushdie's detractors regard the satanic verses story roughly as Western intellectuals regard *The Protocols of the Learned Elders of Zion*. It is, says M. M. Ahsan, "a malicious story coined by the polytheists and picked by orientalists" (6).

4. Of course, it is perfectly possible for a critic to perceive the distinction between fictional characters and historical personages and still find the brothel scene offensive. On this point, see Mazrui: "Rushdie's game of a 'play within a play' is nevertheless a prostitution of the reputations of twelve innocent and respectable women. . . . The real equivalent of comparative blasphemy would be portraying the Virgin Mary as a prostitute, and Jesus as one of her sexual clients. Also comparable would be any novel based on the thesis that the twelve apostles were Jesus' homosexual lovers, and the Last Supper was their last sexual orgy together" (71).

5. On this point, see *Free Speech*. See also Webster, *Brief History*: "The rigidity of some forms of Islamic fundamentalism is real, as is their potential for cruelty. But we should also recognise that absolutist doctrines of freedom are themselves rigid, and that, in the four decades which have passed since the Second World War, we have developed an intellectual culture which has many marks of insensitivity and callousness, and which itself has an enormous potential for cruelty" (134–35).

6. The title of Weldon's tract, *Sacred Cows,* is already highly offensive in its willful confusion of Muslims with Hindus and, one might add, in the disdain for pagan superstitions that the phrase connotes. Some part of the cultural rift comes through strongly in Weldon's further observation that "My novels don't sell in Muslim countries. My particular parables, my alternative realities, don't suit. How could they, being the works of an unclean female unbeliever?" (6).

7. Said, however, points out that the Islamic "cultural context is horrifically and even ludicrously inhospitable to such transgressions." He goes on to say that for Islamic readers *The Satanic Verses* must raise questions: "Why must a Moslem, who could be defending and sympathetically interpreting us, now represent us so roughly, so expertly and so disrespectfully to an audience already

primed to excoriate our traditions, reality, history, religion, language, and origin? Why . . . must a member of our culture join the legions of Orientalists in Orientalizing Islam so radically and unfairly?" (Appignanesi and Maitland 165). Said's article, which is excerpted in Appignanesi and Maitland, appeared in the *Observer* on 26 February 1989 and in the *Washington Post* on 27 February 1989. For other thoughtful uses of the concept of *Orientalism,* see Webster, *Brief History,* and Sardar, "Rushdie Malaise." Webster observes that "Muslims have very good reasons to be especially sensitive to such treatment of their own sacred figures. For both Christian polemicists and Western orientalists sought for centuries to denigrate Islam by attributing to it a fantastic, disreputable or demonic sexuality. And what almost all Muslims know, from their intuitive grasp of their own history, is that there is nothing remotely liberating in this kind of Western fantasy" (40). Sardar similarly points out the problems of the postmodern defense: "magical realism gives the appearance of speaking from the perspective that incorporates the Other but in so doing it merely utilizes that conception of the Other that fits within the Orientalist paradigm. The grotesqueries in *Midnight's Children* could have sat happily in Kipling" (305).

8. This is the theme, to take an example from scholarly criticism, of Feroza Jussawalla's "Resurrecting the Prophet." Jussawalla says that only readers who associate butterflies with "Titli Udi," the "cheap Hindi film song" from *Suraj,* can understand how offensive Rushdie was being when he clothed the modern-day Ayesha in nothing but yellow butterflies (106).

9. If the Rushdie affair raises questions about the political clout of postmodern fiction, it seems to confirm postmodernism's sense of the instability of fact. Two factual issues, the number of people killed in anti-Rushdie protests and the amount of the award offered for Rushdie's death, are impossible to pin down. Appignanesi and Maitland list sixteen deaths: five in Islamabad on 12 February 1989; one in Kashmir on 13 February, and ten in Bombay on 24 February. Daniel Pipes says that "rioters" killed a Pakistani guard at the American Cultural Center in Islamabad on 12 February, "making him the sixth casualty of the day" (24). He claims twelve dead in Bombay on 24 February; "a security guard at the British Council Library in Karachi was killed by a bomb . . . on the 26th. One person was killed in Srinagar on the 27th" (140). Pipes says there was rioting in Srinagar (in Kashmir, presumably the site of the 13 February death Appignanesi and Maitland note) on 14 February, but lists no fatalities. Ahsan and Kidwait list ten dead in Islamabad on 12 February (all protesters, no mention of the Pakistani guard); five dead in Srinagar on 13 February, and thirteen killed in Bombay on February 24. Western sources characterize the demonstrations as riots, whereas Ahsan and Kidwait stress their peaceful nature; everyone agrees that most of the dead were killed by security forces. Similarly, the amount of the reward is open to interpretation. Ruthven writes: "Immediately after the *fatwa* was issued, Hojjat-ul-Islam Sheikh Sanei of the Fifth of June Foundation . . . of-

fered a reward of 20 million tumans (about three million dollars) to any Iranian who would 'punish the mercenary for his arrogance.' Non-Iranians would get the equivalent of one million dollars" (113). Pipes also attributes the reward offer to the Fifth of June group, citing it as 200 million rials, worth three million dollars "at the inflated official rate of exchange" but only $170,000 "on the parallel market" (28). He attributes the second offer of 200 million rials to the hometown of religious leader Akbar Hashemi Rafsanjani (28). In Peshawar, says Pipes, "a preacher offered 500,000 rupees, or $30,000, to the 'young and brave Pakistani who kills the infidel Rushdie'" (139). Weatherby, however, cites the original amount of the reward as "$2.6 million for an Iranian, $1 million for anyone else." According to him, "the next day the reward was doubled" (155). Norman Mailer had the amount at "$5,000,000" in his death-defying speech in New York (Appignanesi and Maitland 163). On 1 November 1992 the Iranian state-run religious charity, the Panzdah Khordad Foundation, increased the reward by an unspecified amount (*New York Times*, 2 November 1992, 9; 4 November 1992, 24). On 12 February 1997 the same foundation reportedly increased the award to $2.5 million, and its head, the Ayatollah Shaikh Hassan Sanei, extended the offer to anyone who killed the "apostate" writer, "including non-Muslims and his bodyguards." At this point President Rafsanjani, who earlier defended the *fatwa*, distanced himself from Sanei, noting that his foundation was a "non-governmental organization and its decisions have nothing to do with the government's policies" (Amnesty International). Britain restored full diplomatic relations with Iran on 24 September 1998 after the Iranian foreign minister, Kamal Kharrazi, pledged that the government of Iran had no intention of threatening Rushdie's life. However, within days 150 of the 270 members of the Iranian parliament had signed "an open letter stressing the edict's utter irrevocability. The Association of Hezbollah University Students announced it would add a billion rials ($333,000) to the reward for Rushdie's assassin, theological students and clerics in the holy city of Qom pledged a month's salary as an additional bounty, and a small village in northern Iran sweetened the pot by offering his executioner ten carpets, 5,400 square yards of agricultural land, and a house with a garden" (Pipes, "Salman Rushdie's Delusions" 52).

10. I am well aware that some thoughtful Islamic writers deplore the use of *fundamentalism,* a term with a long specific history in Christianity, to describe movements within their own religious tradition. "The term 'Islamic fundamentalism' has been imposed rather than chosen by the Muslim proponents of a variety of interpretations of the contemporary meaning of being a Muslim. If the definitional points and doctrinal argumentation of Christian fundamentalism were put to such Muslims they would deny, as articles of their very faith, that they could or should or in fact do subscribe to such notions. To analyse Islamic fundamentalism as if it were a Christian response to the Bible is total nonsense" (Sardar 306). As used here, the term refers to belief in a single vision of truth,

revealed through prophecy and written down in an inerrant text, which must be accepted literally. While fundamentalism is in this sense opposed to the skeptical secular view of, say, postmodern fiction, it is by no means a term of abuse.

11. That is, many Westerners who saw photographs of the Bradford book burnings must have wondered why there was so much fuss about what was, after all, "just a novel." Srinivas Aravamudan has analyzed this problematic position artfully, pointing out that "Western liberal free speech has inscribed itself within certain self-generated limits, idealizing free expression even as it suspends the material effectivity of 'language' in 'the world'" (3).

12. Malise Ruthven sees the Bradford book burning as a similar media event, "the public relations coup of the century" (103), and links it to the experience in dealing with the British media that Bradford Muslims gained during the Ray Honeyford affair. Honeyford, appointed headmaster of the Drummond Middle School in Bradford in 1980, subsequently published a number of articles attacking multicultural and anti-racist policies adopted by the Bradford Council. After an article originally published in the *Salisbury Review* was picked up in the *Yorkshire Post*, Bradford Muslims became incensed at his negative characterizations of Pakistan ("the heroin capital of the world") and such traditional practices as *halal* slaughter of animals (76). They conducted a campaign for his resignation, which eventually was successful when Honeyford agreed to take early retirement. For a full discussion, see 75–80.

13. In Pipes's view, the need for public denunciation of public figures was paramount for Khomeini. He regards those who focus on Khomeini's strictly political motives, such as a desire to find a new focus for nationalist enthusiasm in the wake of the cease-fire with Iraq, as underestimating the power of religious feeling in Islamic countries (97–98).

14. See, for example, Rushdie's protestation that *The Satanic Verses* "is not . . . the book it has been made out to be, that book containing 'nothing but filth and insults and abuse' that has brought people out on to the streets across the world. That book simply does not exist" (*IH* 395).

15. DeLillo told an interviewer that "the photographic image is a kind of crowd in itself, a jumble of impressions very different in kind from a book in which the printed lines follow one another in a linear order. There's something in the image that seems to collide with the very idea of individual identity" (DeLillo, "Interview" 88). For more on the function of the photographs in the text, see Carmichael: "The traumatic photo aspires to an unmediated glimpse of the real and always falls back into the necessary awareness of its own processes of signification. . . . Barthes's description of the photographic image is also uncannily a description of the postmodern intertextual project" (216).

16. "Bill was not an autobiographical novelist. You could not glean the makings of a life-shape by searching his work for clues. His sap and marrow, his soul's sharp argument might be slapped across a random page, sentence by sen-

tence, but nowhere a word of his beginnings or places he has lived or what kind of man his father might have been" (144). In "How to Read Don DeLillo," Daniel Aaron says much the same thing: "No one character in any of his nine novels can confidently be said to speak for him. He is in all of them and none of them, diffused in the eddies of his inventions. DeLillo is the son of Italian immigrants . . . I think it's worth noting that nothing in any of his novels suggests a suppressed 'Italian foundation.'" (67).

17. In this respect she echoes Fredric Jameson, who speaks of "the photorealist cityscape, where even the automobile wrecks gleam with some new hallucinatory splendor," the "exhilaration" of "urban squalor" offered by "these new surfaces" (32–33). In DeLillo's *White Noise,* Murray Jay Siskind, professor of popular culture, lectures about the transformation of car crashes in American film: "the people who stage these crashes are able to capture a lightheartedness, a carefree enjoyment that car crashes in foreign movies can never approach . . . there is a wonderful brimming spirit of innocence and fun" (218–19).

18. In his interview with DeLillo, Anthony DeCurtis remarked on the "men in small rooms" phrase from DeLillo's *Libra* and suggested its resemblance to the author's descriptions of himself as a writer. DeLillo responded by pointing out that Oswald had stated on his application to Albert Schweitzer College that he wanted to be a writer, though he felt the phrase "refers to Oswald much more as an outsider than as a writer" (DeLillo, "Outsider" 52).

2. Eoin McNamee's *Resurrection Man*

1. Allen Feldman has recorded and analyzed oral retellings of the story of the Shankill Butchers in Belfast. For both Protestants and Catholics, the Butchers mark an "outer limit" in which sectarian violence becomes converted into "symbolic genocide" — the killing of people for no other reason than their assumed religion. A UDA (Ulster Defense Association) man reported that after he showed his son Lenny Murphy's grave, an RUC (Royal Ulster Constabulary) man tapped him on the shoulder and asked for identification. "The uneasy surveillance of the grave by the police" suggests its "aura"; "the polarity of the grave . . . in opposition to the police . . . functions as a formulaic expression of paramilitary power" (65). See "Hardmen, Gunmen, Butchers, Doctors, Stiffs, and Ghosts" (Feldman 46–84). The Butchers were back in the headlines on 12 June 1997, when a surviving member, Robert "Basher" Bates, was shot dead at a "drop-in centre" in Belfast for former prisoners. Bates had served a seventeen-year sentence for his role in the group's murders ("Legacy").

2. A Royal Ulster Constabulary press release shows that in 1999 Loyalist paramilitaries committed 47 shootings and 91 assaults, compared to 26 shootings and 42 assaults attributed to Republican paramilitaries. In the year 2000, by 22 May the RUC was attributing 63 "paramilitary style attacks" to Loyalists and

41 to Republicans. In recent years the overwhelming majority of victims have been members of the same community as their assailants. For 1998, the last year for which disaggregated numbers are available, the RUC listed 120 of the 151 Loyalist "paramilitary" attacks as "punishment beatings," sometimes referred to by their apologists as "community justice" (see "Casualties"; "Punishment Beatings").

3. The authors of a recent book would find that McNamee's depiction simply reflects the sober truth. "There is, however, in our view no well-established evidence of a special Irish or Ulster Protestant obsession with the past, or of obsession with those historical events which are held to have shaped key political institutions, or particular patterns of social domination. Knowledge, albeit selective knowledge, and assertions about the past are normal components of most political cultures; so is the stress on decisive, significant historic events. The fact that Northern Irish myths stress historical antagonism between the communities is also not surprising; they reflect current realities rather than a peculiar atavistic celebration of the past" (McGarry and O'Leary 243). Feldman argues that although violence in part stems from ethnic divisions that reflect a history of "an inequitable cultural division of labor. . . . violence can effect autonomous and retroactive interventions in the construction of ethnicity" (5). That is, arson and bombing themselves reinforce ethnic division by driving people into ever more sharply segregated neighborhoods. Such "dynamics attest to the modernist character of political violence in Northern Ireland, despite all popular and easy characterizations of this situation as an archaicized religious or tribal conflict" (5).

4. In this respect Victor Kelly doubtless resembles many other Belfast residents. An anonymous Catholic male resident of North Belfast used a Steven Spielberg film to explain the pervasive terror that kept most Catholics out of Protestant areas while the Butchers were active: "There were places in Belfast you never walked! . . . Just forget about the Oldpark Road. If ET had landed on the Oldpark Road someone would have fuckin' stiffed him! . . . They would have fuckin' cut ET's head off or at least gone after that wee glowing finger of his! ET was definitely a Taig! Aye, wasn't he Green!" (Feldman 61).

5. This particular dialogue, so clearly reminiscent of Jack Gladney's verbal contests with Murray Jay Siskind in *White Noise,* also suggests the extent to which McNamee's style seems influenced by Don DeLillo, another writer preoccupied with conspirators and terrorists. The car salesman in *Resurrection Man* who sees his showrooms as "centres of subliminal knowledge" and the jailed terrorist who notes that a purple and white capsule has the "colours and dimensions," rather than the chemical properties, of "the serious drug capable of producing fundamental changes in the organism" would be at home in DeLillo's America, where the logic of advertising conditions thought (27, 75).

6. Carl Freedman notes that Freud once defined paranoia as "the hyper-cathexis of the interpretations of someone else's unconscious"; in Freedman's gloss, "the paranoiac has an abnormally high investment in the hermeneutic practice which he or she performs on the symptomatic actions of other people" (8). In Lacan's elaboration of Freud, the "ego is structured on a paranoiac basis and . . . human knowledge operates according to a paranoiac principle" (9). Thus Freedman concludes that "Paranoia . . . is no mere aberration but is structurally crucial to the way that we, as ordinary subjects of bourgeois hegemony, represent ourselves to ourselves and embark on the Cartesian project of acquiring empiricist knowledge. In this sense, we can accept Freud's urgency when he insists of certain paranoiac delusions that *'there is in fact some truth in them'*" (10). For a brilliant exposition of paranoia as a motif of postwar American culture, see Melley, *Empire of Conspiracy.*

7. Thomas Luken, a member of a House committee examining the media and diplomacy in the Middle East in 1985; Lawrence Eagleburger, U.S. under secretary of state (quoted in Weimann and Winn 264).

8. On secularization, McGarry and O'Leary's research indicates that there is more violence in urban centers with low church attendance rates than in the more devout rural areas. "A 1986 study by John Darby suggested that Catholic church attendance was only 33% in one Catholic area of Belfast"; in the late 1970s one study of the Shankill neighborhood showed "that Protestant church attendance had dropped to about 15%" (190).

9. An outsider, Frank Burton studied "telling" in Belfast and found that his own skepticism "about the efficacy of signs was shaken when I found myself employing them." Running after a bus without being able to see its number, he correctly concluded that it was the wrong one because all of the people boarding it looked Protestant (69). "When urged a little to give the salient characteristics of being 'Scottish' or 'English' even the most loquacious of respondents became inarticulate. It appeared that such knowledge does not form part of an accountable or reflexive store of information but was more firmly located in a stock of unexamined knowledge" (67). Burton and others emphasize the importance of segregation in Belfast's working-class neighborhood, which increased dramatically after 1969, when threats, bombs, and arson drove people out of areas in which they were an ethnic minority.

10. Another statistic shows civilians making up 37 percent of the people killed by Republican paramilitaries between 1969 and 1989; during the same period over 90 percent of those killed by Loyalist paramilitaries were civilians (McGarry and O'Leary 86). The reason is simple: members of the British Army and the Royal Ulster Constabulary make readily identifiable targets for the IRA, whereas the only noncivilian targets for the Protestants are Republican paramilitaries, who do not go about in uniform or live in easily identified barracks. Mc-

Garry and O'Leary remind us that the "Ulsterization" of the security forces between 1975 and 1985 substantially increased the ratio of local men killed; most Protestants therefore regard attacks on the security forces as sectarian killings (86).

3. Mary McCarthy's *Cannibals and Missionaries*

1. When her attempt failed, McCarthy decided to continue paying her own taxes, believing that refusal to pay taxes would be successful only if large numbers of supporters could be enlisted.

2. When she was in South Vietnam in 1967, a cynical Marine tank commander suggested that McCarthy had written *The Group* to make money and seemed "startled" when she denied having done so: "What do you write for, then?" (McCarthy, *Seventeenth Degree*). This text incorporates *Vietnam* (1967), *Hanoi* (1968), *Medina* (1973), an account of the court-martial of Captain Ernest Medina for the murder of Vietnamese civilians at My Lai, and "Sons of the Morning," McCarthy's review of David Halberstam's *The Best and the Brightest*.

3. The question of the bloodbath is still debated. By Cambodian standards, one can probably agree with Neil Sheehan that there was none. Some 100,000 people spent some time in "reeducation camps" after 1975; about 6,000 died, and as of 1991 all but 120 had, according to the Vietnamese, been released (Sheehan 79). Conditions were harsh, as numerous firsthand narratives attest; prisoners were used to clear minefields, often denied basic medicines such as insulin, and fed a subsistence diet consisting mainly of poor-quality rice. Those imprisoned included not only high-ranking officials of the Saigon government but many doctors, teachers, and other well-educated people who had perhaps served as low-ranking officers in the ARVN, the South Vietnamese army. As for actual executions, accounts vary widely; Shaplen cites a University of California study based on a survey of 831 Vietnamese refugees that claimed that 65,000 people were executed "primarily for political crimes between 1975 and 1983"; such studies are not infallible, but better statistics are unavailable.

The huge exodus of refugees from Vietnam in the 1970s and 1980s obviously attests to great dissatisfaction, and many escapees list the repressive political atmosphere as the major factor. The current Vietnamese regime has reversed a policy of rigid, centralized economic planning that it now believes to have been responsible for some of the hardships of life in the past twenty years. One must remember, however, that wars with Cambodia and China contributed to these hardships. Sheehan says that 58,300 Vietnamese soldiers—or roughly as many as the number of Americans killed in Vietnam—were killed fighting Cambodians and Chinese between 1975 and 1989 (85). After the Vietnamese invaded Cambodia and deposed Pol Pot, a move many might applaud, the U.S. government led an economic boycott of Vietnam joined by all of the Western European countries except Sweden and Finland; much later, after the collapse of the Soviet Union, the Vietnamese lost their only other source of foreign aid. Obviously any isolated Vietnamese government would have had trouble maintaining the standard of living, which has indeed been lowered drastically, at least for reasonably well-educated people. Sheehan, for example, describes squalid hospitals that lack most basic modern equipment, in one of which in 1991 a child lay dying of blood poisoning because the standard antibiotic Keflex could not be bought for any price. In such circumstances the distinction between economic and political refugees is difficult to make.

4. This was an open letter to the Socialist Republic of Vietnam signed by 790 prominent people known for their previous opposition to American policy in Vietnam and including such figures as Cesar Chavez, Nat Hentoff, I. F. Stone, and Daniel Berrigan. After its publication in the *New York Times* Baez was attacked by Jane Fonda; in response, another open letter to the *Times*, signed by Harry Bridges, Joshua Kunitz, Corliss Lamont, and Karen Ackerman, among others, claimed that "Vietnam now enjoys human rights as it has never known in history" (Doan Van Toai and David Chanoff, *Vietnamese Gulag* 341–42). The interviewer was Miriam Gross (McCarthy, "World" 174).

4. Doris Lessing's *The Good Terrorist*

1. Lessing herself provides a similar formulation in the fifth volume of the Canopus series. The youth of Volyen (read Great Britain) owe their enthusiasm for totalitarian Sirius to their inability to find the jobs for which their education has prepared them. As Klorathy explains to Johor, "at the time of your visit, so recently, even in Volyen terms—the young of the expanding upper and middle classes all were educated for, dreamed of, and found a place in the administrative machinery of the Empire. Education matched expectation, expectation matched achievement. But for the last thirty years, since the war, when Volyen . . . fought and won, but at heavy cost, because that 'victory' in fact weakened it and left it unable to recover . . . educated youth have had to face a very difficult future. . . . youngsters emerge from the training establishments with all the equipment, practical but mostly moral, for running, administering, advising, *ruling* others, and find their occupation gone" (*Documents* 78).

2. Lessing's perceptions about the IRA receive confirmation from John Conroy, an American journalist who lived in Belfast for a year and was struck by the amount of teenage vandalism there. In recent years, Conroy reports, the IRA has reduced its numbers to counter British infiltration: the result is a generation that—facing nearly certain unemployment in that devastated city—has no stake "in either normal society or in the underground" (81).

3. One can find confirmation of this perception in newspaper accounts of the December 1983 bombing of Harrods, which Lessing claims was the model for

the car bombing in her novel. The IRA's claim that the Harrods bombing was unauthorized (although it "accepted responsibility") was reported but largely ignored in the spate of anti-Irish publicity that culminated in Denis Thatcher's braving the heavily damaged store the Monday after the bombing. Clutching his Christmas shopping bags, the prime minister's husband was quoted as saying that "No damned Irish murderer is going to stop me going there" (*Times*, 20 Dec. 1983, 1). Numerous suspects have been questioned in the bombing, but no one has ever been convicted of it. On 8 March 1985 the *Times* reported that a Dublin IRA member, Natalino Vella, claimed that he had been sent by his organization to "find out why it happened." Vella, who had himself been charged with the bombing in June 1984 (and who was given a fifteen-year prison sentence for possession of explosives), claims that one Paul Kavenagh, given a life sentence on 7 March 1985 for his part in a series of fatal bombings in London in 1981, was the person responsible.

4. Are real-life terrorists the mad bombers of popular and even literary stereotype? Certainly one can find experts who think so; as an example one can cite Martin Jay's "The Fictional Terrorist," an essay that uses Karen Horney's analysis of neurotics who create fictional identities for themselves to argue that "from Booth to Sirhan, terrorists and assassins have murdered as a way of seizing their victims' lives and turning them into identities of their own" (69). However, many would disagree. While psychologists such as Joseph Dowling, Anthony Storr, and Oleg Zinam agree with Richard Rubenstein that certain broad social conditions increase the likelihood that terrorism will break out, they are far less certain that one can define a terrorist personality, let alone pathology. Lawrence Freedman says, "A psychological profile of a model terrorist cannot be drawn. The personalities are disparate. The context and circumstances within which terrorism, both political and ecclesiastical, has been carried out are diverse in chronology, geography, and motive" (quoted in Rubenstein 6). Another noted expert, Brian Jenkins, entertains the notion that terrorists may suffer from "anonymity, deprivation, and a sense of powerlessness" and seek in violence "not only attention but intimacy with the powerful figures of society" (173). However, he concludes that "We do not know at this point whether terrorists in general suffer from some common psychosis, or from any psychosis at all. Wilfried Rasch, a psychiatrist who has the opportunity to observe and interview many of Germany's terrorists, believes they do not. We do not know whether there is a common terrorist personality or a common mindset" (174).

5. Lessing says that the Harrods bombing of Christmas 1983 in which six people were killed was the immediate source of her plot; she also says that she was in Ireland when Lord Mountbatten was assassinated in 1979 (Donoghue 3).

6. A 1990 Foreign Policy Research Institute book, *KGB: Masters of the Soviet Union*, coauthored by a former KGB agent, echoes Goren's argument. After not-

ing specific evidence for KGB funding of the Baader-Meinhof group and of the Red Brigade, the authors tell us that "similar evidence links the Irish Republican Army and the Palestine Liberation Organization to the KGB as well as to the Romanians" (Derabian and Bagley 359). We do not learn what that evidence is. Andrew and Gordievsky make a more nuanced argument that in the 1980s Moscow developed "a growing distaste for some of its terrorist associates in the Third World" (632). They note an exaggerated fear in the Kremlin that the Soviet Union was becoming a terrorist target. As of December 2000, the Royal Ulster Constabulary puts the total number of deaths in the Irish Troubles at 3,313, of which 526 occurred after 1989 ("Deaths").

5. J. M. Coetzee's *The Master of Petersburg*

1. *The Master of Petersburg*, as one might expect, contains many other allusions to Dostoevsky's work. Joseph Frank notes that the fictional Dostoevsky's sense of *déja vue* in the police station, which is accompanied by a vague memory of fainting, recalls Raskolnikov's collapse when, summoned to the police station to pay an IOU, he overhears talk of the murder he has just committed. Frank notes the origins of the fictional affair between the writer and Anna Sergeyevna in a Dostoevsky story called "The Landlady"; when Coetzee's Dostoevsky embraces Nechaev, kissing him on both cheeks, Frank finds an echo of Christ's embrace of the grand inquisitor. Coetzee's Nechaev also quotes a legend about the mother of God going on "a pilgrimage to hell to plead for the damned" that Dostoevsky used in *The Brothers Karamazov* (*Master* 53–54).

2. The story that "Stavrogin's sin" was Dostoevsky's had already reached Tolstoy in 1883. One version has Dostoevsky rushing into Turgenev's room to make his confession; Frank cites a Soviet scholar, V. N. Zakharov, who tracked down its printed variants and concluded that they are inconsistent and contradictory. Zakharov believes that Turgenev invented the story "as a satirical anecdote" to characterize the man who had savaged him in *Demons* and that it became fact in the retelling (*Dostoevsky* 432.) Frank also quotes a letter from Dostoevsky that offers an alternative to the view that the author had an unwholesome preoccupation with child molestation. The letter notes that as a child Dostoevsky was sent to find his father, a doctor, to treat a nine-year-old girl, a friend of the future author, who had been raped by a drunken man. The child's terrible hemorrhaging could not be stopped, and she died: "All my life this memory has haunted me as the most frightful crime, the most terrible sin, for which there is not, and cannot be, any forgiveness, and I punished Stavrogin in *The Devils* with this very same terrible crime" (22).

3. If "African" means anything more specific than "dark-haired person for whom I feel contempt," it presumably means "North African." Aimée describes

Dostoevsky's first wife as being "part Mameluke," a term with a variety of meanings, the closest of which seems to be "Islamic slave of Caucasian or Asian descent."

4. Dostoevsky's grief for his daughter Sofya and his son Alyosha, both of whom died in early childhood, is movingly depicted in Joseph Frank's biography. Sadly, however, there is a more personal dimension to the theme of the bereaved author; Coetzee's son Nicolas died in an automobile accident in 1989 at the age of twenty-three (Gallagher 194).

6. Friedrich Dürrenmatt's *The Assignment*

1. Bethami Dobkin agrees that "television news reproduces an ideology of counterterrorism that justifies an approach to international conflict guided by symbolic gestures and overt military force." Yet she adds a note of caution, "by reinforcing and legitimizing official constructions of terrorism, television news contributes to a cycle of responses that may ultimately serve . . . the terrorist" (9). More recently, Tamar Liebes argues that around-the-clock disaster reporting, such as the seventy-two hours of continuous live coverage that followed the Hamas bombing of three city buses in Jerusalem and Tel Aviv in March 1996, actually works against the government's interest. "From the media's point of view, stories of disaster invite a hermeneutic search for the culprit, someone to whom to assign the blame"—in her view, usually those in power when the disaster struck. Also, since TV is biased toward "visual, personalized stories," the "frame of 'disaster' calls for people who scream the most . . . the louder, the less controlled, the better." Television has adopted a new convention, "victims as policy experts," which encourages viewers to conflate the "personal tragedy of the victims with a catastrophe for the whole of society" (70). As proof, she points to the election of a new Likkud government in May 1996—one guaranteed to take a harsher line with Palestinians than the Peres government.

2. In 1998, according to the State Department, twelve U.S. citizens died in "international terrorist attacks," all of them in the 7 August bombing of the U.S. embassy in Nairobi; there were no international terrorist attacks in the United States (U.S. Department of State 1). Between 1990 and 1999, the State Department counts 89 U.S. deaths from international terrorism, with the largest number, 25, in 1996. Between 1982 and 1997, there were 183 terrorist incidents in the United States; in 1995 a single domestic terrorist incident, the bombing of the Murrah Federal Building in Oklahoma City, killed 168 people ("Casualties resulting from international terrorism involving U.S. citizens," Table 3.192, and "Terrorist incidents," Table 3.191, *Sourcebook*). The Oklahoma City bombing was by far the most deadly incident of domestic terrorism in recent U.S. history; by comparison, Theodore Kaczynski, arrested in 1996 as the much publicized "Unabomber," is accused of killing 3 people over a seventeen-year period.

One need not trivialize these figures to see the stark contrast with other casualties from violence in the United States: In 1998, 25 percent of the 1,531,044 violent crimes reported in the country involved handguns (U.S. Department of Justice 10–11). In 1997, according to the Centers for Disease Control, the homicide rate in the United States, 9 per 100,000, was 4–9 times the rates in comparison countries (Canada, Denmark, England and Wales, France, Israel, New Zealand, Norway, Scotland, and the Netherlands). "In all the countries except the United States, the firearm deaths were primarily (51–93%) suicides. In the United States the majority of the firearm-related deaths (62%) were homicides" (Fingerhut 2). One might argue, however, that the U.S. media have devoted more attention to death from firearms, even before the wave of school shootings in small-town America that began in the fall of 1997, than Zulaika and Douglass suggest. Rather like terrorist incidents, each of the school shootings received massive and repetitious media coverage, resulting in criticism that the press was in effect encouraging disturbed teenagers to imitate the accused killers.

3. Critics frequently cite the British Prevention of Terrorism Act of 1974 and the Northern Ireland (Emergency Provisions) Act of 1973 as examples of such curtailment of civil liberties because they "not only enact a significant disparity between the legal treatment of terrorism compared to other crimes but they do so through a legal circumscription of the normal process of law and 'common law values'" (Hocking 104). Once an organization such as the Ulster Volunteer Force (UVF) or Irish National Liberation Army (INLA) has been proscribed, simply joining it is a crime, and the burden of proof is borne by those accused. Suspects may be detained for interrogation for seven days without arrest; the right to trial by jury is suspended in cases involving accusations of terrorism. With the possible exception of hijacking, not a major tactic of Irish revolutionaries, "terrorist" crimes—theft, illegal weapons possession, assault, murder, arson —are regularly committed by people without political motives, yet "legislation . . . assumes enormous divergence between terrorism and other crimes" (Hocking 104).

In a similar move, the U.S. Congress passed the Clinton administration's Effective Counterterrorism Act in April 1996, over the bitter opposition of, among others, the American Civil Liberties Union (ACLU) and the National Association of Criminal Defense Lawyers. The act expands the wiretapping authority of the federal government and empowers it to detain aliens indefinitely on the basis of classified information. Such persons have "no right to judicial review, including application for a writ of *habeas corpus*," except for violations of their limited constitutional rights. Once the secretary of state and the attorney general designate a group as a "foreign terrorist organization," U.S. citizens are banned from donating money to it, a crime punishable by up to ten years in jail. The power to label groups as "terrorist organizations" is, in the ACLU's opinion, "virtually unfettered" since the definition is so loose as to include charitable and educational subgroups of organizations vaguely designated as having "engaged in any 'terrorism activity' at any time" (American Civil Liberties Union). The U.S. National Commission on Terrorism report to Congress on 5 June 2000 raises similar concerns. The report proposes setting aside the ban on CIA and military action within the nation's borders in the event of a major terrorist attack on U.S. soil. It also "recommended expanding a regional pilot program for tracking foreign students that could alert officials whenever a foreign student changes his or her major from, say, 'English literature to nuclear physics'" (Loeb A19).

4. On this point see also Annamarie Oliverio's analysis of U.S. media responses to the hijacking of TWA Flight 847 in 1985 and comparable Italian responses to the *Achille Lauro* incident a few months later. She begins with the premises that "terrorism is . . . a discursive practice in the constitution of nation-states" and that analyzing the "'conventional' . . . language of the media" enables us to observe the "practical, political production of . . . the social reality constituting terrorism and violence" (16, 24).

5. Hubert Lyautey, marshal of France (1854–1934), served in Northern Africa, French Indo-China, and Madagascar. For the novel's purposes it is probably most important that he was resident-general in Morocco from 1912 until 1916, when he joined the French cabinet as minister of war. See André Maurois, *Lyautey.*

6. Robert Helbling suggest another possible source of D.'s name when he notes the "unobtrusive projection of the narrator's persona into the characters of the logician D. (Dürrenmatt?), the film-producer F. (Friedrich?) as well as Polyphemus, who embodies the type of *Augenmensch* represented by his visually oriented creator, the writer/painter/cartoonist Dürrenmatt" (181).

7. For an interesting gloss on this passage see Franz Hebel (43): "Die Realität, die F. aufzuzeichnen meint, als ob sie vorhanden wäre, wird von ihr erst produziert" [The reality that F. wishes to record, as if it were already at hand, must first be produced by her].

8. But Jennifer Michaels is quite right to point out the ironic resemblance between F.'s project and Dürrenmatt's 1971 play *Portrait of a Planet,* also an attempt to put "together a complete portrait of our planet by creating a whole out of chance scenes" (144).

7. Philip Roth's and Robert Stone's Jerusalem Novels

1. For further discussion, see also Siegel-Itzkovich.

2. Alive and well in Gaza, Abbas called the hijacking a mistake in 1996 ("Leader"). However, the *Boston Globe* quoted him contending in a 1998 interview that Klinghoffer "created troubles. He was handicapped but he was inciting and provoking the other passengers" ("Achille Lauro").

3. Robert Alter sees the double in *Operation Shylock* "not as the embodiment of a hidden self . . . . [but] as a kind of retribution exacted from the novelist. . . . The second Philip Roth is also an ideological extrapolation, rather than a psychological excavation, of the first" (32).

4. Everyone who writes about *Operation Shylock* struggles with "Philip Roth," the name of the author, his protagonist, and the protagonist's double. I've chosen to refer to Roth the character as "Roth" and to call the double Moishe Pipik, the nickname "Roth" gives him.

5. "Roth" expresses a similar view of Anne Frank's diary. In the draft of his introduction to Klinghoffer's diaries, he speculates that Jews would be as boring as anyone else without their persecutors: "Without the Gestapo and the PLO, these two Jewish writers (A.F. and L.K.) would be unpublished and unknown" (329).

6. The novel, then, gets its name from an intelligence "operation" that it suppresses. See Shostak (748).

7. "Thus, German Jews in Israel are called yekkes, not tekkes; the Jewish marketplace in Jerusalem is Machaneh Yehuda, not 'Machaneh'; a non-Hasidic European Jew is a mitnaged, not a mitnag; the initial consonant in the Hebrew word kavan . . . is not 'glottalized'; . . . the numerical value of the Hebrew letter kuf is 100, not 19" (Halkin 4). "The Jerusalem he brings to life here ultimately amounts to little more than a caricature, but it does possess all the cacophony and chaos of the New Orleans of his first novel, *A Hall of Mirrors*" (Mahler). *Operation Shylock* attracted similar criticism: "there is still little of the Israel I know that is recognizable in these pages" (Merkin 44).

8. By 1917, Lenin was already constrained to argue that the phrase "wither away" should not be interpreted too hastily, that is, to deny the importance of "violent revolution" and the "dictatorship of the proletariat": "democracy is *also* a state and . . . consequently . . . will *also* disappear when the state disappears" (17).

9. For example, after the publication of *Damascus Gate*, "two Christians were detained by Israeli authorities . . . when they tried to enter the country. The pair of Americans, reportedly members of a fundamentalist cult . . . were planning to carry out an attack on the Islamic holy site the Temple Mount in order to 'precipitate Armageddon'" ("Israel's Next Nightmare" 2).

8. Volodine's *Lisbonne dernière marge*

1. Lisbon: 'last margin' (the French word, rather like its English counterpart, can refer to the 'margin' of a text or the 'border' or 'edge' of a cloth and metaphorically indicates 'freedom, latitude, scope'). Translations in this chapter are my own.

2. Putting aside commonplace names such as "Müller" and "Kurt," we can see that at least eight characters or communes in the novel have names that appear in accounts of the Red Army Faction:

1. Ingrid Vogel: Probably after Cornelia Vogel, who, having met Thorwald Proll at an anti-Vietnam War congress, reluctantly allowed him, Andreas Baader, Gudrun Ensslin, and Horst Söhnlein to stay at her apartment in early April 1968; they used it as a base of operations for their bombing of two department stores.

2. Silke Proll: In Volodine's novel, the name of a writers' commune. See Thorwald Proll, above; after the department store bombers were convicted in 1969, Astrid Proll, his sister, fled the country with Baader and Ensslin, after purposely losing Thorwald in Strasbourg because his resolve appeared to be weakening.

3. Katalina Raspe: After Jan-Carl Raspe, a member of Berlin's Kommune II; tried at Stammheim with Baader, Ensslin, and Meinhof.

4. Suzanne Speitel: In the novel, a writers' commune; in real life, Volker Speitel was a prominent member of the RAF.

5. Elise Dellwo: The fieriest of the writers' communes in the novel; Heinz Dellwo stood trial as a member of the Holger Meins Commando; he also belonged to Dr. Huber's Therapy-through-Violence movement, or Bomb-for-Mental-Health, Kill-for-Inner-Peace (Becker 278).

6. Verena Goergens: Another of the writers' communes in the novel; Becker calls Irene Goergens a protegee of Ulrike Meinhof; arrested 8 October 1970 with Horst Mahler.

7. Eva Rollnik: In the novel, the name of a workers' group falsely accused of responsibility for circulating a new experimental form of poetry; Gabriele Rollnick, a sociology student, was charged with kidnapping Peter Lorenz; she escaped from Lehrter Strasse prison in Berlin in 1976.

8. Irene Schelm: In the novel, a writers' commune; Petra Schelm was killed in a shootout with police in 1971.

Information on these individuals was drawn from Becker and Wright. For a readable, if highly conservative, discussion of the Frankfurt School's relation to the RAF, see Becker, 52–62. Although the students of the Free University of Berlin who founded the radical movement that eventually became the Red Army Faction admired Theodor Adorno, Jürgen Habermas, and Herbert Marcuse, all three disappointed them by refusing to support actual violence. In response to a speech by Rudi Dutschke, Habermas famously predicted a "fascism of the left." Marcuse, whose theories about repressive tolerance and consumer terrorism were widely quoted by the group, appeared before cheering crowds when he came to Berlin to visit Rudi Dutschke in the hospital, but he was booed for being too theoretical. Becker cites speculation that Adorno's death was hastened by the abuse heaped on him by students at the Free University. Though not a novelist, Ulrike Meinhof was a writer. She was associated with a newspaper called *konkret* for ten years, working as editor-in-chief from 1962 to 1964. In a study of Meinhof's published essays, Arlene Teraoka makes the case for a continuity between her writing and her later acts of terrorism; both failed to "reach a proletarian audience," she concludes, because they are "historically and perhaps generically impaired by the privileged education and learning that they continue to presuppose" (220). On 20 April 1998, German security sources announced that an eight-page fax sent to Reuters, claiming that the RAF was disbanding, was authentic. See "Red Army Faction" and "Red Army Faction Gives Up."

3. *Guele* [animal's mouth] is slightly vulgar slang for the human mouth, jaw, or face, as in *Ferme ta guele* [Shut up]. *Lune* not only means 'moon' but can mean, as Cassells puts it shyly, 'posterior.' Given Volodine's penchant for puns, it may be relevant that *Se metter dans la guele du loup* means 'to throw someone to the wolves,' while *guele-de-loup* is a 'snapdragon.'

Epilogue

1. *USA Today* reported that the one of the killers of James Byrd Jr., an African American man dragged behind a car and decapitated near Jasper, Texas, on 6 June 1998 had made the comment, "Let's start *The Turner Diaries* now" before he and two of his friends set out to find a black man to kill (Jones). At a critical point in the fictional Organization's revolution, when people outside its protected enclaves are suffering from hunger, white men are allowed inside only on the production of "the head of a freshly killed Black or other non-white" (Macdonald 207).

2. In 1996, after coverage of the Oklahoma City bombing had given *The Turner Diaries* a new lease on life, Barricade Books brought out the first trade edition of the novel. Predictably, the publisher, Lyle Stuart, wrote an introduction claiming that the public has "the right to know what the enemy is thinking." Morris Dees of the Southern Poverty Law Center led a crusade to publicize Barricade's decision and its obvious financial advantages for Pierce and the National Alliance ("Amid Controversy").

3. Jacob Young's documentary about Pierce features a scene filmed at a Cosmotheist worship service in which a baritone soloist sings a hymn apparently titled "Race of Whiteness" to the tune of "Rock of Ages." Machine-made fog rolls over the singer, eerily suggesting that he is being swallowed up in sulphurous clouds.

4. The killings at Columbine High School near Denver occurred on 20 April 1999.

5. On Pierce's modernist aesthetics, see also an essay reproduced on his web site in which he claims *The Turner Diaries* "doesn't advocate killing innocent women and children . . . it is not a book of advocacy at all, but a novel" (Pierce). Conveniently, the author draws the veil over his views on killing, say, African American men.

Pierce also draws pedantic distinctions between his book and the Oklahoma City bombing. "The bomb described for the destruction of the FBI headquarters was made of ammonium nitrate and heating oil. The bomb which destroyed the federal building in Oklahoma City was made of nitromethane, ammonium nitrate and PETN.

"Furthermore the structure of the two bombs was different and the engineering of the bombings were different in the two cases. . . . So a blueprint may have been used for the Oklahoma City bombing, but that blueprint could not have come from *The Turner Diaries*. . . . Furthermore, the motives were different. The motives described for the fictional bomb was to destroy a bank of supercomputers in the basement of the FBI building, which were to be used for an internal passport system. In Oklahoma City, the motive for the bombing seems to have been a desire for revenge against the government for the Waco massacre two years earlier" ("*Turner Diaries*").

6. In the relevant scene, fifty thousand "light-skinned" African Americans, along with a group of Jews and "unclassifiable mongrels from various Asian and southern climes," are marched into a canyon. "I have a suspicion their trip into that canyon will be a one-way affair!" chortles Turner (158). These particular people are killed first because the Organization fears they will "confuse" the racial issue and might even "pass" for white. Dark-skinned African Americans will be kept alive a little longer because they can be used to increase the pressure on whites in parts of the United States still controlled by its elected government.

7. The *Washington Post* also noted that Mark David Chapman, who killed John Lennon, was obsessed with *The Catcher in the Rye* and that John W. Hinckley Jr., would-be assassin of President Reagan, was "consumed" by the film *Taxi Driver* (Kovaleski 2). Pinning a murder rap on Holden Caulfield seems harsh; the article does not explain how this verdict was reached.

Bibliography

Aaron, Daniel. "How to Read Don DeLillo." In *Introducing Don DeLillo*, ed.
   Frank Lentricchia, 67–81. Durham, NC: Duke UP, 1991.
Abramowitz, Leah. "The Jerusalem Syndrome." *Israel Review of Arts and Letters*
   103 (1996). <http://www.israel- mfa.gov.il/mfago.asp?MFAH01xu0> (21
   July 2000).
"Achille Lauro Mastermind Says Klinghoffer 'Provoked' Terrorists to Murder
   Him." *Zionist Organization of America*. Press release. 14 July 1998.
   <http://www.zoa.org/pressrel/19980714a.htm> (8 Sept. 2000).
Ahsan, M. M. "The Orientalists' 'Satanic Verses.'" In *The Kiss of Judas: Affairs of
   a Brown Sahib*, ed. Munawar A. Anees, 6–10. Kuala Lumpur, Malaysia:
   Quill, 1989. Originally published in *Hamdard Islamicus* 5.1 (1988).
Ahsan, M. M., and A. R. Kidwait. *Sacrilege and Civility: Muslim Perspectives on
   the Satanic Verses Affair*. Leicester, England: Islamic Foundation, 1990.
Alter, Robert. "The Spritzer." Review of *Operation Shylock: A Confession*, by
   Philip Roth. *New Republic* 208.14 (5 April 1993): 31–34.
Althusser, Louis. "Ideology and Ideological State Apparatuses." In *Lenin and
   Philosophy*, trans. Ben Brewster, 127–86. New York: Monthly Review Press,
   1971.
American Civil Liberties Union. "ACLU Background Briefing: House to Con-
   sider Ominous Counter-Constitution Act (Also Known as the Omnibus
   Counterrorism Act)." 31 March 1995. <http://www.wolfenet.com/
   ~danfs/aclu.txt> (retrieved 2 May 1997; no longer accessible).
"Amid Controversy, Barricade Fast-Tracks *The Turner Diaries*." *BookWeb*. American Booksellers Association. 29 April 1996. <http://www.bookweb.org/
   bookweb/btw/042996/art2.html> (retrieved 5 June 1998; no longer
   accessible).
Amnesty International. "Iran: Eight Years of Death Threats to Salman
   Rushdie." Amnesty International Report MDE 13/17/97. May 1997.
   <http://www.amnesty.org/ailib/aipub/1997/MDE/51301797.htm> 21
   July 2000).

Andrew, Christopher, and Oleg Gordievsky. *KGB: The Inside Story.* New York: HarperCollins, 1990.

Anesko, Michael. *"Friction with the Market": Henry James and the Profession of Authorship.* New York: Oxford UP, 1986.

Appignanesi, Lisa, and Sara Maitland. *The Rushdie File.* Syracuse, NY: Syracuse UP, 1990.

Aravamudan, Srinivas. "'Being God's Postman Is No Fun, Yaar': Salman Rushdie's *The Satanic Verses.*" *Diacritics* 19.2 (1989): 3–20.

Armstrong, Nancy, and Leonard Tennenhouse, eds. *The Violence of Representation.* London: Routledge, 1989.

Attwell, David. *J. M. Coetzee: South Africa and the Politics of Writing.* Berkeley: U of California P, 1993.

Bakhtin, M. M. *The Dialogic Imagination.* Ed. Michael Holquist. Trans. Caryl Emerson and Michael Holquist. Austin: U of Texas P, 1981.

Bar-El, Yair, et al. "Psychiatric Hospitalization of Tourists in Jerusalem." *Comprehensive Psychiatry* 32.3 (May–June 1991): 238–44.

Baudrillard, Jean. *Selected Writings.* Ed. Mark Poster. Stanford: Stanford UP, 1988.

———. *In the Shadow of the Silent Majorities.* Trans. Paul Foss, John Johnston, and Paul Patton. Foreign Agents Series. New York: *Semiotext(e),* 1983.

Becker, Jillian. *Hitler's Children: The Story of the Baader-Meinhof Terrorist Gang.* Philadelphia: J. B. Lippincott, 1977.

Benjamin, Walter. "Theses on the Philosophy of History." In *Illuminations,* trans. Harry Zohn, 253–64. New York: Schocken Books, 1968.

Bennahun, David. "Fly Me to the MOO: Adventures in Textual Reality." *Lingua Franca* 4.4 (May–June 1994): 1, 22–36.

Berthaud, Jacques. *Joseph Conrad: The Major Phase.* Cambridge: Cambridge UP, 1978.

Borrill, Rachel. "Former British Officer's Case Strengthened." *Irish Times,* 10 October 1996.

Breckinridge, Carol A., and Arjun Appadurai. "On Fictionalizing the Real." Editors' Comments. *Public Culture* 1.2 (spring 1989): i–v.

Brightman, Carol. *Writing Dangerously: A Critical Biography of Mary McCarthy.* New York: Clarkson Potter, 1992.

Bronson, Bertrand. "Strange Relations: The Author and His Audience." In *Facets of the Enlightenment: Studies in English Literature and Its Contexts,* 298–325. Berkeley: U of California P, 1968.

Bruce, Steve. *The Red Hand: Protestant Paramilitaries in Northern Ireland.* Oxford: Oxford UP, 1992.

Burton, Frank. "Ideological Social Relations in Northern Ireland." *British Journal of Sociology* 30 (1979): 61–80.

Carmichael, Thomas. "Lee Harvey Oswald and the Postmodern Subject:

History and Intertextuality in Don DeLillo's *Libra, The Names*, and *Mao II*. *Contemporary Literature* 34.2 (summer 1993): 204–18.

Casanova, Pascale. "Pour le plaisir de se perdre." *La quinzaine littéraire*, no. 563 (1–15 Oct. 1990): 13.

"Casualties as a Result of Paramilitary Style Attacks." Royal Ulster Constabulary. Press release. 22 May 2000. <http://www.ruc.police.uk/press/statistics/punbeat2.htm> (22 July 2000).

Cave, Terence. *Recognitions*. Oxford: Clarendon, 1988.

Churchill, Winston. *The World Crisis: The Aftermath*. New York: Scribner's, 1929.

Coetzee, J. M. *The Master of Petersburg*. New York: Viking, 1994.

Collins, James, et al. "The Weight of the Evidence." *Time*, 28 April 1997, 37–42.

Conrad, Joseph. *The Secret Agent*. 1907. Rpt., New York: Anchor-Doubleday, 1953.

———. *Under Western Eyes*. 1910. Rpt., New York: Anchor-Doubleday, 1963.

Conroy, John. *Belfast Diary*. Boston: Beacon Press, 1987.

Cordes, Bonnie. "When Terrorists Do the Talking: Reflections on Terrorist Literature." In *Inside Terrorist Organizations*, ed. David C. Rapoport, 150–71. New York: Columbia UP, 1988.

Davan, Daniel, and Elihu Katz. *Media Events: The Live Broadcasting of History*. Cambridge: Harvard UP, 1992.

"Deaths Due to the Northern Ireland Security Situation." Royal Ulster Constabulary. Press release. <http:/www.ruc.police.uk/press/statistics/deaths2.htm> (28 Dec. 2000).

DeLillo, Don. "An Interview with Don DeLillo." Interview by Maria Nadotti. Trans. Peggy Boyers. *Salmagundi* 100 (fall 1993): 86–97.

———. *Libra*. New York: Viking, 1988.

———. *Mao II*. New York: Penguin, 1992.

———. *The Names*. New York: Knopf, 1982.

———. "An Outsider in This Society: An Interview with Don DeLillo." By Anthony DeCurtis. In *Introducing Don DeLillo*, ed. Frank Lentricchia, 43–66. Durham, NC: Duke UP, 1991.

———. *White Noise*. New York: Viking, 1985.

De Man, Paul. "The Resistance to Theory." In *Modern Criticism and Theory*, ed. David Lodge, 354–71. London: Longman, 1988.

Derabian, Peter, and T. H. Bagley. *KGB: Masters of the Soviet Union*. New York: Hippocrene Books, 1990.

Derrida, Jacques. "Some Statements and Truisms about Neo-Logisms, Newisms, Postisms, Parasitisms, and Other Small Seismisms." In *Modern Literary Theory: A Reader*, ed. Philip Rice and Patricia Waugh, 3d ed., 368–78. London: Arnold, 1996. Originally published in *The States of 'Theory': History, Art, and Critical Discourse*, ed. David Carroll, 81–94. New York: Columbia UP, 1990.

Dillon, Martin. *The Shankill Butchers: A Case Study of Mass Murder.* Foreword by
   Conor Cruise O'Brien. London: Hutchinson, 1989.

Dixit, J. P., et al. "Deliberate Provocation." In Ahsan and Kidwait, eds., *Sacrilege
   and Civility,* 83–84. Originally published in *Indian Express* 17 (October
   1988).

Doan, Van Toai, and David Chanoff. *The Vietnamese Gulag.* New York: Simon
   and Schuster, 1986.

Dobkin, Bethami. *Tales of Terror: Television News and the Construction of the
   Terrorist Threat.* New York: Praeger, 1992.

Donoghue, Denis. "Alice, the Radical Homemaker." Review of *The Good Terrorist,* by Doris Lessing. *New York Times Book Review,* 22 Sept. 1985, 3, 29.

Dooley, Brian. "Cardinals Speak on Rushdie but Pope Is Silent." In Ahsan and
   Kidwait, eds., *Sacrilege and Civility,* 127. Originally published in *Catholic
   Herald,* 3 March 1989.

Dostoevsky, Aimée. *Fyodor Dostoyevsky: A Study.* New Haven: Yale UP, 1922.

Dostoevsky, Fyodor. *Demons.* 1871–1872. Rpt., trans. Richard Pevear and Larisa
   Volokhonsky, New York: Knopf, 1994.

Dowling, Joseph A. "Prolegomena to a Psychohistorical Study of Terrorism." In
   Marius Livingston, ed., *International Terrorism in the Contemporary World,*
   223–30.

Dürrenmatt, Friedrich. *The Assignment; or, On Observing the Observer of the
   Observers.* Trans. Joel Agee. New York: Random House, 1988.

Emerson, Ralph Waldo. "The Transcendentalist." In *The Portable Emerson,* ed.
   Carl Bode in collaboration with Malcolm Cowley, rev. ed., 92–110. Harmondsworth: Penguin, 1980.

Engels, Friedrich. *Herr Eugen Dühring's Revolution in Science.* Trans. Emile
   Burns. Ed. C. P. Dutt. New York: International, 1966. Originally published
   as *Anti-Dühring,* 1876.

"FBI Suspects Alleged Unabomber Based His Life on Conrad." *All Things
   Considered.* National Public Radio. 14 July 1996. (Transcript available)

Feldman, Allen. *Formations of Violence: The Narrative of the Body and Political
   Terror in Northern Ireland.* Chicago: U of Chicago P, 1993.

Fingerhut, Lois, Christine Cox, and Margaret Warner. *International Comparative
   Analysis of Injury Mortality Findings from the ICE on Injury Statistics: Advance
   Data from Vital and Health Statistics of the Centers for Disease Control and Pre-
   vention.* Hyattsville, MD: U.S. Dept. of Health and Human Services, 1998.

Foucault, Michel. "The Life of Infamous Men." Trans. Paul Foss and Meaghan
   Morris. In *Michel Foucault: Power, Truth, Strategy,* ed. Meaghan Morris and
   Paul Patton, 76–91. "Working Papers," Collection 2. Sydney, Australia:
   Feral, 1979.

———. "Truth and Power." In *Power/Knowledge: Selected Interviews and Other
   Writings,* ed. Colin Gordon and trans. Colin Gordon et al., 109–33. New
   York: Pantheon, 1980.

Frank, Joseph. *Dostoevsky: The Miraculous Years*. Princeton: Princeton UP, 1995.
———. "The Rebel." Review of *The Master of Petersburg*, by J. M. Coetzee. *New Republic* 213.16 (16 Oct. 1995): 53–54.
Freedman, Carl. "Toward a Theory of Paranoia." In *Philip K. Dick: Contemporary Critical Interpretations*, ed. Samuel J. Umland, 7–17. Westport, CT: Greenwood, 1995.
Free Speech: Report of a Seminar Organised by the Commission for Racial Equality and the Policy Studies Institute. London: Commission for Racial Equality, 1989.
Fukuyama, Francis. *The End of History and the Last Man*. New York: Free Press, 1992.
Fussell, Edwin Sill. *The French Side of Henry James*. New York: Columbia UP, 1990.
Gallagher, Susan V. *A Story of South Africa: J. M. Coetzee's Fiction in Context*. Cambridge: Harvard UP, 1991.
Geismar, Maxwell. *Henry James and the Jacobites*. Boston: Houghton Mifflin, 1963.
Gerbner, George. "Symbolic Functions of Violence and Terror." In *In the Camera's Eye: News Coverage of Terrorist Events*, ed. Yonah Alexander and Robert G. Picard, 3–9. Washington, DC: Brassey's U.S., 1991.
Gordon, Mary. *Good Boys and Dead Girls: And Other Essays*. New York: Viking, 1991.
Goren, Roberta. *The Soviet Union and Terrorism*. Ed. Jillian Becker, with an introduction by Robert Conquest. London: Allen and Unwin, 1984.
Greene, Gayle. "Bleak Houses: Doris Lessing, Margaret Drabble and the Condition of England." *Forum for Modern Language Studies* 28.4 (Oct. 1992): 304–19.
Grosscup, Beau. *The Explosion of Terrorism*. Far Hills, NJ: New Horizon Press, 1987.
Gubar, Susan, and Sandra Gilbert. *The Madwoman in the Attic: The Woman Writer and the Nineteenth Century Literary Imagination*. New Haven: Yale UP, 1979.
Halkin, Hillel. Review of *Damascus Gate*, by Robert Stone. *New Republic* 218.21 (25 May 1998): 29–32.
"Heart of Darkness." *Dateline*. National Broadcasting Company. 16 April 1996. (Transcript available)
Hebel, Franz. "Technikentwicklung und Technikfolgen in der Literatur: Timm, *Der Schlangenbaum* / Eisfeld, *Das Genie* / Dürrenmatt, *Der Auftrag* / Wolf, *Störfall*." *Der Deutschunterricht* 41.5 (1989): 35–45.
Helbling, Robert. "'I Am a Camera': Friedrich Dürrenmatt's *Der Auftrag*." *Seminar: A Journal of Germanic Studies* 24.2 (1988): 178–181.
Hocking, Jenny. *Beyond Terrorism: The Development of the Australian Security State*. Sydney: Allen and Unwin, 1993.

"Israel's Next Nightmare: Doomsday Nuts Want Armageddon in Jerusalem!"
  Tabloid. <http://www.tabloid.net/1998/10/22/jerusalemdoom981022.
  html> (21 July 2000).
Jacobson, Marcia. *Henry James and the Mass Market.* U of Alabama P, 1983.
James, Caryn. "Time Out for Realism." *New York Times Book Review,* 22 Sept.
  1985, 3.
James, Henry. *Henry James: Letters.* Ed. Leon Edel. 4 vols. Cambridge: Belknap
  Press of Harvard UP, 1974–84.
———. *The Princess Casamassima.* 1886. Rpt. Harmondsworth: Penguin, 1986.
  (The text is that of the first edition.)
Jameson, Fredric. *Postmodernism; Or, The Cultural Logic of Late Capitalism.*
  Durham, NC: Duke UP, 1991.
Jay, Martin. "The Fictional Terrorist." *Partisan Review* 55.1 (1988): 69–81.
Jellicoe, The Right Honourable Earl. *Review of the Operation of the Prevention
  of Terrorism* (Temporary Provisions) Act 1976. London: Her Majesty's
  Stationery Office, 1983.
Jenkins, Brian. "Research in Terrorism: Areas of Consensus, Areas of Igno-
  rance." In *Terrorism: Interdisciplinary Perspectives,* ed. Burr Eickelman,
  David Soskis, and William Reid, 153–77. Washington, DC: American
  Psychological Association, 1983.
Jones, Charisse. "Race Killing in Texas Fuels Fear and Anger." *USA Today,* 11
  June 1998, 1A.
Jussawalla, Feroza. "Resurrecting the Prophet: The Case of Salman, the Other-
  wise." *Public Culture* 2.1 (fall 1989): 106–17.
Kermode, Frank. *The Art of Telling.* Cambridge: Harvard UP, 1983.
Kiernan, Frances. "Group Encounter." *New Yorker* 69.16 (7 June 1993): 56–61.
Kovaleski, Serge. "1907 Conrad Novel May Have Inspired Unabomb Suspect."
  Washington Post, 9 July 1996, A01.
Kubiak, Anthony. *Stages of Terror: Terrorism, Ideology, and Coercion as Theatre
  History.* Bloomington: Indiana UP, 1991.
Laqueur, Walter. *The Age of Terrorism.* Boston: Little, Brown, 1987.
———. *The New Terrorism.* New York: Oxford, 1999.
"Leader in Achille Lauro Hijacking Apologizes." *Detroit News,* 23 April 1996.
Lee, Alan J. *The Origins of the Popular Press in England: 1855–1944.* London:
  Croom Helm, 1976.
Lee, Alison. *Realism and Power: Postmodern British Fiction.* London: Routledge,
  1990.
"Legacy of 'Shankill Butchers' Survives." *Irish Times.* 12 June 1997.
Lenin, Vladimir. *State and Revolution.* 1917. Rpt., New York: International, 1943.
Lessing, Doris. *Documents Relating to the Sentimental Agents in the Volyen Empire.*
  New York: Vintage-Random, 1984.
———. *The Four-Gated City.* 1969. Vol. 5 of *Children of Violence* series. Rpt., New
  York: Bantam, 1970.

———. *The Good Terrorist.* New York: Vintage-Random, 1986.

———. *Shikasta.* New York: Knopf, 1979.

———. "The Small Personal Voice." In *A Small Personal Voice: Essays, Reviews, Interviews,* ed. and introduction by Paul Schlueter, 3–21. New York: Knopf, 1974.

Lévi-Strauss, Claude. *Tristes Tropiques.* Trans. John and Doreen Weightman. New York: Atheneum, 1974.

Liebes, Tamar. "Television's Disaster Marathons: A Danger for Democratic Processes." In *Media, Ritual, and Identity,* ed. Tamar Liebes and James Curran, 71–84. London: Routledge, 1998.

Livingston, Marius, ed., with Lee Bruce Kress and Marie Wanek. *International Terrorism in the Contemporary World.* Contributions in Political Science no. 3. Westport, CT: Greenwood, 1978.

Loeb, Vernon. "U.S. Is Urged to Preempt Terrorists." *Washington Post,* 4 June 2000, A1+.

Lurie, Alison. "Bad Housekeeping." Review of *The Good Terrorist* and *The Diaries of Jane Somers: The Diary of a Good Neighbour* and *If the Old Could . . . ,* by Doris Lessing. *New York Review of Books,* 19 Dec. 1985, 8–10.

Lyotard, Jean. *The Postmodern Condition: A Report on Knowledge.* Minneapolis: U of Minnesota P, 1984.

Maas, Peter. "Generations of Torment." *New York Times Magazine,* 10 July 1988, 29–33, 36–37.

Macdonald, Andrew [pseud. of William Pierce]. *The Turner Diaries.* 2d ed. Hillsboro, WV: National Vanguard, 1980.

MacGregor, Brent. *Live, Direct and Biased? Making Television News in the Satellite Age.* London: Arnold, 1997.

Mahler, Jonathan. "Plots and Prophets in the Holy City." Review of *Damascus Gate,* by Robert Stone. *Wall Street Journal,* 24 April 1998, W4.

Mansergh, Nicholas. *The Unresolved Question: The Anglo-Irish Settlement and Its Undoing, 1912–72.* New Haven: Yale UP, 1991.

Marc, David. *Bonfire of the Humanities: Television, Subliteracy, and Long-Term Memory Loss.* Syracuse, NY: Syracuse UP, 1995.

Marx, Karl. *The Eighteenth Brumaire of Louis Bonaparte.* 1852. Rpt., Moscow: Foreign Languages, 1948.

Maurois, André. *Lyautey.* New York: Appleton, 1931.

Mazrui, Ali A. "Satanic Verses or a Satanic Novel?" In *The Kiss of Judas: Affairs of a Brown Sahib,* ed. Munawar A. Anees, 61–90. Kuala Lumpur, Malaysia: Quill, 1989.

McCarthy, Mary. *Cannibals and Missionaries.* 1979. New York: Harvest Books, Harcourt Brace, 1991.

———. *Ideas and the Novel.* New York: Harcourt Brace, 1980.

———. "Living with Beautiful Things." In *Occasional Prose,* 101–26. New York: Harcourt Brace, 1985.

————. *The Seventeenth Degree.* New York: Harcourt Brace, 1974.

————. "A World out of Joint." Interview by Miriam Gross. In *Conversations with Mary McCarthy,* ed. Carol W. Gelderman, 170–78. Jackson: UP of Mississippi, 1991. Originally published in *Observer,* 14 Oct. 1979, 35.

McGarry, John, and Brendan O'Leary. *Explaining Northern Ireland: Broken Images.* Oxford: Blackwell, 1995.

McNamee, Eoin. *Resurrection Man.* 1994. New York: Picador, 1995.

"McVeigh Obsessed with Weapons." *Denver Post,* 2 May 1997. <http://www.denverpost.com> (21 July 2000).

Mehlman, Jeffrey. *Revolution and Repetition: Marx/Hugo/Balzac.* Berkeley: U of California P, 1977.

Melchiori, Barbara. *Terrorism in the Late Victorian Novel.* London: Croom Helm, 1985.

Melley, Timothy. *Empire of Conspiracy: The Culture of Paranoia in Postwar America.* Ithaca: Cornell UP, 2000.

Merkin, Daphne. In "Philip Roth's Diasporism: A Symposium." Ed. Sidra DeKoven Ezrahi. *Tikkun* 8 (May–June 1993): 41–45, 73.

Michaels, Jennifer E. "Through the Camera's Eye: An Analysis of Dürrenmatt's *Der Auftrag.*" *International Fiction Review* 15. 2 (1988): 141–47.

Miller, D. A. *The Novel and the Police.* Berkeley: U of California P, 1988.

Miller, Karl. *Doubles: Studies in Literary History.* Oxford: Oxford UP, 1985.

Miller, Martin. "The Intellectual Origins of Modern Terrorism in Europe." In *Terrorism in Context,* ed. Martha Crenshaw, 27–62. University Park: Pennsylvania State UP, 1995.

Montrose, Louis. "Professing the Renaissance: The Poetics and Politics of Culture." In *The New Historicism,* ed. H. Aram Veeser, 15–36. New York: Routledge, 1989.

Moore, Chris. *The Kincora Scandal: Political Cover-Up and Intrigue in Northern Ireland.* Dublin: Marino-Mercier, 1996.

Moore, Lorrie. "Look for a Writer and Find a Terrorist." Review of *Mao II,* by Don DeLillo. *New York Times Book Review,* 9 June 1991, 7.

Morgan, Robin. *The Demon Lover: On the Sexuality of Terrorism.* New York: Norton, 1989.

Murray, Nicholas. "Mr. Evans, Mr. Rushdie, and the White Settlers." *New Welsh Review* 3.11 (winter 1990–91): 51–52.

Mustapha, Muhammad. *An Islamic Overview of "The Satanic Verses."* Trinidad and Tobago: T. K. Industries, 1989.

Nguyen Ngoc Ngan, with E. E. Richey. *The Will of Heaven: The Story of One Vietnamese and the End of His World.* New York: Dutton, 1982.

Olivera, Annamarie. *The State of Terror.* Albany, NY: SUNY P, 1998.

"On Fictionalizing the Real." Editor's comments. *Public Culture* 1.2 (spring 1989): i–v.

Orr, John. "Terrorism as Social Drama and Dramatic Form." In *Terrorism and Modern Drama*, ed. John Orr and Dragan Klaic, 48–63. Edinburgh: Edinburgh UP, 1990.

Orr, John, and Dragan Klaic. "Terrorism and Drama: Introduction." In *Terrorism and Modern Drama*, ed. John Orr and Dragan Klaic, 1–12. Edinburgh: Edinburgh UP, 1990.

Paletz, David L., and Alex P. Schmid, eds. *Terrorism and the Media: How Researchers, Terrorists, Government, Press, Public, and Victims View and Use the Media.* Newbury Park, CA: Sage, 1992.

Pfeil, Fred. *Another Tale to Tell: Politics and Narrative in Postmodern Culture.* London: Verso, 1990.

Picard, Robert G. *Media Portrayals of Terrorism: Functions and Meaning of News Coverage.* Ames: Iowa State UP, 1993.

Pierce, William. "Remember What Happened to Anwar?" *Free Speech* 3.6 (June 1997). <http://www.natvan.com/free-speech/fs976b.html> (7 Aug. 2000).

Pipes, Daniel. *The Rushdie Affair: The Novel, the Ayatollah, and the West.* New York: Birch Lane, 1990.

———. "Salman Rushdie's Delusions, and Ours." *Commentary* 106.6 (Dec. 1998): 51–53.

Prendergast, Christopher. *The Order of Mimesis.* Cambridge: Cambridge UP, 1986.

"Punishment Beating and Exile." BBC News Online Network. 31 Aug. 1999. <http://news6.thdo.bbc.co.uk/hi/english/static/northern_ ireland/understanding/themes/punishment_beatings/stm> (7 Aug. 2000).

"Red Army Faction." This Is Baader-Meinhof: Germany in the Post-War Decade of Terror, 1968–1977. 2 January 2000. <http://www. baader-meinhof. com> (7 Aug. 2000).

"Red Army Faction Gives Up the Fight." BBC News Online Network. 21 April 1998. <http://news6.thdo.bbc.co.uk/low/english/world/europe/newsid_81000/81124.stm> (7 Aug. 2000).

Rodinson, Maxime. *Mohammed.* 1968. Rpt., trans. Anne Carter, New York: Pantheon, 1971.

Roth, Philip. *Operation Shylock: A Confession.* 1993. New York: Vintage International, 1994.

———. "Philip Roth Sees Double." Interview by Esther B. Fein. *New York Times,* 9 March 1993, C13+.

Rubenstein, Richard. *Alchemists of Revolution: Terrorism in the Modern World.* New York: Basic Books, 1987.

Rushdie, Salman. *Imaginary Homelands: Essays and Criticism, 1981–1991.* New York: Penguin, 1992.

———. *The Satanic Verses.* New York: Viking, 1989.

Ruthven, Malise. *A Satanic Affair: Salman Rushdie and the Rage of Islam*. London: Chatto and Windus, 1990.

Safer, Elaine. "The Double, Comic Irony, and Postmodernism in Philip Roth's *Operation Shylock*." *Melus* 21.4 (winter 96): 157–72.

Said, Edward. "The Essential Terrorist." In *Blaming the Victims: Spurious Scholarship and the Palestinian Question*, 149–58. London: Verso, 1988.

Sardar, Ziaddin. "The Rushdie Malaise: A Critique of Some Writings on the Rushdie Affair." In Ahsan and Kidwait, eds., *Sacrilege and Civility*, 278–309. Originally published in *Muslim World Book Review* 11.1 (1990): 3–19.

Sartre, Jean-Paul. Introduction to *Poésies*, by Stéphane Mallarmé. Paris: Lucien Mazenod, 1952.

Schimmel, Annemarie. *Islam: An Introduction*. Albany: SUNY P, 1992.

Schlagheck, Donna. *International Terrorism: An Introduction to the Concepts and Actors*. Lexington, MA: Lexington Books, D. C. Heath, 1988.

Schmid, Alex P., and Janny de Graaf. *Violence as Communication: Insurgent Terrorism and the Western News Media*. London: Sage, 1982.

Seltzer, Mark. *Henry James and the Art of Power*. Ithaca: Cornell UP, 1984.

Serrano, Richard. *One of Ours: Timothy McVeigh and the Oklahoma City Bombing*. New York: Norton, 1998.

Shaffert, Richard. *Media Coverage and Political Terrorists: A Quantitative Analysis*. New York: Praeger, 1992.

Shahabuddin, Syed. "Yes, Mr. Rushdie, We Shall Not Permit Literary Colonialism, Nor Religious Pornography." In Ahsan and Kidwait, eds., *Sacrilege and Civility*, 152–55.

Shaplen, Robert. *Bitter Victory*. New York: Harper and Row, 1986.

Sheehan, Neil. *After the War Was Over: Hanoi and Saigon*. New York: Random House, 1992.

Sheftel, Yoram. *Defending Ivan the Terrible: The Conspiracy to Convict John Demjanjuk*. 1993. Rpt., trans. Haim Watzman, Washington, DC: Regnery, 1995.

Shinbaum, Myrna. "Q & A on *The Turner Diaries*." Anti-Defamation League. 16 May 1996. <http://www.adl.org/presrele/militi%5F71/2737%5F71.html> (21 July 2000).

Shostak, Debra. "The Diaspora Jew and the 'Instinct for Impersonation': Philip Roth's *Operation Shylock*." *Contemporary Literature* 38.4 (winter 1997): 726–54.

Showalter, Elaine. *A Literature of Their Own: British Women Novelists from Brontë to Lessing*. Princeton: Princeton UP, 1987.

Siegel-Itzkovich, "Israel Prepares for 'Jerusalem Syndrome.'" *British Medical Journal* 318.7182 (20 Feb. 1999): 484.

Silke, Andrew. "In Defense of the Realm: Financing Loyalist Terrorism in Northern Ireland—Part One: Extortion and Blackmail." *Studies in Conflict and Terrorism* 21.3 (July–September 1998): 331–61.

Simon, Jeffrey D. *The Terrorist Trap: America's Experience with Terrorism.* Bloom-
    ington: Indiana UP, 1994.
Smith, M. R. L. *Fighting for Ireland? The Military Strategy of the Irish Republican
    Movement.* London: Routledge, 1995.
Sourcebook of Criminal Justice Statistics Online.
    <http://www.albany.edu/sourcebook/1995/pdf/t3192.pdf> (8 Aug.
    2000).
Spark, Muriel. *Mandelbaum Gate.* New York: Knopf, 1965.
Spivak, Gayatri Chakravorty. "Reading *The Satanic Verses.*" *Public Culture* 2.1
    (fall 1989): 79–99.
Spurr, David. "Terrorism in the News Media." *Works and Days* 4.2 (1986):
    93–105.
Stein, William Bysshe. "*The Secret Agent*: The Agon(ies) of the Word." *Boundary
    2* 6.2 (winter 1978): 521–40.
Stone, Robert. *Damascus Gate.* 1998. New York: Scribner's, 1999.
———. "We Are Not Excused." In *Paths of Resistance: The Art and Craft of the
    Political Novel,* ed. William Zinsser, 17–38. Boston: Houghton Mifflin, 1989.
Storr, Anthony. "Sadism and Paranoia." In Marius Livingston, ed., *International
    Terrorism in the Contemporary World,* 231–39.
Stuckey, J. Elspeth. *The Violence of Literacy.* Portsmouth, NH: Boynton/Cook
    Publishers, 1991.
Suleri, Sara. "Contraband Histories: Salman Rushdie and the Embodiment of
    Blasphemy." *Yale Review* 78.4 (1989): 604–24.
Tahourdin, Adrian. "Atlantis Transplanted." *Times Literary Supplement,* 4 Oct.
    1991, 28.
Taussig, Mick. "Terror as Usual: Walter Benjamin's Theory of History as a State
    of Siege," *Social Text* 23 (fall/winter 1989): 3–20.
Teachout, Terry. "Mad Loner Builds Perfect Bomb." *New York,* 13 July 1996,
    15, 19.
Teicholz, Tom. *The Trial of Ivan the Terrible.* New York: St. Martin's, 1990.
Teraoka, Arlene A. "Terrorism and the Essay: The Case of Ulrike Meinhof." In
    The Politics of the Essay: Feminist Perspectives, ed. Ruth-Ellen Boetcher Joeres
    and Elizabeth Mittman, 209–24. Bloomington: Indiana UP, 1993.
Thornton, Thomas Perry. "Terror as a Weapon of Political Agitation." In *Internal
    War: Problems and Approaches,* ed. Harry Eckstein, 71–99. New York: Free
    Press, 1964.
Trilling, Lionel. *The Liberal Imagination.* New York: Doubleday, 1950.
"*Turner Diaries* Author William Pierce." *Time/CNN's IMPACT:* Discussion
    Transcript Archive. 1 June 1997. <http://www.pathfinder.com/time/
    community/transcripts/chattr060197.html> (21 July 2000).
Updike, John. "Recruiting Raw Nerves." Review of *Operation Shylock,* by Philip
    Roth. *New Yorker* 69.4 (15 March 1993): 109–12.

Uris, Leon. *Exodus*. New York: Doubleday, 1958.

U.S. Dept. of Justice. Federal Bureau of Investigation. *Uniform Crime Reports, 1998*. Section 2, "Crime Index Offenses Reported." <http://www.fbi.gov/ucr/98cius.htm (21 July 2000).>

U.S. Dept. of State. *Patterns of Global Terrorism 1998*. Washington, DC: Dept. of State, 1999.

Volodine, Antoine. *Alto solo*. Paris: Minuit, 1991.

———. *Lisbonne dernière marge*. Paris: Minuit, 1990.

Walker, Christopher. "Israelis on Alert for Millennium Suicide Invasion." *Times* (London), 22 Oct. 1998, 23.

Weatherby, W. J. *Salman Rushdie: Sentenced to Death*. New York: Carroll and Graf, 1990.

Webster, Richard. *A Brief History of Blasphemy: Liberalism, Censorship, and "The Satanic Verses."* Southwold, Suffolk: Orwell Press, 1990.

Weimann, Gabriel, and Conrad Winn. *The Theater of Terror: Mass Media and International Terrorism*. New York: Longman, 1996.

Weldon, Fay. *Sacred Cows*. London: Chatto and Windus, 1989.

Weir, David. *Anarchy and Culture: The Aesthetic Politics of Modernism*. Amherst: U of Massachusetts P, 1997.

Welsh, Alexander. *George Eliot and Blackmail*. Cambridge: Harvard UP, 1985.

Widdowson, Peter. "Terrorism and Literary Studies." *Textual Practice* 2.1 (spring 1988): 1–21.

Wittebols, J. H. "Words and Worlds of Terror: Context and Meaning of a Media Buzzword." *ETC: A Review of General Semantics* 48.3 (fall 1991): 336–442.

Woodcock, George. "Henry James and the Conspirators." *Sewanee Review* 60 (1952): 219–29.

Wright, Joanne. *Terrorist Propaganda: The Red Army Faction and the Provisional IRA, 1968–1986*. New York: St. Martin's, 1991.

Yeats, William Butler. "The Man and the Echo." *Collected Poems*, 337–39. New York: Macmillan, 1951.

Young, Jacob. *Dr. No?* Videotape. Morgantown, WV. WNPB, 1991.

Zinam, Oleg. "Terrorism and Violence in the Light of a Theory of Discontent and Frustration." In Marius Livingston, ed., *International Terrorism in the Contemporary World*, 240–65.

Zulaika, Joseba, and William A. Douglass. *Terror and Taboo: The Follies, Fables, and Faces of Terror*. New York: Routledge, 1996.

Index

Oklahoma City bombing, 156–59,
   176n, 181n, 182n
O'Leary, Brendan, 50
Olympics, Munich, 12, 125
Orientalism, 23, 166
Orr, John, 77, 189
Orwell, George, 10, 192

Palestine, 43, 51, 125, 128, 175
paranoia: and plotting of terrorist fic-
   tion, 37, 46; Freud on, 171n. *See also*
   conspiracy theory
parody, 22, 26, 37, 56, 136
Pfeil, Fred, 25, 189
Pham Van Dong, 66, 68
Photography, 117
Picard, Robert, 12, 186, 189
Pierce, William, 157, 158, 161, 181,
   182, 189, 191
Pipes, Daniel, 24, 166, 167, 189
PLO, 125, 126, 130, 179n
Prendergast, Christopher, 46,
Prevention of Terrorism Act, 84, 177n
Pynchon, Thomas, 26

RAF (Red Army Faction), 140, 142,
   180n, 181n
Reagan, Ronald, 84, 90, 182
Roth, Philip, 15, 124, 126–31, 179n
Royal Ulster Constabulary, 41,
   169–71n, 175n
Rubenstein, Richard, 71, 75, 76, 85,
   174n
Rushdie, Salman, 19, 21–36, 164–66n
Russian Revolution, 10, 103
Ruthven, Malise, 21n, 164n, 166n,
   168n

Said, Edward: fictional depictions of
   30, 128; Orientalism 23, 166n; on
   manipulations of terrorist threat, 1,
   83, 109, 126; Rushdie Affair 165,
   166n
Salinger, J. D., 26, 32
Sardar, Ziaddin, 21, 165–67n

Sartre, Jean-Paul, 11, 77
SAS (British Special Air Service), 136
Schmid, Alex, 13, 79, 163n
Second World War, 1, 11, 45
Serrano, Richard, 157, 158
Shahabuddin, Syed, 21
Shinbaum, Myrna, 157
Shining Path, 28, 97
Showalter, Elaine, 78
Sinn Fein, 85
Soviet Union, 5, 85, 86, 133, 173–75n
Spark, Muriel, 124, 125, 131
Spivak, Gayatri, 23
Spurr, David, 109
Stade, George, 160
Stein, William Bysshe, 78
Stockholm syndrome, 32
Stone, Robert, 15, 124, 131–38
Stowe, Harriet Beecher, 4, 155
Suleri, Sara, 23

Tahourdin, Adrian, 139
Taussig, Mick, 109, 112, 119
Teachout, Terry, 160
Tennenhouse, Leonard, 164n
Teraoka, Arlene, 181n
terrorism: computers and, 118, 119; —,
   defined, 5–7; —, discourse, 108–10;
   —, as fashion statement, 34; —, and
   global electronic revolution, 14, 24,
   25, 28–31, 38, 45–49, 53, 91, 152–54,
   156. *See also* terrorism, computers
   and: terrorism, journalism and;
   futility of, 86, 87, 123, 137, 138, 153,
   154; history, 5, 6, 11–13; journalism
   and 4, 5; 12–13, 77–80; —, newspaper, 4–6, 53, 156, 157, 173–74n; —,
   television news 12–14, 126, 161,
   168n, 171n, 176–78n; —, romanticism and 4, 9, 10, 31, 107, 133, 139; as
   threat to novel, *see* novel, death of
Terrorist organizations, *see* Baader-
   Meinhoff, Hamas, Irgun, INLA,
   IRA, PLO, RAF, Shining Path, UDA,
   UDF, UVF